CROSSING THE
DOUBLE-CROSS

ELIZABETH A. MEESE

CROSSING THE DOUBLE-CROSS

THE PRACTICE OF FEMINIST CRITICISM

The University of North Carolina Press

Chapel Hill and London

Copyright © 1986 The University of North Carolina Press

All rights reserved

Manufactured in the United States of America

Library of Congress Cataloging-in-Publication Data

Meese, Elizabeth A., 1943–
Crossing the double-cross.

Bibliography: p.
Includes index.

1. American literature—Women authors—History and
criticism.   2. Feminism and literature—United States.
3. Feminist literary criticism.   4. Women in literature.
I. Title.

PS152.M44   1986   810'.9'9287   85-20920
ISBN 0-8078-1683-3
ISBN 0-8078-4149-8 (pbk.)

The author is grateful for permission to reproduce passages from the following:

Emily Dickinson, poem no. 670, from *The Complete Poems of Emily Dickinson*, edited by
Thomas H. Johnson. Copyright © 1914, 1929, 1935, 1942 by Martha Dickinson Bianchi;
copyright © 1957, 1963 by Mary L. Hampson. Used by permission of
Little, Brown and Company.

Adrienne Rich, *The Will to Change, Poems 1968–1970* (copyright © 1979 by W. W. Norton and
Company, Inc.), and *The Dream of a Common Language, Poems 1974–1977* (copyright © 1978
by W. W. Norton and Company, Inc.). Used by permission of the author and
W. W. Norton and Company, Inc.

Chapter 1, "Sexual Politics and Critical Judgment," appeared in a slightly different version in
After Strange Texts: The Role of Theory in the Study of Literature, edited by Gregory S. Jay and
David L. Miller, and is reprinted here by permission of the University of Alabama Press.

Cover photograph by Gay Burke.

dŏu′ble-cross, *v.t.*
to betray (a person) by doing the opposite of, or intentionally failing to do, what one has promised; cheat. [Slang.]

cross′ing.

cross, *v.t.*
1. to make the sign of the cross over or upon.
2. to place across or crosswise; as, *cross* your fingers.
3. to lie or cut across; intersect, as, Broadway *crosses* Seventh Avenue at Times Square.
4. to draw or put a line or lines across.
5. to pass over; go from one side to the other of; go across; as, [s]he *crossed* the ocean.
6. to carry (troops, etc.) across.
7. to extend or reach across; as, the bridge *crosses* a river.
8. to meet (each other) in passing.
9. to thwart; oppose; go counter to; as no one likes to be *crossed.*
10. to interbreed (animals or plants); hybridize; cross-fertilize.

—Webster's New Twentieth Century Dictionary

CONTENTS

PREFACE

The chapters of this book have been written during a period of turmoil and excitement in both critical theory and feminist scholarship. The book charts a journey that, perhaps more than anything else, maps a difference within. This development shows itself plainly in the distance between the first chapter, "Sexual Politics and Critical Judgment," which reviews the problem of the feminist critic and writer within literary criticism, and later ones, "Crossing the Double-Cross: The Concept of 'Difference' and Feminist Literary Criticism" and "In/Conclusion: Feminism and Critical Theory," which explore the question of a direction for the feminist project in relation to contemporary critical theory. While we expect books, like journeys, to begin and to end, this text refuses to realize its own conclusion.

Feminist criticism can be represented in the figure standing at an intersection grown complex because the paths through the territory and the obstacles on the way have been more clearly specified. The critical wilderness of Geoffrey Hartman is already civilized and homo-geneous, without the entangling snares of different voices, whereas feminist criticism's wild complexity supplements Virginia Woolf's imprisonment as the daughter of an educated man with Audre Lorde's prisons of racial oppression, Adrienne Rich's jungle of heterosexism, and Tillie Olsen's silenced ghettos of the poor. This book, therefore, refuses to compress the problematics of feminist criticism into a single theory, not because these kinds of arguments cannot be or are not being made, but out of the belief that such constructions prematurely delimit the possibilities of our intellectual and social projects. At present, the variety of women's experiences that would have to be comprehended in a single theory cannot be reduced to simplicity without encoding in that theory the terms of its own undoing. Indeed, these mistakes of identity, where a part is taken for the whole, have been the problem with much feminist theorizing to date.

I begin here in indecision because I cannot reconcile the terms, the differences within myself, feminist criticism, and critical theory. My text makes only tentative explorations of the territory, forays out and back, displaying in that process—without doubt unwittingly—my complicity as a white academic feminist. I have no reason to believe that what I do here does not also ask for its own undoing, especially since, in the act of writing, I totalize feminist criticism and critical theory. In fact, if what I say is true, what I say is not true. Because of the arbitrary inevitability of who I am, I share the sense of value Spivak finds in deconstruction: "The aspect that interests me most is . . . the recognition, within deconstructive practice, of provisional and intractable starting points in any investigative effort; its disclosure of complicities where a will to knowledge would create oppositions; its insistence that in disclosing complicities the critic-as-subject is herself complicit with the object of her critique; its emphasis upon 'history' and upon the ethico-political as the 'trace' of that complicity—the proof that we do not inhabit a clearly defined critical space free of such traces; and, finally, the acknowledgment that its own discourse can never be adequate to its example."[1] At this particular critical moment, then, I believe it is intellectually more important to explore the possibilities of a relationship between feminism and critical theory than to construct a coherence of view within feminist criticism that will betray itself and its readers through the discovered traces of our own complicity. Thus, the text moves only tentatively from readings conducted at the crossroads of multiple contradictions, desiring what I deny it: to choose a pathway out of the wilderness of critical indeterminacy on a road toward an inclusive theory of feminist liberation with attendant theories of cultural and literary interpretation.

In order to practice feminist criticism, I am always taking positions but I am never comfortable with them. My resistance to conclusion leads me to refuse to construct a theory of feminist criticism, preferring instead to enact theorizing as a process (a way of understanding informed by certain values) that inhabits certain readings and to display aspects of theory (ways of reading that reflect those understandings and values). Rewriting Jane Gallop's desire in *The Daughter's Seduction* to bring feminism and psychoanalysis "each to its most radical potential,"[2] I would like to provoke critical theory, particularly American manifestations of deconstruction, to be more radically political, and feminism to be more self-consciously polyvocal and destabilizing in its theorizing.

At the moment, there is no single work that addresses the quarrel feminism has with recent critical theory and the disputes within feminism as seen in relation to critical theory, especially deconstruction. The book takes the form it does—discussions of critical texts and positions and analysis of literary texts —in the hope that the potential inherent in this constructed relationship between the two major terms will be made more palpable and compelling to both deconstructors writing without feminism and to feminists who still speak from a presumedly unassailable center of "truth." This work is not intended for those schooled in the intricate debates of feminism and contemporary critical theory; rather, it is offered as a prologue for readers wishing to understand their own work in terms of a relationship between these two projects, or as a description of one way into the dialogue. I am, therefore, in the uncomfortable position of asking for patience from all quarters.

While I assume that deconstruction needs to accommodate feminism, I do

Preface

not believe that feminist criticism should compromise its goals in order to achieve a reconciliation with deconstruction. However, the political analysis that occasioned and inhabits deconstruction makes it a more promising strategy than others for feminist critics to consider. Deconstructive criticism seeks the otherness of texts—that is, their "difference from what is already dealt with by the cultural models of literature as an institution."[3] This is an otherness that is repressed in interpretive or constructive acts as they "naturalize" texts according to genre, gender, culture, or models of behavior and personality—the implicit understandings and assumptions that produce the analogies we need in order to read. In this sense, then, deconstruction is compatible with feminist criticism, and when gender is the focus for examining difference, deconstructive criticism might even be said to be identical with the feminist project.

Feminist criticism does not need ideology as dogma in the guise of theory, and deconstruction equips us to detect and unravel our own and others' masquerades with a certain skill. Still, feminist criticism does need theory as a strategic process of conceptualization that relates various instances of practical criticism and enables us to explain ourselves to each other and to a larger critical audience. I am suggesting that feminist critical theory is a means to a vaguely specified but nonetheless powerfully compelling end; that it be construed as ideas that assist us and then disappear, as opposed to a codification that restricts or determines what can be said, by whom, and about what, thereby circumscribing our sociocultural projects just as we prepare to move into the uncertain future.

Further, as I hope this work demonstrates, theorizing is an interactive process among critics and texts, progressing in a not so systematic tension between the difficult demands of practical exercises and the illuminating force of abstract generalizations. The book as a whole is constructed to illustrate the necessary ways in which the practical plays within the theoretical, as in chapter 7, and how the development of theory reveals itself in the practice of close reading, displayed in chapters 2, 3, 4, and 6.

Without doubt, the chapters are unified in their common concern with the problems of sex, class, race, and sexual preference. The restrictions at work historically within each of these categories mark writers, texts, and readers. They constitute the unwritten or unspoken assumptions dictating who and what is read, how a work is read, and why. Therefore, in addition to disclosing their own preoccupations, the chapters of this book can be read as dialogues with critical theorists and practitioners. They frequently advance by exploration and critique: for example, chapter 1 works with Stanley Fish's *Is There a Text in This Class?*; chapter 2 demonstrates how Freeman and her critics determine a tradition of misreading; several engage aspects of Derrida's work; and still another considers the usefulness of Terry Eagleton's *Literary Theory*

Preface

to feminist criticism. In essence, the feminist critic's relationship to critical texts resembles the feminist writer's relationship to cultures' texts.

To be without conclusion or destination is not, however, to be without purpose. All of the chapters concern themselves with what Woolf called "the difference of view," resulting from woman's position in a patriarchal culture sustained by phallocentrism. My principle demonstration, best shown in chapters 6 and 7, involves the ways in which feminist writers, taking account of sexual politics, stage their own deconstructions of prescribed roles within the phallocentric economy. Furthermore, I examine the ways in which feminist writing, as Mary Jacobus describes it in "The Difference of View," "[t]hough necessarily working within 'male' discourse . . . work[s] ceaselessly to deconstruct it: to write what cannot be written."[4] Concerned with explications of what is revealed and what is concealed, the chapters construct implicit and explicit terms for relating writers of the past—Freeman, Woolf, and Hurston—to those of the present—Robinson, Olsen, and Walker respectively.

These efforts to stage one's resistance to the prescriptions of patriarchal culture, to exorcize the oppressor's consciousness, to construct oneself as a speaking subject, are the province, not of "woman," but of feminism's radical potential to escape what Audre Lorde calls the greatest danger of all, particularly for white women: "the pitfall of being seduced into joining the oppressor under the pretense of sharing power."[5] I am claiming the term "feminist" for this hypothetical woman who, not completely possessed by man and not fully alienated from herself as woman, attempts to define herself as a speaking/writing subject. Thus, this work reaffirms the idea of a feminist tradition of defiance—though it is not always transformative—within literature by suggesting the common motive that feminist writers share with us as we stand together in conscious, self-conscious and unconscious resistances to certain apparently ubiquitous effects of power as exercised by phallocentric cultures. Feminist strategies of the past can have both applicability and force in the present, as we continue to transgress the boundaries of gender, race, class, and sexual preference by crossing the double-cross of difference.

ACKNOWLEDGMENTS

Many people over the years deserve mention here. In particular I would like to thank David L. Miller for his careful readings and useful suggestions. Shelton Waldrep and Carol Argo kindly contributed hours of assistance. The inter-library loan services provided by Kay Jones and her staff at the University of Alabama's Gorgas Library were indispensable.

I am grateful to Claudia Johnson for her unfailing belief in my work. For years of conversation on issues of feminist criticism, and for the example of her life, I am indebted to Alice Parker, whose encouragement and incisive observations have always been generously offered and gratefully accepted.

This work could not have been possible without the time and opportunities provided by The University of Alabama College of Arts and Sciences—first, by Dean Douglas Jones who supported my sabbatical request, and then by Dean Richard E. Peck who encourages all of us through his ability to write and enjoy it. Finally, for thoughtful attention throughout the editorial process, I want to thank Sandra Eisdorfer and Pamela Upton, who were there in advance of every turn.

CROSSING THE DOUBLE-CROSS

Feminism "is a commitment [to exploring the ways of being a woman] involving a double movement: on the one hand, there is a desire to understand how it is that women as a sex are subordinated; on the other hand, there is a desire to challenge the very idea of natural sex roles. The problem is that of understanding the position of women as a sex without presuming that being a sex entails forms of natural behaviour and position. . . . The contradictoriness of this position is, however, only apparent."

Rosalind Coward, *Patriarchal Precedents*

SEXUAL
POLITICS
AND
CRITICAL
JUDGMENT

Literature is no one's private ground; literature is common ground. . . . Let us trespass freely and fearlessly and find our own way for ourselves.

—Virginia Woolf, "The Leaning Tower"

A new scientific truth does not triumph by convincing its opponents and making them see the light, but rather because its opponents eventually die, and a new generation grows up that is familiar with it.

—Max Planck, *Scientific Autobiography*

From the beginning, women have been trespassers in the world's literary communities. We receive a vision of ourselves skating around the edges of groups of artistic and intellectual men, striking occasional relationships, enjoying fleeting patronages or glimmers of momentary recognition. Regardless of the literary mode or style we choose for our self-expression, regardless of our level of accomplishment, we remain the outsiders among insiders, the "Other" in Simone de Beauvoir's sense of the term. In a 1960 letter published eighteen years later in *The Winner Names the Age*, Lillian Smith offers a paradigmatic view of the woman writer's position in relation to the literary establishment:

> I have been curiously smothered during the past nine years; indeed, ever since *Killers of the Dream* [1949]. When writers about "race" are discussed, I am never mentioned; when southern writers are discussed, I am never mentioned; when women writers are mentioned, I am not among them; when best-sellers are discussed, *Strange Fruit* (which broke every record for a serious book) is never mentioned. This is a curious amnesia; I have smiled at it, have laughed it; but I know what it has done to me in sales and in prestige.
>
> This is frank talk. Do not, I beg you, be embarrassed by it. I can still laugh it off most of the time; but now and then, I truly wonder. Whom, among the mighty, have I so greatly offended![1]

Smith aptly and painfully captures the woman writer's situation: an overriding condition of invisibility resulting from sexual politics, exacerbated in her case by attitudes toward region and race. Unlike the works of some women, Smith's were at least published and read, but like most, they are only now beginning to command the critical attention they deserve.

Of late it has become something of a commonplace among critics to acknowledge the political nature of the literary judgments used in constituting "good literature" and in determining a writer's inclusion in or exclusion from the literary canon. There are politics of authorship (race, sex, ethnicity, and class), of form (undervaluation of short stories, letters, diaries, essays, oral testimonies), of region (every place but New York, California, and Boston), and of content as it reflects nonheterosexism, nonobjectivism, nonphallocentric heroism, or any other nonexclusivist concern. (Clearly, I find it easier to say what is not allowed, thus producing a reactive criticism, a criticism written from exclusion, than to elaborate what might be valued under a more radical feminist politics of literary judgment.) The catalogue of injustices, abuses, and misrepresentations cited over the last decade by feminist critics is extensive.[2] While it bears repeating, ritualistically, in the way of chants and evocations, here I want to reassert a motive for feminist criticism by looking at the

5

way criticism regards women writers with respect to establishing the literary canon (its exemplars of value), and what limits feminist critics in their attempts to change the fundamental politics imbedded in the tradition of method and judgment. I hope that, in presenting this particular view of the critical process, a clearer understanding of the challenge confronting feminist criticism might emerge.

How the critical community establishes reputation, as evidenced by inclusion in the literary canon, is the crux of the problem for women writers and feminist critics. Obviously, certain writers such as Chaucer and Shakespeare enjoy permanence, but there are numerous others whose reputations remain in a state of flux, waxing and waning in accord with the prevailing interests of the critical moment. In "Literature as an Institution," Leslie Fiedler cynically observes: "We all know in our hearts that literature is effectively what we teach in departments of English; or conversely, what we teach in departments of English is literature. Within that closed definitional circle, we perform the rituals by which we cast out unworthy pretenders from our ranks and induct true initiates, guardians of the standards by which all song and story ought presumably to be judged."[3] Basically, works included in the literary canon deserve critical attention (while others don't), and critical attention needs to be paid to works in the canon because they are, by definition, important. The effect of this kind of exclusiveness is transparent: it places literature almost entirely in the service of white, male, elite culture.[4] The significance of works by writers outside of the mainstream is effectively diminished; as Tillie Olsen explains, "the rule is simple: whenever anyone of that sex, and/or class, and/or color, generally denied enabling circumstances, comes to recognized individual achievement, it is not by virtue of special capacity, courage, determination, will (common qualities) but because of chancy luck, combining with those qualities."[5] Feminists and other radical critics of the past decade have noted the ironic circularity at work here: what is not valued is not studied (canonized); what is not studied is not valued.

In a profound sense, the writer and the critic have been at odds with one another for centuries—at least since the secularization of literary forms, the increasing divergence of intellectual prose from other modes of discourse, and the changing function of criticism.[6] It remains the artist's role to challenge social conventions and to destroy artistic constraints in the process of making art. Unlike the artist, the critic too often serves the institutions of culture by assimilating the dissenting voices within only narrowly circumscribed limits; thus, George Stade notes:

> That literature has social functions is no longer news, although storytellers often deny it. They deny it because their private interests in their stories are at odds with the institutional ones—for humans differ from

animals in that the interests of the individual human . . . are often at odds with the interests of the group. Among such interests is the interest in stories. The private functions of literature . . . are at odds with the institutional functions, or there would be no need for critics, whose institutional function is to coopt private subversiveness for the public interest.[7]

Lagging behind, as categorizer, interpreter, ameliorator, as reactive rather than active, the traditional (masculinist) critic is, at worst, a conservator of Culture, a perpetuator of the very traditions the artist is in the process of attacking. Frank Lentricchia takes issue with this view in *Criticism and Social Change*, where he argues on behalf of the "radical literary intellectual"[8] who, by retrieving his "outsider's experience," works to break the inertia sustaining social conservators. Lentricchia nonetheless betrays himself as a conservator of sex and race relationships by excluding the words of women and black men from his own text (there are 229 footnotes to works by white men).[9] There is a circularity in the relationships of artists and critics, too: by attacking old traditions, the artist creates the material out of which new traditions emerge; without a text, the critic has nothing to do; the artist without a critic (or worse, without a publisher) is silenced until one emerges, and the possibility of transforming tradition is mute. Both have their respective arenas of power.

If we are to expand the consideration of literary value as reflected in the traditional literary canon, either by opening the canon to other works or by destroying such an exclusive, bias-ridden concept, we need to understand the critical dynamics underlying the perpetuation of conventions. In his collection of essays, *Is There a Text in This Class?*, Stanley Fish presents a view of critical judgments as issuing from an interpretive community; this view, when examined from a feminist perspective, provides a useful means of describing the nature of critical bias. Perhaps inadvertently, Fish helps us to see clearly the construction of a strong insider-outsider dynamic, a gender-based literary tribalism, that comes into play as a means of control. Critics who permit the possibility of variations in critical interpretation and value judgments, as opposed to those seeking the *Ur*-reading or a "universal" standard of value, immediately face the problem of closing ranks against the extremes of relativism in interpretation. Otherwise, the authority of the mainstream literary tradition could be seriously threatened. Fish guards against this by invoking the concept of "community": "What will, at any time, be recognized as literature is a function of a communal decision as to what will count as literature. All texts have the potential of so counting. . . . The conclusion is that while literature is still a category, it is an open category, not definable by fictionality, or by a disregard of propositional truth, or by a predominance of tropes and figures, but simply by what we decide to put into it."[10] While it is

Crossing the Double-Cross

true that Fish represents only one somewhat conservative current in today's confluence, other critics who disagree with him in some respects accept the concept of the authoritative community. Harold Bloom assumes such a community;[11] it lurks in the appeals to "common knowledge" and "common sense" (reminiscent of the "reasonable man" standard in legal and philosophical discourse) advanced by Frank Kermode and Gerald Graff. M. H. Abrams, in "How to Do Things with Texts," observes: "Stanley Fish seems to me right in his claim that the linguistic meanings we find in a text are relative to the interpretive strategy we employ, and that agreement about meanings depends on membership in a community which shares an interpretive strategy."[12] Abrams then asserts his own position, maintaining that the text, invested with the author's meaning, is the source of control over the interpretations produced by the critic. Such a view grows problematic when the notion of the critic as the writer's linguistic heir suggests as well that some have been disinherited.

This idea of membership, of belonging to the "insider's club," is attractive to mainstream critics; it is similarly appealing to many feminist critics and might in fact be a human desire—neither to be locked out nor locked in, as Woolf puts it. The club preserves and affirms control while offering the illusion of admissibility to the powerless. Still resonant today is the outsider's view expressed by Woolf in *Three Guineas* (Olsen calls this work a "savage" essay emerging from "genius brooding on . . . exclusion,"[13] and epitomized in her fictitious "Outsiders' Society," an anonymous and secret society for the daughters of educated men. In the passage that follows, Woolf's persona is ironically the "insider" (occupant of domestic space) looking "sidelong from an upper window" at the "solemn sight" of the male community in all its awesome symbolic and real power, enrobed and ascendant.[14] They move freely, related to each other in the procession of generations: "There they go, our brothers who have been educated at public schools and universities. . . . It is a solemn sight always—a procession, like a caravanserai crossing a desert. Great-grandfathers, grandfathers, fathers, uncles—they all went that way, wearing their gowns, wearing their wigs, some with ribbons across their breasts, others without."[15] They are self-perpetuating in their authority, these generations of powerful men. The ones who drop out of the procession are excluded in much the same way as women. They are cloaked in silence, distant; or, divested of robes, wigs, and ribbons, they wear shabby clothes and hold only menial jobs.

Critics such as Fish, Bloom, and Abrams genuinely believe in their community of critics; they march in the procession, speaking the truth from their own positions of privilege but suggesting other truths to feminists, Marxists, and critics of the nonmajority culture. Radical critics understand that the "interpretive community" is really the "authoritative community." Even though Fish regards criticism as an "open category," we are forced to see it, like his version of community, as a closed system that excludes us from the arena of its authority. The fact that literature is simply another cultural institution requiring protection dictates this process of critical circumscription.

Interpretive communities, like tribal communities, possess the power to ostracize or to embrace, to restrict or to extend membership and participation, and to impose norms—hence their authority. The system is mutually reinforcing, designed and chosen to mirror a structure of power relationships inextricably bound up with knowledge. Thus, Fish states explicitly that credible interpretations issue not from just any critic but from members of the club: "The reader is identified not as a free agent, making literature in any old way, but as a member of a community whose assumptions about literature determine the kind of attention he pays and thus the kind of literature 'he' 'makes'. . . . The act of recognizing literature . . . proceeds from a collective decision as to what will count as literature, a decision that will be in force only so long as a community of readers and believers continues to abide by it."[16] His remarks contain the answer to the question, why the failure of so many feminist commentaries aimed at demonstrating to mainstream critics the stature of neglected works by women?

In the introduction to *Is There a Text in This Class?*, Fish argues that various critics of a text share the same reading experience, but "that their critical preconceptions lead them either to ignore or devalue it."[17] Although in principle critical argument occurs on the level of rational discourse, judgments are undeniably built upon affective responses, learned or spontaneous, and they are conditioned by sociohistorical realities. It is difficult to imagine, for example, any feminist reader who could "value" Norman Mailer's judgment in *Advertisements for Myself*, the classic representation of man "thinking through his body":

> I have a terrible confession to make—I have nothing to say about any of the talented women who write today. . . . I can only say that the sniffs I get from the ink of the women are always fey, old-hat . . . too dykily psychotic, crippled, creepish, fashionable, frigid . . . or else bright and still-born. Since I've never been able to read Virginia Woolf, and am sometimes willing to believe it can conceivably be my fault, this verdict may be taken fairly as the twisted tongue of a soured taste, at least by those readers who do not share with me the ground of departure—that a good novelist can do without everything but the remnant of his balls.[18]

Unlike many writers of criticism, Mailer makes his fundamental assumptions explicit. He is not obligated to feign objectivity. The object of his ridicule is viewed similarly by others who might not make such a bold or public declaration but agree with him nonetheless.

Mailer's pronouncement points to the problem in Fish's scheme: the importance placed on persuasion in establishing consensus as to what constitutes our shared assumptions. Fish knows that this is the sticking point (all puns intended), although he has found no way around it. He realizes that standards issue from assumptions that then determine the course of critical debate: "Assumptions do not stand in an independent relationship to verifying procedures, they determine the shape of verifying procedures, and if you want to persuade someone else that he is wrong you must first persuade him to the assumptions within which what you say will be convincing."[19] By extension, assumptions do not exist in an independent relationship to literary judgments, yet few things are harder to change than beliefs forged around such fundamental factors as sex, race, class, and sexual preference, perhaps because these attitudes issue from the critic's personal and sometimes unarticulated (and even unarticulable) belief system. This imaginary exchange between Virginia Woolf and Stanley Fish (it would do no good to talk with Mailer, the spokesman of phallic criticism) throws the problem into relief. Woolf claimed in *A Room of One's Own* that "when a subject is highly controversial—and any question about sex is that—one cannot hope to tell the truth. One can only show how one came to hold whatever opinion one does hold."[20] However, this self-disclosure is precisely what Mailer did in the passage above. Fish and Woolf agree: when the differences are so basic, the arguments go unheard. It is comparable to shouting across the Grand Canyon.

In her paper, "Not-So-Gentle Persuasion," Annette Kolodny stages her own dialogue with Fish on the problem of persuasion. We agree every day, Fish maintains, on what interpretations are acceptable and unacceptable, and likewise, I would assume, on what constitutes "great" literature. He argues for a "limited plurality" of meanings determined by the subcommittees recognized by the reigning literary-critical establishment.[21] But this particular way around the critical impasse of conflicting interpretations returns the feminist critic to the same point of requiring communal legitimization, and this only in terms of the reigning politics of truth: one only gains acceptance and recognition for what the community is willing to accept. In an observation that underscores the essential relationship between feminist literary criticism and the broader goals of a feminist political revolution, Kolodny summarizes the situation as follows: "We have failed to alter the belief system of our profession in such a way as to make others see *as evidence* what it is we feminists are incapable of ignoring as evidence."[22] The more vigorously Fish argues to allay his colleagues' fears of rampant interpretive anarchy and an open admission policy, the more clearly the feminist critic perceives the power held by members of this interpretive community. I see that they are speaking to one another about me; and that they inevitably control the admissibility of facts, texts, and evidence, as well as the norms constitutive of reasonableness in argumentation. Out of a commitment to the illusion of objectivity, they miss an essential distinction that Camus apprehended: "There are crimes of passion and crimes of logic. The boundary between them is not clearly defined."[23]

Fish very cleverly catches us up in his critical net. Like it or not, we all play the game because, for him, there is no other. Even if we reject the rules, we are still participants because the rules themselves include the rejection of the rules—an inauspicious position for those who are not members of the authoritative community. We become a member when the community makes us one, and not necessarily by virtue of how well we perform critical acts. The truth that Fish refuses to disclose is that membership is a privilege (conferred by those in power) rather than a right (earned by skill).

Although Kolodny (and Showalter as well) is certainly correct in her objection that Fish and other contemporary critical theorists continue to focus their attention on the "major" (male) figures of Western culture, Fish's work is useful to feminist critics because he redirects attention from the mystique of the text—from arguments concerning "facts," "truth," "beauty," and "universality"—toward the more political considerations of the ways in which literary value is legislated and culture thereby shaped. Because he speaks as a member of the authoritative community whose arguments in any contest of persuasion are invested with undeniable value, if not validity, he can believe in his own claim that disputes are settled by persuasion, that there is no position of privilege, and that one's arguments will be considered (if not accepted). In contrast, the trespassers find themselves on shifting ground. They are trained on the one hand to construct arguments from textual and contextual evidence, which then have little impact, and on the other, to avoid unseemly debates—in reality the fundamental ones—predicated upon "extra-literary" assumptions concerning the nature of social and political reality, or the sexual politics of literary judgment. Ishmael Reed expresses the outsider's frustration from the viewpoint of the black writer caught in the same system of judgment: "Art is what white people do. All other people are 'propagandists.' "[24] Still, Kolodny insists that feminist criticism should center its concern on effective persuasion: "Our task is to persuade our nonfeminist colleagues of the value and validity of the ideological premises from which our work proceeds. We need to find ways, for example, of putting our nonfeminist colleagues in possession of those assumptions, those interpretive strategies which will make women's texts available to them in the same way they are to us."[25]

This exploration of the background of feminist criticism raises a number of significant concerns. The first of these inheres in the question of persuasion: Is this the direction feminist criticism ought to take? The emphasis on persuasion suggests that we value a desire for membership. In spite of her life-long psychic and artistic struggle against "being despised," Virginia Woolf, like some later feminist critics, was never certain that women should join the authoritative community even if we could: "We have to ask ourselves, here and now, do we wish to join that procession, or don't we? On what terms shall we join that procession? Above all, where is it leading us, the procession of educated men? . . . The questions must be answered; and they are so important that if all the daughters of educated men did nothing, from morning to night, but consider that procession, from every angle, if they did nothing but ponder it and analyse it, and think about it and read about it and pool their thinking and reading, and what they see and what they guess, their time would be better spent than in any other activity now open to them."[26] Woolf has not been the only feminist writer to explore the price of inclusion and the benefits of exclusion, though she has done it with an acute honesty that I will discuss further in chapter six. Inclusion requires participation in the perpetuation of what Michel Foucault aptly terms a " 'regime' of truth."[27] Lillian Smith, whose words formed the basis for Adrienne Rich's later analysis in "Disloyal to Civilization: Feminism, Racism, Gynephobia," elaborates on the situation as follows: "Freud said once that woman is not well acculturated; she is, he stressed, retarded as a civilized person. I think what he mistook for her lack of civilization is woman's lack of *loyalty* to civilization."[28] By virtue of this kind of separateness, women may develop resistances to different ideological positions (segregation for Smith) and freedom from certain behavioral and attitudinal compulsions (war-making for Woolf, racism and heterosexism for Rich and Lorde). In the best instances, a valuable perspective and critique of culture issue from feminist disengagement.

Because of their disloyalty, their positions in the margins, feminist critics challenge the relative homogeneity of male critics whose views center criticism's authoritative communities. The "phallic" critics have produced extremely narrow views of what great literature is and how to interpret it, not so much because they enjoy seeing reflections of themselves and their values in what they praise (though this is partially true), but because they close ranks— through pretenses to equality, objectivity, and universality—in the service of maintaining masculinist values. In terms suggested by Camus, and developed much more extensively by French feminists discussed in later chapters, such a hegemony fosters dissent by employing "a theoretical equality [that] conceals great factual inequalities."[29] The fundamental assumptions underlying judgments are disguised, even from those who adhere to them, and they produce distortions in the act of reading that are replayed in the judgments constructed. Margaret Atwood offers a characteristic description of the woman writer's experience with phallic criticism: "A man who reviewed my *Procedures for Underground* . . . talked about the 'domestic' imagery of the poems, entirely ignoring the fact that seven-eighths of the poems take place outdoors. . . . In this case, the theories of what women ought to be writing about, had intruded very solidly between reader and poems, rendering the poems themselves invisible to him."[30] The effect of such a critical bias is a need to consider

Sexual Politics and Critical Judgment

everything anew, in a complete re-vision of literature from text to interpretive theory. Furthermore, it illustrates the need to persuade nonfeminist readers to revise their basic assumptions about women and women's writing. Feminist critics perform acts of reclamation; like salvage archaeologists, we work back through the texts of different cultures.

By virtue of the masculinist claims to objectivity, literary critics have created the need for a criticism of advocacy, espousing special perspectives based on gender, sexual preference, race, and class. The charge of advocacy, a pejorative term in the academic world, is always leveled at those whose ideological position differs from one's own. The mistake is believing that any criticism is "apolitical" in theory, judgment, or interpretation. Stanley Fish is at least cognizant of the difficulty of persuading critics to change the beliefs that shape their interpretations and values; for after all, at issue is an ideology masked in a critical paradigm. He comments: "It is always possible to entertain beliefs and opinions other than one's own; but that is precisely how they will be seen, as beliefs and opinions *other than one's own*, and therefore as beliefs and opinions that are false, or mistaken, or partial, or immature, or absurd."[31] Fish does not take this reasoning far enough. He clearly perceives the interplay between conflicting structures of belief, but stops short of questioning its implications. At that point, his position of privilege in the authoritative community appears to undercut his sense of urgency.

Even without obstacles to persuasion, feminist criticism remains a monumental undertaking which involves changing the very structure/sex of knowledge. It wants to liberate criticism from what Diana Hume George calls an "operational model that artificially, or even necessarily, dualizes intellectual activity and sexuality,"[32] or to help us see how this model, as Barbara Johnson suggests, reflects one set of fictions inhabiting another. The problem confronting us is both epistemological and political—each term significant and inseparable from the other. For years feminist critics have grappled with this dilemma. On the one hand, we want to believe in that "theoretical equality": our right to earn a place within our interpretive communities and to persuade others of the validity of the feminist project. On the other hand, we fear the capitulation to an oppressive system of values symbolized in terms of the insider/outsider metaphor, as well as the fragmentation from within that could result from a more precise definition and articulation of feminist methodology (an inchoate ideological map that threatens to separate women from men and from the institutions of culture, and in doing so, to separate women from one another).

Recent developments in critical theory hold out the promise of an analysis that, because it has the potential for encompassing the literary, political, and epistemological dimensions of texts, could permit us to address (though not to resolve) these dilemmas more effectively. Deconstructive criticism's interest in meaning, difference, and identity relate directly to some of feminism's most pressing concerns. In the mid-seventies, however, very few feminist critics were sympathetic with the tentative explorations of "difference." Attention to certain constructions of the idea of difference still threatens those who wish to argue for "sameness" in the interest of gaining equality. The rising prominence of post-structuralism has provoked feminists to reconsider our earlier resistance. Elizabeth Abel explains: "The notion of difference has only recently emerged as a focus of feminist criticism. Initially, feminist theorists bolstered claims for equality with claims for similarity." The value she sees in this renewed attention is that it affords "the feminist critic a position closer to the mainstream of critical debate."[33] This strikes me as a weak motive: now through "difference" we are to achieve the illusory sameness and equality. More persuasive reasons than the dream of acceptability need to be offered with respect to the potential value of the concept of "difference" if we are to abandon our former rejection of the concept's figuration. Because of deconstruction's nature and texts (its preoccupation with the "classics" of Western literature and philosophy), feminist critics should engage this current preoccupation cautiously, considering its source and our motives. Certainly, I am not arguing against deconstruction or its interest in difference—indeed, it influences all of the chapters that follow; rather, I am suggesting that feminist critics need to examine carefully the relationship between the goals of both feminism and deconstructive criticism before we link our energies with this other trespasser. In any case, the motive of feminist criticism cannot be acceptance; it must be resistance in the interest of social transformation through interpretation.

Feminist criticism has made some advances in the last decade. In addition to the many new books which have been issued, it is, for example, the subject of graduate courses; convention sessions on the topic offer standing room only, and Jonathan Culler devotes a section to "Reading as a Woman" in his important book, *On Deconstruction*. But it remains as difficult to escape cynicism as to determine its appropriate object. I wonder why we are permitted to do what we do. Fiedler, observing the "ultimate irony" of the situation, asks why members of "the elite guard" have volunteered to entertain this attack on their values: "Can it be because they believe in tolerance more? Or are they, on the off chance that one or more of us dissenters may be right, cannily hedging their bets? Or do they suffer us gladly, knowing that at this point, all dissent, whether populist, feminist, Marxist, or Third World, can be assimilated, neutralized, sterilized. . . ?"[34] Fiedler poses nagging questions that return us to another question of importance to feminist criticism today: Do we want to install feminism at the center of critical debate, and if not, or if so, how can we ever expect to transform assumptions and judgments? Some critics and philosophers do espouse a commitment to change, as Lentricchia has argued. Fish,

Sexual Politics and Critical Judgment

for example, reveals the potential for radical subversion inhabiting his conservativism when he suggests that the critic is not "trapped forever in the categories of understanding at one's disposal (or the categories at whose disposal one is), but that the introduction of new categories or the expansion of old ones to include new (and therefore newly seen) data must always come from the outside or from what is perceived, for a time, to be outside."[35] Still, it is never clear how criticism itself, employing its own favored methodologies and working within its own constraints, ever transforms the "extrinsic" into the "intrinsic," or displaces the opposition of margin and center that confers the power of persuasion.

Some proponents of post-structuralism, engaged in their own attack on the ideological character of discourse, maintain that criticism has finally freed itself of its orientation toward objectivity and universality. It is tempting to regard the post-structuralist position as pervasive, characteristic of contemporary criticism. And yet, far from representing critical activity today, post-structuralists have made only a beginning in their attack on the historically rooted traditions of criticism. In his discussion "Conventional Conflicts," Hayden White suggests the complexity of efforts to reform the theory and practice of criticism: "Any appeal to the 'interpretive community' must fail for the more fundamental reason that there is no such thing as *the* interpretive community but rather a hierarchy of such communities, each with its own conventions and all more or less antagonistic to the rest."[36] White's observation discloses the inherent limitation of basing revisionary efforts on a monolithic approach to the critical community. His point further reinforces the view that the only real common denominator underlying today's various interpretive schools is the white patriarchal substructure of the discipline of criticism as a whole. The political nature of the struggle is further heightened when coupled with the realization that, as White puts it, "it is the privilege of devotees of dominant conventions either to pay attention or not to any new practice appearing on the horizon of a discipline."[37] Just as the masters are never obliged to learn the language of the slaves, the hierarchies within our critical communities will continue to resist criticism by feminists, in addition to that of gays, blacks, and Marxists (who may or may not be feminists), as long as the power/knowledge configurations upon which the establishment rests remain undisturbed.

Nonetheless, there is a certain hope that can be seen in post-structuralism's potential to appeal to those critics (the radicals named above) harboring a critique of criticism's cultural hegemony. The records of the new and newly seen are accumulating in a swiftly mounting challenge to the old structures of knowledge. As Foucault suggests in *Power/Knowledge*, "The essential political problem for the intellectual is . . . that of ascertaining the possibility of constituting a new politics of truth. The problem is not changing people's consciousnesses—or what's in their heads—but the political, economic, institutional régime of the production of truth."[38] In other words, prevailing paradigms reflect and are reflected in the current regime of truth. Truth holds no independent relationship to systems of power. It results from or is coincident with the very power that inhabits knowledge itself. Thus, our effort as feminist critics necessarily becomes highly political when approaching a paradigm from the outside. Foucault explains, "It's not a matter of emancipating truth from every system of power (which would be a chimera, for truth is already power) but of detaching the power of truth from the forms of hegemony, social, economic and cultural, within which it operates at the present time."[39] Foucault's observation speaks directly to those functioning on the margins of the literary critical establishment. It is clear that those excluded from the terms of truth are the very ones who perceive the inadequacies of the paradigm and experience the sense of urgency required to address it. A diffusion of the experience of discontinuity, beyond the ring of outsiders/trespassers, is needed before significant changes can occur. Such a generalized discomfort—the guilt or uncertainty that includes at least one novel by a woman in a course or invites feminist and other minority critics to the English Institute—marks a transitional phase toward paradigm revolution.

It has never been the obligation of literary critics, masked by the pretense of objectivity, to explicate the political origins and implications of their judgments. Feminist critics must continue to develop strategies that question vigorously the methods and techniques of the inherited critical tradition. Fish, for example, represents the limits of the tradition. In his notion of the interpretive (authoritative) community, he proffers equality: literature is an open system, admitting any text (within reason); variations in interpretation are permitted (within reason); and persuasion is the means by which (reasonable) critics establish consensus. When he reinvests the authority for determining the limits of the reasonable in the profession as it is now constituted, Fish reinscribes the politics of exclusion that he might have undone by defining literature as an open category and (dis)locating the interpretive power/knowledge relationship. But inherent in Fish's approach is the fact that the right to reason and the power of determination are located where power and reason have always rested in Western civilization—within the community of elite white men. He thereby preserves theoretical access at the expense of actual change. It makes sense to suspect, as Marxist critics have always noted from their vantage point, that our conceptual frameworks mirror ideology. The principle task of feminist criticism, in providing a necessary re-vision of the politics of "truth," is to make its own ideology explicit. If we seek to transform the structures of authority, we must first name them, and in doing so, unmask and expose them for all to see. Likewise, we should be suspicious of gaining our "equality" within an undisturbed hierarchical system. The future of feminist criticism rests on defying the oppositional logic currently sustaining the concept of privilege. As we forge a new criticism, our theories and assumptions must stay clear of a hegemonic role reversal that results in an infinite series of upended oppositions such as male/female, insider/outsider and center/margin, where the second term simply replaces the first in an unending regression within an oppressive economy of Sameness. Because of the language within which we think and speak, we inevitably inscribe the tension of the member who is not, the outsider who is not, implicating ourselves as we attempt to extricate ourselves, and vice versa.

Luce Irigaray warns us of the failure to resist this phallocentric system that Culler describes as the consolidation of "an interest in patriarchal authority, unity of meaning, and certainty of origin."[40] Women, she argues, will simply tell each other the same story that men have told or told about them for centuries.[41] Phallocentrism, like any system, is driven by the desire to perpetuate itself. By fulfilling its prescription, by speaking as we are required to speak, we contribute to our own oppression. The transformation of literature and criticism as cultural institutions demands a language of defiance rather than the silent or unquestioning mimetic complicity expected of us in order to sustain phallocentrism. If it is any good, feminist criticism, all feminist writing, and from my view all criticism, is guaranteed to offend the mighty. Its contrariness is essential to its value, a barometer of its ultimate effectiveness. A new politics, based not on negation but on the positive deconstruction and reconstruction of woman through the efforts of feminist practitioners, should change theory as well as praxis. My concern in the following chapters is how critical theory, and particularly deconstruction, can clarify, obstruct, and facilitate this project, and how feminist criticism can challenge and politicize the enterprise of critical theory.

Having reached the crossroad again, I return to the epigraphs. We are trespassing and creating our own way, as Woolf advises. The territory grows more certain and the journey more urgent when the assumptions masking the political within the theoretical are exposed—the case of Woolf versus Fish. The second epigraph talks about the process of profound change in scientific knowledge, other fictions fused with power. Max Planck's remark could be taken as a comment on the questions of persuasion and revolution posed repeatedly in this chapter but never answered. These epigraphs that figure fearless trailblazing toward a new, unspecified truth might better serve as postscripts, reminders of what is required of us in the work ahead.

CHAPTER 2

SIGNS OF UNDECIDABILITY

RECONSIDERING THE STORIES OF MARY WILKINS FREEMAN

It is not, in the final analysis, what you don't know that can or cannot hurt you. It is what you don't know you don't know that spins out and entangles "that perpetual error we call life."

—Barbara Johnson, *The Critical Difference*

Ourself behind ourself, concealed—
should startle most—

—Emily Dickinson, "One need not be a Chamber. . . ."

The most fortunate circumstance of women's writing in the western world has been that its production—though ignored, devalued, suppressed, or misrepresented—could never be completely extinguished. Women could be denied education, publication, and critical recognition, but as Woolf keenly observed, ink and paper were the cheapest, most readily available tools for the practice of one's trade. She immediately detected this essential feature of the "profession of literature": "There is no head of the profession; no Lord Chancellor . . . no official body with the power to lay down rules and enforce them. We cannot debar women from the use of libraries; or forbid them to buy ink and paper; or rule that metaphors shall only be used by one sex, as the male only in art schools was allowed to study from the nude; or rule that rhyme shall be used by one sex only as the male only in Academies of music was allowed to play in orchestras."[1] Women could not be programmed or policed thoroughly enough to stop their literary activity. We have been saved by the very nature of the craft: the act of writing is solitary, accessible to almost anyone who is literate (still a fact of its elitism), and as such the institution of literature admits its own subversion.

Recent developments in critical strategies for approaching texts and new understandings of how the patriarchal regime of truth plays within criticism equip us for the defensive, resistant re-reading of women's writing that critics like Annette Kolodny and Judith Fetterley urge us to undertake. By exposing the masculinist misreadings upon which criticism has relied, we can begin to understand more specifically what it means for women writers to become feminist writers. The case of the New England local colorist Mary Wilkins Freeman, who published from 1881 to 1918, illustrates a transitional phase when the interplay of feminism and antifeminism are textually inscribed, and responses to her work demonstrate how this struggle is both suppressed and simplified through misreading.

Although she was one of the women writers who managed to "ascend" to the novel, Freeman's twelve volumes of short stories are of particular interest because they present works that typify the writing done by women during the reign of the local color tradition in the late nineteenth and early twentieth centuries. Just as certain genres are undervalued, so are some literary historical periods—perhaps, in the case of the local color tradition, because of the predominance of the short story genre, or even because so many women wrote and published at the time. One of the many local colorists whose works have been undervalued and even misrepresented, Freeman gives us more than most critics after William Dean Howells have led us to believe. Few writers of equivalent, albeit modest, stature have elicited so many erroneous, personal attacks masquerading as literary criticism. She deserves renewed and careful consideration.

Crossing the Double-Cross

Whether through malice or narrowness of view, traditional (masculinist) critics have interpreted Freeman's work as though she structured a determinate and decidedly negative view of her characters, their relationships, and settings. They feel the need to pass judgment on these obscure women struggling with their relationships to the social institutions that attempt to command their loyalties. I would like to propose another view of Freeman's response to the content of her work: her own experience of sexual politics led her to represent the interplay of forces through undecidable or purposefully "unreadable" images that both affirm and negate, sometimes alternately and at other times simultaneously, but always resisting a determination of the text's meaning. A strong argument can be made for Freeman's strategic approach to these complexities and for her persistent refusal to inscribe within her fiction the simple or singular judgment of her female characters that her role as a writer within her sociohistorical context might have dictated and that later critics seem to want. These signs of undecidability, then, can be read as demonstrations of how the author reflects the conscious and unconscious experiences of her personal inner life and her perception of the public expectations for women in society; their differential treatment, privilege, and status, as presented in the external world; and the differences between the social codes for women and for writers. These discrepancies form the site of more or less conscious tension, alienation, and dissonance, creating a break within an otherwise self-perpetuating, self-confirming system.

It is easy to take my point to mean "ambivalence" on Freeman's part, and doubtless some psycho-social dynamic informs the author's unsettling production. If readers sum up and settle her position again, even in the self-contradictory term "ambivalence," they attempt to close the textual gaps, thereby denying the ambiguities of language and reducing the infinite play of signification, by substituting another form of consistent (insistent) narrative authority. With respect to such discursive conflicts as we find in Freeman, Paul de Man notes: "No contradiction or dialectical movement could develop because a fundamental difference in the level of explicitness prevented both statements from meeting on a common level of discourse; the one always lays hidden within the other as the seen lies hidden within a shadow, or truth within error."[2] In the record of language proceeding from conflicting codes (cultural and literary, personal and social, private and public), Freeman allows us to represent the problematics of gender in its complexity rather than through a reductive, controlling simplicity.

Freeman's undecidable or unreadable texts demand that we read and re-read or "write" as we produce her texts and ours. Explaining Barthes' distinction between the readerly and writerly text, Barbara Johnson remarks: "The readerly is defined as a product consumed by the reader; the writerly is a process of production in which the reader becomes a producer; it is 'ourselves writing.' The readerly is constrained by considerations of representation: it is irreversible, 'natural,' decidable, continuous, totalizable, and unified into a coherent whole based on the signified. The writerly is infinitely plural and open to the free play of signifiers and of difference, unconstrained by representative considerations, and transgressive of any desire for decidable, unified totalized meaning."[3] Read from this perspective, Freeman's writerly texts contain the strongest arguments against the positions they attempt to take. The same can be said of the texts her critics make.

In view of her own departure from conventional role expectations and of the changing cultural norms for women, Freeman creates a more than 'realistic' scene by producing irreconcilable and unresolvable oscillations between the positive and negative features of women's lives in the New England villages of the period. By means of this effect, she presents the impossibility of fixing the text's meaning according to prescribed gender role and gives us an allegory for reading new possibilities for women. In other words, she simultaneously undermines and develops, (dis)articulating the roles of the period. Thus, Freeman's questioning of her milieu's representation of women's sexual decidability offers us a bridge between women's writing of the past and feminist texts today.

As is often the case, a review of the major critical appraisals Freeman has received demonstrates the course of significant misunderstandings. There are at present two book-length critical works on Freeman—Edward Foster's *Mary E. Wilkins Freeman* and Perry D. Westbrook's *Mary Wilkins Freeman*— and a number of commentaries and articles, the most important among them by Ann Douglas Wood, Susan Toth, Alice Brand, Leah Blatt Glasser and Josephine Donovan.[4] Both Foster and Westbrook assume a conventional view of the local color genre and Freeman's preoccupations as a writer working in that mode. Foster's overview of the author's relationship to place and time situates her between the Puritan village as it survived in Randolph, with its rigid, decaying environment, and the idealistic milieu issuing from the Concord community. As the first to construct a major bio-critical work, Foster confronts significant difficulties that shape his interpretation and the readings of many critics after him.

In his determination to produce a chronicle of the relationship between Freeman's life and works, Foster relies on the comments of friends, neighbors, and only a few scraps of concrete written evidence in the form of letters and essays. The absence of concrete evidence is a common problem for biographers of women writers, including those writing of major as well as minor figures. The manuscript material Foster cites is of considerable value, as is the basic biographical chronology that he manages to reconstruct. Still, the skeletal nature of this outline frequently requires his inventiveness, through which he constructs his subject according to his image of Freeman-as-woman. The problem of Freeman's late marriage at forty-eight plagues him from the outset. When Freeman returned from Mount Holyoke at nineteen, Foster explains that family finances necessitated that she marry soon: "It was not that Miss Wilkins disliked young men in general; she thought and dreamed in a normally romantic way. It was that she could not imagine herself falling in love with any of the boys who came her way in Brattleboro; they seemed to her dull, clumsy, self-conscious, and appallingly young. It was fun for her to sit demurely and let them babble while she peered beneath the youthful swagger; she could not take them seriously."[5] And a variation on the theme later in Freeman's life: "She was devoted to her friend [Mary John Wales], but was she quite ready to put aside all thought of marriage? That must have been the question she was asking, for by this time she was forty-five."[6] More serious problems issue from the way Foster reads Freeman's characters through his construction of the author's attitudes. Depicting Freeman, perhaps correctly, as a woman who was fiercely uncertain in her judgment of the characters in her stories, the villages where the stories are set, and the relationships between female and male characters, Foster broaches the essential question: Was she or wasn't she ambivalent about her subjects? But in his eagerness to advance his answer, he betrays the writer and her works.

Perhaps the most damaging refrain in Foster's book, anticipating Marder's view of Woolf's *Three Guineas*, is his characterization of Freeman as a neurotic woman: "She was at once within and outside the spirit of the culture from which she drew her themes and characters; she loved—and almost hated the people of whom she wrote. Out of this partially neurotic ambivalence comes much of her intensity and her deepest insight into her characters."[7] In this description, it is Freeman's feminism, her double-edged view of sexual politics, combined with Foster's own judgment of her characters that earns her the label of "neurotic." Foster's misreading stems from the conflicting codes inscribed in her texts and his desire to fix Freeman's position on the basis of gender-biased judgments concerning her life and relationships as elaborated in the biographical fiction he creates in order to situate and control his subject. Suffering not so much from neurotic ambivalence as multiplicity of view, Freeman sees a complex realism in the village's prescribed conventions and alternative possibilities that are not without cause or consequence. Foster's position creates a lasting critical problem, reinforced by his easy identification of Freeman herself with the first-person narrative voice in "The Shrew," an unpublished manuscript fragment. The unfinished work opens as follows: " 'I am a rebel and what is worse a rebel against the Over-government of all creation. . . . I even dare to think that, infinitesimal as I am . . . I, through my rebellion, have power. All negation has power. I, Jane Lenox, spinster, as they would have designated me a century ago, living quietly, and apparently harmlessly in the old Lennox homestead in Baywater, am a power.' "[8] Foster calls the fragment a "story," but echoing the narrator's words, he ends his discussion by asking: "Was Miss Wilkins indeed a 'monster'?"[9] In the absence of substantial autobiographical evidence, Foster's general propensity for seeing Freeman's fiction as "lightly disguised" autobiography, read as a "man" reads a "woman," creates especial problems for later critics. For example, Wood, spinning her own fiction, refers to this same fragment which seems to her "almost like a witch's confession. . . . Witches were popularly supposed to have the power to blight life, and this power, Freeman, who had lost a lover, a sister, a mother and a father within a short space of time in her young womanhood, must surely have felt was hers."[10] Witches also have other power; they are power—a truth hidden in the shadow of Wood's text which suggests itself as her text tries to deny it. Wood's interpretation suggests how Foster's view, when combined with the attendant misreadings of some of the texts, fixes Freeman's place as one of New England's large cast of "striving neurotics."[11] Through his approach to the undecidability inherent in Freeman's texts, Foster poses lasting critical problems that create a tradition of (mis)interpretation that later feminist critics seek to supplant but, in their own singlemindedness, also tend to perpetuate.

While critics after Foster contribute to our understanding of Freeman's works, the unquestioned allegiance some hold to a particular view of the author herself or to their own understanding of women's roles (feminist and nonfeminist) determine their readings of her work. Deriving his biographical perspective from Foster, Westbrook frequently compares Freeman to the "old maids" and "spinsters" of her fiction. Wood characterizes the local colorists as displaying "what seems to a modern observer a nearly neurotic fixation on one or both of their parents"; although she lists Freeman among these, she cites neither example nor source for her asssertion.[12] Wood depicts local color writers as reflecting "attenuation, even impoverishment" in their lives, careers, and fiction.[13] (I prefer to see some of them in Willa Cather's terms: "Miss Jewett wrote of the people who grew out of the soil and the life of the country near her heart, not about exceptional individuals at war with their environment. This was not a creed with her, but an instinctive preference. She once laughingly told me that her head was full of dear old houses and dear old women, and that when an old house and an old woman came together in her brain with a click, she knew that a story was under way."[14])

An examination of Foster's interpretation of "A New England Nun," a reading that remains largely unqualified or uncontested, will illustrate my point. Foster characterizes Louisa Ellis's existence as a "neatly sterile design for living" and describes the story as "Miss Wilkins' definitive study of the New England spinster."[15] He refuses in this case, however, to equate the author with her character whom he believes, out of his own predilection, she "roundly condemned," concluding, rather, that "in 'A New England Nun,' she exorcised an image of atrophy which may have been deeply disturbing."[16] All of the critics writing after Foster—with the exception of Susan Toth, who doesn't cite his work at all, and Michele Clark and Josephine Donovan, who make reference to it but employ an exclusively feminist optic—rely on his basic characterization of Freeman's life and values. Larzer Ziff, in *The American 1890s*, also mentions "A New England Nun," advancing the view that Freeman "clearly presents the single state as a frustrated existence, since in it a woman is deprived of what Mrs. Freeman considers to be her birthright—a man."[17]

Freeman's own staunch indeterminacy of view creates these interpretive problems. In *Blindness and Insight*, Paul de Man explains how the text, any text, stages "the necessity of its own misreading": "It knows and asserts that it will be misunderstood. It tells the story, the allegory of its misunderstanding: the necessary degradation of melody into harmony, of language into painting, of the language of passion into the language of need, of metaphor into literal meaning. In accordance with its own language, it can only tell this story as a fiction, knowing full well that the fiction will be taken for fact and the fact for fiction; such is the necessarily ambivalent nature of literary language."[18] Taking Freeman's best known story, "A New England Nun," as a case in point, I want to illustrate the author's refusal to center her work in the value system of her contemporaries, electing instead to display the shadows of her own doubt, foreshadowings of feminist deconstructions of the sexual politic, through the imagery she employs and the characters she draws. Her refusal to judge— women, the aged, the poor, and the culture of New England villages—renders her meaning "unreadable." In the case of Louisa Ellis, Freeman constructs the reflection of possibility in women's roles as a result of indeterminacy or the impossibility of determining an appropriate role or meaning for women's experience (and hence, the meaning of her own fiction).

Critics, feminist and nonfeminist alike, who make the choice the author refuses to make by determining the indeterminate, limit the richness of the text and its value to later readers. Only Leah Glasser and Josephine Donovan, through their feminist views, resist this arbitrarily delimiting move. It is as though most critics fear the possibilities embedded in the text's complexity, in its contrariness that, when pushed to the extreme, challenges the phallocentric economy in which the story and its readers are situated. The kind of reading or interpretation one gives to the text depends ultimately upon which imagistic strain the reader takes most seriously. In effect, the meaning is created by the reader as much or more than it is by the writer or the text. "Such unreadability," Jonathan Culler argues, "does not result simply from a central ambiguity or choice but from the way in which the system of values in the text both urges choice and prevents that choice from being made."[19] Furthermore, if

Freeman passes judgment on her characters, she simultaneously judges herself: by refusing their choices, she risks restricting her own.

Our knowledge of Louisa Ellis begins with the story's title, in which the author calls her "A New England Nun," but the significance of that superficially pejorative designation remains to be shown in the working out of the fiction itself. Louisa is suspended between states: solitude and marriage, control and chaos, harmony and disorder. We enter the story following Louisa's fourteen-year separation from her betrothed, Joe Daggett, and just before their subsequently resumed courtship. When she is alone, Louisa's internal and external worlds are in harmony: "There seemed to be a gentle stir arising over everything for the mere sake of subsidence—a very premonition of rest and hush and night."[20] This stir is also the stirring action of the narrative, a premonition of peace that evokes the possibility of its disturbance.

Louisa's life and house are in order. The house doesn't seem to be the "rocklike prison" or "claustrophobic trap" of Wood's description; perhaps it is, in this case, "a frail refuge from a world more frightening than any prison."[21] Freeman shows us something more like Jewett's idea of a house in the solitary, but pleasant and colorful, surroundings of her character's daily activities. The author's description is not without its negative associations: Louisa looks older than she is, her motions are slow and deliberate, her routines have no apparent meaning or value, except to the character herself. Freeman tells several stories and leaves the ultimate interpretation to her readers. When Joe enters, he brings disorder to the house, to the canary in its cage (doubtless an analogue to Louisa), and to Louisa. He has "heavy feet" and an "uneasiness" about him, but despite the comic disarray he occasions, one suspects Joe's natural ease in his disdain for rigidity, especially when we encounter him later in another context. In Louisa's presence, however, "he was afraid to stir lest he should put a clumsy foot or hand through the fairy web, and he had always the consciousness that Louisa was watching fearfully lest he should" (p. 84). Through the juxtaposition of Louisa and Joe, Freeman thematizes difference, rematerializing the story's opening in another register: "It was late in the afternoon, and the light was waning. There was a difference in the look of the tree shadows out in the yard" (p. 79).

The reader soon learns that Louisa set out on this unlikely course toward marriage through "falling into the natural drift of girlhood," from which perspective she regarded marriage "as a reasonable feature and a probable desirability of life" (p. 86). With gentle encouragement from her mother, Lousia unhesitatingly fulfills her socially prescribed role by accepting Joe's proposal of engagement and marriage. Although Joe leaves for fourteen years in order to secure his fortune, Louisa has always envisioned marriage as the "inevitable conclusion of things." Freeman, however, refuses to subscribe to any such inevitability. As Louisa projects her marriage "so far in the future that it was almost equal to placing it over the boundaries of another life" (p. 86), Freeman, in fact, projects it beyond the boundaries of her story, thereby subverting the socially desired outcome and the power of marriage as a social institution.

During Joe's absence, Lousia becomes a woman, free from the control of her own mother. She determines an alternative course. Her "feet had turned into a path, smooth maybe under a calm, serene sky, but so straight and unswerving that it could only meet a check at her grave, and so narrow that there was no room for any one at her side" (pp. 85–86). The author preserves her character's way of life, forestalling Louisa's need to leave "her neat maidenly possessions" in order to merge her home with her betrothed's old family homestead. On the brink of consigning Louisa to life with Joe and his aged mother, a "domineering, shrewd old matron" (p. 88), Freeman stages a break from tradition and extends Louisa's alternative course. She saves both of her characters from the mutually disturbing fate of making a future with one another. Taking a moonlight stroll one night, Louisa overhears Joe's declaration of love to another woman, Lily Dyer, and his simultaneous vow to honor his commitment to Louisa. When, through Louisa's agency, each liberates the other from the determined course, they discover more tenderness for each other than they had experienced before. Freed from the arbitrariness of social prescription, they achieve a new authenticity of affection. That night, Louisa "wept a little" (p. 96); whether these are tears of sorrow or relief, Freeman refuses to disclose. In the morning, the character awakens feeling "like a queen," reigning undisturbed over her peaceful domain with no apparent regrets.

In her concluding passages, Freeman offers the following summary: "If Louisa Ellis had sold her birthright she did not know it, the taste of the pottage was so delicious, and had been her sole satisfaction for so long. Serenity and placid narrowness had become to her as the birthright itself" (pp. 96–97). Confronting the assertion of what Louisa did not know, readers must wonder what they themselves in fact know. Did the character sell her birthright to marriage and a man? Meaning pivots on the initial word: "If. . . ." There is not enough, or perhaps there is too much here to know. In the story's final sentences, Freeman fuses the imagistic and symbolic strains—the rosary of the nun and the harmony of the external world set "right" again, that is, under Louisa's control: "She gazed ahead through a long reach of future days strung together like pearls in a rosary, every one like the others, and all smooth and flawless and innocent, and her heart went up in thankfulness. Outside was the fervid summer afternoon; the air filled with the sounds of the busy harvest of men and birds and bees; there were halloos, metallic clatterings, sweet calls, and long hummings. Louisa sat, prayerfully numbering her days, like an uncloistered nun" (p. 97). The ending satisfies us; it is neat, like Louisa's life. But what judgment is Freeman making? What story is she telling? Is it that classic indictment of the New England spinster for which the author is best known? I don't believe it is so simple.

An examination of the text itself reveals the sense in which all readers are only partially attentive and fundamentally misled if they choose to read the story as a tale of either the "profound disillusionment and hostility" in the "counterfeit" and "self-mutilative" lives of Freeman's characters like Louisa,[22] or "the positive drive towards . . . fulfillment of what they believe to be their own true selves . . . a measure of individual freedom."[23] Westbrook sees a mitigating aspect to Louisa's gesture, but cannot resist invoking the old categories: "But Louisa, realistically assessing the ingredients of her own and the others' happiness, emerges as the strongest of the trio, pitiable though the barrenness of her own existence may be. Louisa has allowed her life to slip into paralysis over a period of fifteen years; for this she is culpable and for this she pays. As things now are, she will be happier, or less miserable, single than married. . . ."[24] Clark takes a more judicious course by focusing on Freeman's ability "to empathize with" and "to understand how a woman's character adapted to being without a man, because *she* was learning to adapt."[25] And Donovan reads Freeman's ambivalence in the price Louisa pays for order and control: "eternal restriction to a limited sphere."[26]

Indirectly, Freeman discloses her level of empathy with Louisa in a letter written to Marian Allen in 1907. Having spent the summer supervising the construction of her new house, Freeman says: "Sometimes I wish I could have a little toy house, in which I could do just as I pleased, cook a meal if I wanted to, and fuss around generally. . . . If I had my little toy house nobody could say anything, and if I get what I may for this serial [*The Shoulders of Atlas*] I don't know but I shall have it."[27] The resemblance between Freeman's toy house and Louisa's (as well as Edna's in *The Awakening*) is provocative, the resonances of desire and value deep enough—inhabiting Foster's own text—to unsettle his one-dimensional view of the author's story. Is she presenting an image of ordered meaninglessness, sterility, and sublimation? Is she creating a version of woman's assertion of control, independence, and autonomy? Is there something in both views, or in the difference between or within them?

By expanding my consideration to include other critics and stories, I would like to explore additional ways in which Freeman's texts stage the drama of critical (mis)readings. I have chosen to focus on three other stories, from among many, which call into question Freeman's attitudes toward female characters confronting social expectations. Alice Glarden Brand selects "A Conflict Ended" to illustrate her thesis concerning Freeman's misanthropy: "Freeman's stories were . . . an exposé of contempt for men's impotence, incompetence, and aggression and for women's passivity, dependence, and rage."[28] Susan Toth uses "Arethusa" to demonstrate that many of Freeman's critically neglected stories explore the "urge toward self-fulfillment and . . . insist upon an individual's inviolable right to his [*sic*] own personality."[29] And, finally, I choose "The Revolt of 'Mother,'" instructive because its reception caused Freeman later to deny her defiance and her text's artistic integrity.

In "A Conflict Ended," Freeman creates at least three stories—two parallel, interactive tales that explore the difference between men and women, and a third story (or is it the only one?) that contains the interplay of the two. One strand follows Esther Barney and Marcus Woodman, lovers whose relationship is never consummated because it remains frozen in a contest of will between the two of them and between Marcus and the new minister; both standoffs are further circumscribed in a shadowy projection of the townspeople's attitude. The second strand explores the relationship between younger lovers, George and Margy, who are similarly arrested by the demand that George's mother be housed with them. These two stories lead us to ask whether or not Margy and George are simply enacting an inevitable recapitulation of the older lovers' earlier fate. Through these two narrative strands, Freeman poses the dilemma of relationships between men and women by exposing the difference between relationships and locating it within individuals in relationship.

Brand needs to claim that the men Freeman creates are impotent and the women passive. Marcus, who is more fully characterized than George, is paralyzed by the force of his will. An old feud concerning the selection of a new minister with a different approach to doctrine results in Marcus's decision never to set foot in the church. He has spent ten years on the front steps as a gesture of his own rigid determination. While his is a religious dispute dignified by New England history, Marcus's behavior finally entraps him; resistance becomes a way of life, perpetuating itself beyond the point of sense and affection. Marcus resigns his prospective bride, personal happiness, and community standing as long as he allows his will to determine his behavior. Esther also refuses compromise—she is afraid to wed the town's laughing stock. In the other pair, Margy, determined not to live with George's old, domineering mother, resigns her own lover rather than compromise. George, similarly, remains singlemindedly committed to inflicting his mother on his prospective bride (though his position is the most highly sanctioned social responsibility in the story).

Through her interpretation, Brand simplifies these contests, defusing their moral value by undoing the tensions inherent within and between them. Without rationale, she represents Marcus's principled stand as "consummate mulishness" and describes his character as one of "stubborn blandness or ignorant indignation," while she views Margy's ultimate capitulation to her lover's desire as an outrageous compromise "in order to see the young heroine achieve the exalted state of matrimony." She describes marriage for Marcus as "the ultimate punishment for his impotence." Esther, whom Brand characterizes as calculating and full of guile, is motivated exclusively by her "nagging sense of the social premium on marriage."[30] Freeman provides Esther with a more complex decision, which Brand might have seen paralleled in a different reading of Louisa's circumstance: "She was more fixed in the peace and pride of her old-maidenhood than she had realized, and was more shy of disturbing it. Her comfortable meals, her tidy housekeeping, and her prosperous work had become such sources of satisfaction to her that she was almost wedded to them, and jealous of any interference."[31] Exploring the tensions between autonomy and compromise, Freeman places a certain value on these acts of will; without them life and character would be bland, unprincipled.

Like all of us, Brand is blind to the inconsistency inhabiting her own judgment: Marcus cannot be condemned for adhering to his willfulness and Margy castigated for abandoning hers. Freeman plays off these parallels to force the larger, more complex issue of the relationship between individual will and human affection. The older characters represent the extreme fate of those who confuse what they think they have to do, and what others expect them to do, with what they really want. Esther's description of Marcus illustrates this view: " 'No, he ain't crazy; he's got too much will for his common sense, that's all, and the will teeters the sense a little too far into the air. I see all through it from the beginning. I could read Marcus Woodman jest like a book' " (p. 326). The reader too reads Marcus like a book, though his contrariness makes the reading difficult.

As we have seen in "A New England Nun," Freeman has no compulsion to resolve conflicts or to valorize marriage. Each of her characters in "A Conflict Ended" sees marriage for love as a prerequisite for personal happiness but loses sight of its importance when it is complicated by an act of will. Margy's ability to weigh what she really wants against everything else undoes the conflict between herself and George, and ultimately frees Esther and Marcus as well. Freeman gives Margy her reward—George's mother goes to live with his brother—the author's way of suggesting that Margy has done what was needed to construct a positive relationship.

The writer frees the past from its paralysis and projects a future, not without conflict since tensions recapitulate themselves, but with the capacity for human resolution. Thus, she grants Marcus "the grand mien of a conqueror" as he mounts the steps to enter the church: "He trembled so that the bystanders noticed it. He actually leaned over toward his old seat as if wire ropes were pulling him down upon it. Then he stood up straight, like a man, and walked through the church door with his wife" (pp. 334–35). Here the tensions in content and form snap as Freeman resolves her narrative in a few closing sentences. A reading such as this, which attributes some integrity to the characters' actions, calls into question Brand's conclusions concerning Freeman's misanthropy and cynicism. It is no longer possible to view the women as "lemmings, invariably committing some form of suicide at the hands of men," or as people without "life-affirming experiences . . . inexorably drawn to stasis within predatory or parasitic relationships."[32] The characters are characters in a book, whose life stories play out fictional struggles for us to interpret as we can, reading their drama within ours.

To extend the scope of my discussion, I want to supplement Brand's view with Susan Toth's antithetical position, which she presents through the little discussed "Arethusa." Freeman bases this tale on the mythic story of the river god Alpheus and his beloved, the nymph Arethusa, whose name was taken for the rare, spring-blooming wild orchid. Freeman writes at the outset: "But it is seldom that any man sees the flower arethusa, for she comes rarely to secluded places, and blooms to herself. . . . She is the maiden."[33] Against this backdrop, Freeman draws obvious parallels between the etiology of arethusa provided in the tale of the nymph and water god and the story of the shy country maiden Lucy Greenleaf and her suitor Edson Abbott.

Lucy's character presents no model of strength for emulation. The small, delicate Lucy is as ethereal as the flower and the mythic prototype to which the author links her: "Everything about the girl except her hair seemed fluttering and blowing. She wore ruffled garments of thin fabrics, and she walked swiftly with a curious movement of her delicate shoulder-blades, almost as if they were propelling her like wings" (p. 148). Lucy has almost no corporeality. An ephemeral, gauze-like presence, with a spiritual rather than a physical reality—if she has any reality at all—Lucy spends most of the story in flight: "She half amused, half terrified herself with the sound of imaginary footsteps behind her. When she reached the green marsh, she felt safe, both from real and imaginary pursuers" (p. 150). She acquiesces to others and to life itself, with no more interest in the realities of daily life than the marsh orchid. She insists correctly that the flower should not be picked, for it would die. The reader cannot escape the fear that someone will inadvertently "pick" Lucy, reaping analogous mortal consequences because of the identification between character and flower (recalling the dying women of Hawthorne's allegorical tales). The feeling is reinforced by the belief that marriage is as inappropriate for Lucy as it was for Artemis' follower Arethusa.

Freeman draws Lucy in strict contrast to her mother, "a farmer's widow, carrying on a great farm with a staff of hired men and a farmer. She was shrewd and emulative, with a steady eye and ready elbow for her place in the ranks" (p. 149). Mrs. Greenleaf's love for her daughter creates a fragile bridge between these very different women and forms Lucy's fundamental link to reality—a less subtle version of the relationships Hurston examines in *Their Eyes Were Watching God* or Marilynne Robinson constructs in *Housekeeping*.

In Freeman's story, the mother's principle task is to transfer her protective function to a husband. Mrs. Greenleaf's view of marriage, which she shares with Sarah Penn, is precisely what we might expect of someone in her situation: "This woman . . . had been insensibly trained by all her circumstances of life to regard a husband like rain in its season, or war, or a full harvest, or an epidemic, something to be accepted without question if offered, whether good or bad, as sent by the will of the Lord, and who had herself promptly accepted a man with whom she was not in love, without the least hesitation, and lived as happily as it was in her nature to live ever after" (p. 153). However, her limitations are tempered by the pragmatic anxiety that a caretaker must be found for her unworldly daughter.

What makes this story work is not so much the elusive, unchanging Lucy—who doesn't like men, wishes to live with her mother forever, and believes God will take care of her—but the genuine affection of Mrs. Greenleaf and the sensitive perseverance of Edson Abbot, who represents Freeman's ideal male. Mrs. Greenleaf is not one of the mothers Donovan describes, who "are trying to keep their daughters 'home,' in a female world."[34] Edson sees Lucy as a challenge, abandoned by other men in the village because of her strangeness, and he assumes the role played by Margy in the previous story. He is flexible, understanding, and certain in his knowledge of what it is he wants for himself. He pursues his goal of marriage with diplomacy, courting Lucy as one would a wild, timid animal, humoring her despite her peculiarities. Exercising complete restraint, "he could always keep a straight course on the road to his own desires" (p. 159).

To disturb the reading of "Arethusa" as a heterosexist tale, in which the man is motivated by his desire to bring the "wild," free female into his sphere of control, to civilize her, Freeman reinforces the positive aspect of Lucy's betrothal and impending marriage. In this, the author grants more value to compromise than Toth can afford to admit. Lucy benefits from her relationship with Edson, becoming more clever and functional: "She seemed to take a certain pleasure in her new tasks, and she thrived under them. She grew stouter; her cheeks had a more fixed color" (p. 163). The results are unquestionably felicitous. Her character is not transformed substantially, however, as Lucy precipitates a crisis by choosing the moment of her wedding to search the swamp for arethusa. Gestures such as this in Freeman's fiction challenge Donovan's general observation that "Mary E. Wilkins seems to have imbibed a moral atmosphere which assumes the male prerogative."[35] Rather, the author offers a resolution that, by retaining its own complexity, appears to compromise no one. Edson gets his bride, Mrs. Greenleaf provides for her daughter's future, and Lucy still pays solitary annual visits to arethusa. And in a gesture of authorial resistance to this perfect patriarchal arrangement, Freeman carefully undercuts Edson's power over Lucy: "In his full tide of triumphant possession he was as far from the realization of the truth as was Alpheus, the fabled river god, after he had overtaken the nymph Arethusa, whom, changed into a fountain to elude his pursuit, he had followed under the sea, and never knew that, while forever his, even in his embrace, she was forever her own" (p. 169).

But Freeman does not end the story here "with an ironic thrust at Lucy's self-satisfied husband,"[36] as Toth argues. The author makes it clear that Edson differentiates himself from other men by indulging what he unwittingly regards as his wife's "harmless idiosyncrasy" (pp. 168–69), despite his blindness to the spiritual substructure of Lucy's attachment. Although provided for in life, Lucy remains true to her own nature as exemplified in the orchid, "clad in her green leaf": "This soul, bound fast to life with fleshly bonds, yet forever maiden, anomalous and rare among her kind, greeted the rare and anomalous flower with unending comfort and delight. It was to her as if she had come upon a fair rhyme to her little halting verse of life" (p. 169). These final lines underscore what Toth perceives as "Freeman's vision of an inviolable personality,"[37] but her interpretation is limited in that she never applies this consideration to Edson in order to extend her interpretation of "Arethusa." By seizing one side of the dilemma of identity and desire, the critic diminishes the story's power.

Similarly misunderstood, Freeman's "The Revolt of 'Mother' " is a story the author was asked to comment on frequently during her lifetime. Her renunciation of the defiance she created inevitably confuses the feminist reader. I believe that in fiction Freeman assumes an authentic position (that is, she "authorizes" the conflicting codes) and in nonfiction she constructs a duplicitous story concerning her view of Mother's action and herself as a writer. The work and its circumstances epitomize the ways in which Freeman stages our (mis)readings. The story begins with a man's intention to construct another barn on a site where he had promised forty years ago to build his family a new house. He conceives of and begins to execute his plan without informing his wife and daughter. The ensuing conflict results in another contest of wills between the men and women of Freeman's world. "Mother," or Sarah Penn, is a small, benevolent woman whom Freeman likens to "one of the New Testament saints."[38] She nonetheless perceives the unmistakable inequity in her husband's housing of his animals in contrast with his family. The daughter recognizes this too, but Sarah, upholding the mother's role, defends Father (Adoniram Penn) as a good provider, albeit one who sees the world differently from the women. Freeman is not kind to Father, whom she presents through animal imagery. A man of action, Adoniram "ran his words together, and his speech was almost as inarticulate as a growl" (p. 116). His identity manifests itself in his barns and livestock and is perpetuated in his inarticulate son Sammy.

The feminist critic's interest in this story, the reason it was chosen as the title piece for the recent Feminist Press collection of Freeman's selected stories, derives from the phenomenal act of defiance at its center. For the first time in forty years of marriage, Sarah Penn oversteps the bounds of her role as silent companion and domestic servant to her husband. Her first transgression is " 'to talk real plain' " to him (p. 124), the fuller ramifications of which we will consider in the works of Hurston and Walker. Comparing the Penn house with the larger ones of less prosperous neighbors, Mother presents the final charge that their daughter Nanny, too weak to perform all of the household tasks, will have to go somewhere else when she marries. Time after time, Father reiterates his refrain—" 'I ain't got nothing' to say' "—and the narrator concludes that in spite of Mother's impressive performance, "her opponent employed that obstinate silence which makes eloquence futile with mocking echoes" (p. 126). (Adoniram plays the resistant critic to Mother's feminist interpretation of her text.) Freeman backs Father into a corner. Having refused to reconsider his plan, he expects his wife to accept it, but the story that Freeman chooses to tell requires Mother's rejection of the plan—a notion that has never occurred to Adoniram. In response to Nanny's gently mocking suggestion that her wedding be held in the new barn, Sarah Penn conceives a plan of her own.

For a woman in one of Freeman's New England villages, and for some women today, the only thing worse than objecting to her husband's decision is acting to oppose it. Sarah Penn allows a maxim to form in her mind: " 'Unsolicited opportunities are the guide-posts of the Lord to the new roads of life' " (p. 130). Just as the new barn is finished, providence assists her by calling Adoniram away on business. Then Sarah Penn moves out of her house and into the new barn—dishes, stove and all. Her children are awe-struck: "There is a certain uncanny and superhuman quality about all such purely original undertakings as their mother's was to them" (p. 133).

As with any feminist resistance to patriarchal authority, Sarah Penn's action receives complete disapproval from the town chorus. Freeman well knew the interpretations that would be offered: "Some held her to be insane; some, of lawless and rebellious spirit" (p. 134). The minister comes to invoke the moral force of institutionalized religion, only to elicit the following, incontrovertible response: " 'I've got my own mind an' my own feet, an' I'm goin' to think my own thoughts an' go my own ways, an' nobody but the Lord is goin' to dictate to me unless I've a mind to have him' " (p. 135). Upon his return, Adoniram is shocked into amazed and even more inarticulate bewilderment. Through action, Sarah's meaning makes itself plain to him, and he finally understands what the new house means to her. Both are overcome by this reversal—Adoniram weeps and Sarah covers her face with her apron. Accentuating the effect, Freeman summarizes the attack: "Adoniram was like a fortress whose walls had no active resistance, and went down the instant the right besieging tools were used" (p. 139).

Though the surface of the story seems far from ambiguous, some critics still manage to delimit the narrative's power. Foster's basic approach to the story as a "comic folk tale" seems completely misdirected. He observes: "We are amused by the battle of the sexes—anywhere; and we cheer when any worm turns."[39] I can't agree with his assumption that "we" are amused. While Westbrook admits a truth beyond probability of event and locates it in the fiercely individualistic New England character, he undercuts his position and Freeman's story with the following assertion: "The greatest disservice done to this story was President Theodore Roosevelt's comment in a speech that American women would do well to emulate the independence of Sarah Penn. From then on, the story was removed from the category of comic fantasy where it belongs and placed before the public as a serious tract on women's rights, which it surely is not."[40] The masculinist critics deny Freeman's imaginary defiance of sex roles by relegating it to comic fantasy, another way of saying that Sarah Penn's revolt need not be taken seriously; it is fun, and we should enjoy it.

Westbrook's comment points to the notoriety and discomfort "The Revolt of 'Mother'" brought its author. In 1917, near the end of her writing career, Freeman wrote of the story:

> In the first place all fiction ought to be true and "The Revolt of Mother" is not true. . . . There never was in New England a woman like Mother. If there had been she certainly would not have moved into the palatial barn. . . . She simply would have lacked the nerve. She would also have lacked the imagination. New England women of the period coincided with their husbands in thinking that the sources of wealth should be better housed than the consumers. . . . I sacrificed truth when I wrote that story, and at this day I do not know exactly what my price was. I am inclined to think coin of the realm.[41]

This passage is often quoted, puzzled over, and qualified by critics. None of them offers the qualifying vision of Blanche Colton Williams, who cites two other passages from the same article in *Saturday Evening Post* (8 December 1917).[42] One shows how Freeman situated the disclaimer by first voicing her frustration that "people go right on with almost Prussian dogmatism, insisting that the Revolt of Mother is my one and only work. It is most emphatically not. Were I not truthful, having been born so near Plymouth Rock, I would deny I ever wrote that story. I would foist it upon somebody else."[43] The story's disproportionate fame, resulting from its treatment as a tract, reduces Freeman's entire project. When she is called upon publicly to pass judgment on Sarah Penn, a gesture she refuses within her fictions, she protects her right to create the possible by denying the probability of Sarah's action. Assiduously resisting efforts to limit her story to a treatise on women's rights, Freeman plays the nonfeminist reader who interprets the story according to the period's social realities, the realm of the status quo rather than of defiant possibilities—a position the story itself advances in the view of Sarah's actions as uncanny and "superhuman" (p. 133).

Freeman's renunciation of the ending may be read as the ultimate reclamation of text and author by the dominant, phallocentric discourse. In her statement, Freeman at once denies the truth-value (the desire for defiance) and affirms the fictive quality of Sarah Penn's action. The questioning strikes too close to home, for it was Freeman, after all, who had the imagination, the rebellious capacity, to construct Sarah Penn's revolt. A citizen of the world she chronicles, Freeman takes a position similar to the one Flannery O'Connor adopts later. When her friend Maryat Lee encourages her to see James Baldwin in Georgia, O'Connor refuses: "In New York it would be nice to meet him; here it would not. I observe the traditions of the society I feed on—it's only fair. Might as well expect a mule to fly as me to see James Baldwin in Georgia."[44] By refusing overt declaration, the writer imagines she can protect her position as artist and social critic. Again only Blanche Williams included Freeman's additional comment from the *Post* article that women in New England villages often hold the household reins, and for good reason: "They really can drive better."[45] Once more Freeman expresses a less compromised view and preserves the freedom purchased through her unyielding undecidability. The reader knows from the beginning that Sarah's revolt is a fiction, that the text of the story and the text of the disclaimer are equally true and untrue.

If we are to read Freeman's fiction in the tradition of her best known critics, we substitute our own desire for narrative authority for the author's persistent denials and evasions and for the text's own essential subversiveness. The reader/critic's dilemma is inescapable. No one is to blame. The rhetoric of Freeman's texts places us in what Culler describes as "impossible situations where there is no happy issue but only the possibility of playing out roles dramatized in the text."[46] The beauty of Leah Glasser's article on Freeman rests in her struggle to read the writer as she finds her rather than as Glasser, representative of the contemporary feminist reader, would like her to be. Glasser allows herself to confront the troubling ambiguities of Freeman's " 'slavery' as well as her 'rebellion.' "[47] Roland Barthes' comments on Greek tragedy apply equally well to the task of interpreting Freeman's work; he describes the texts as "being woven from words with double meanings that each character understands unilaterally (this perpetual misunderstanding is exactly the 'tragic'); there is, however, someone who understands each word in its duplicity and who, in addition, hears the very deafness of the characters speaking in front of him [or her]—this someone being precisely the reader (or here, the listener)."[48] It is not easy (or perhaps even possible) to be the reader upon whom nothing is lost. However, we make less rather than more of the fiction when we play the character's part and resolve the tensions inherent in the task of formulating moral judgments during a time of change and possibility—a choice that Freeman's perception of internal and external realities would not permit her to make. Her view demanded both sides of the situation, as opposed to an unqualified depiction of gender roles, aging, poverty, and rural life of the period.

Each strand of meaning requires the existence of the other and is inhabited by its opposite, making it impossible to choose between them or to decide what Freeman really meant for us to understand. The text's meaning does not reside in story "A" or "B"; instead it is "A" and "B" and the combination of the two. The effect of the human compulsion to choose a resolution is to illustrate Culler's point that "texts thematize, with varying degrees of explicitness, interpretive operations and their consequences and thus represent in advance the dramas that will give life to the tradition of their interpretation. Critical disputes about a text can frequently be identified as a displaced reenactment of conflicts dramatized in the text, so that while the text assays the consequences and implications of various forces it contains, critical readings transform this difference within into a difference between mutually exclusive positions."[49]

As Freeman's readers, we follow suit, continuing to play out the text's struggles in our interpretive debates. By reducing the critical drama to a contest between simple oppositions, criticism perpetuates itself. But Freeman, in a necessary strategy, outwits us all. She anticipates us, encouraging and demanding our differences of view by encoding them within her fictions. She constructs us as she did her characters, particularly in her refusal to write an easy solution to the problematics of gender. Through her insistence on this complexity she stages the text's resistance to temporality. But returning for a moment to Barthes' view of the tragic, I cannot deny the relationship between Freeman's renunciation of "The Revolt of 'Mother' " and the characters in a Greek play who limit their understanding of what they hear and say as they stage the text's misunderstandings. In her nonfiction Freeman accepts the role in which woman has been cast (as O'Connor accepts southern racism) when she denies Sarah's rebellion. She retreats from her own feminist moment and plays the "woman," exposing her personal inability to escape temporality. The price of denial is great, as we shall see implicitly in the contrast between Freeman's work and Zora Neale Hurston's uncompromising challenge to racial and sexual politics through her character Janie in *Their Eyes Were Watching God.*

CHAPTER 3

ORALITY AND TEXTUALITY IN ZORA NEALE HURSTON'S *THEIR EYES WERE WATCHING GOD*

who told you anybody wants to hear from you?
you aint nothing but a black woman!

    —hattie gossett, *This Bridge Called My Back*

Ah got de law in my mouth.

    —Zora Neale Hurston, *Mules and Men*

Through her novel *Their Eyes Were Watching God*, Zora Neale Hurston presents a forceful resistance to black women's oppression in a sexist and racist society. She does so by means of her own artistic accomplishment, which she shares with her character Janie Crawford. The work has attracted varied attention since it was first published in 1937. June Jordan called it the greatest novel of Blacklove ever written. Alice Walker has explored its place in Hurston's presentation of herself as a role model for black women artists. A host of critics have discussed the significance of Janie as a black woman who creates herself in her own image. Not all of the commentary, however, has been positive. Ignoring her critique of sexual politics, some writers have criticized Hurston's political views, comparing her unfavorably with Richard Wright and Ralph Ellison and describing her as an opportunist and a reactionary. While we have finally developed a fuller understanding of Hurston's work, critics still feel obliged to begin their discussions by reconstructing the author's life and works, continually reestablishing their right to undertake the more specialized literary analysis this black feminist writer deserves. Few critics have talked at any length about the literary value and construction of meaning in *Their Eyes Were Watching God*, one of the century's finest works of fiction.

Hurston remains something of an enigma. She incited jealousy, dedication, love, and anger in her friends and associates; later writers have shared these responses in varying degrees. Certainly no one is immune to them because Hurston's position, like Freeman's, refuses a one-dimensional reduction. Her defiant individualism frequently displays itself in the bias, equivocation and obliquity of her critics' commentaries. In her exceptional essay, "On Refusing to Be Humbled by Second Place in a Contest You Did Not Design: A Tradition by Now," which serves as the Dedication to the Feminist Press edition of Hurston's selected writings, Alice Walker summarizes the puzzle surrounding the author and her work:

Is *Mules and Men* racist? Or does it reflect the flawed but nonetheless beautiful creative insights of an oppressed people's collective mythology? Is "Gilded Six-Bits" so sexist it makes us cringe to think Zora Neale Hurston wrote it? Or does it make a true statement about deep love functioning in the only pattern that at the time of its action seemed correct? Did Zora Neale Hurston never question "America" or the status-quo, as some have accused, or was she questioning it profoundly when she wrote phrases like "the arse-and-all of Democracy"? Is Janie Crawford, the main character in *Their Eyes Were Watching God*, light-skinned and silken-haired because *Hurston* was a colorist, as a black male critic has claimed, or because Hurston was not blind and therefore saw that

41

black men (and black women) have been, and are, colorist to an embarrassing degree?

Is Hurston the messenger who brings the bad news, or is she the bad news herself? Is Hurston a reflection of ourselves? And if so, is that not, perhaps, part of our "problem" with her?[1]

Through the use of countervailing questions, Walker defends the writer against her critics and provides us with a badly needed corrective in her re-membering of Hurston. Walker concludes her litany of questions by cautioning us to restrict our comments to Hurston's artistry.

Obviously, this is an injunction that is difficult for Walker to heed. She cites a Wellesley College student's comment: " '*What does it matter what white folks must have thought about her?*' "[2] Aside from Hurston's association with and patronage by liberal whites, and the influence they exerted on the shape of her art and career,[3] we must ask an equally pressing question with respect to the development of her reputation as an artist: What does it matter what black men thought about Hurston? Sharing her oppression as a black American, black male critics read Hurston the way most men read women. The need to construct a defense against those male critics has preoccupied black women writing on her. Langston Hughes's comment in *The Big Sea* exemplifies the problem. Rivaling Hemingway's remarks on Stein, Hughes writes his sense of jealous competition with Hurston between the lines: "In her youth she was always getting scholarships and things from wealthy white people, some of whom simply paid her just to sit around and represent the Negro race for them, she did it in such a racy fashion. . . . To many of her white friends, no doubt, she was a perfect 'darkie,' in the nice meaning they give the term—that is a naïve, childlike, sweet, humorous, and highly colored Negro."[4] Hurston, along with her character Janie, transgresses the boundaries of gender roles. In "Zora Neale Hurston: A Woman Half in Shadows," Mary Helen Washington criticizes Darwin Turner and Nathan Huggins for confusing the personal with the artistic as a means of dismissing Hurston's contribution to literature.[5] Larry Neal's remarks have escaped much qualification. Discussing Hurston's view of the South, he describes her as "an inveterate romantic" who managed to avoid the oppressive forces that characterized the region for political radicals such as Wright. He supports this assertion with the observation: "Perhaps it was because she was a black woman, and therefore not considered a threat to anyone's system of social values."[6] Black women who have written about Hurston adopt a very different position, reflecting the awareness they share with her of the effects of male power.

Hurston, as a black woman, poses a double threat. In her article, " 'This Infinity of Conscious Pain': Zora Neale Hurston and the Black Female Literary Tradition," Lorraine Bethel assesses Hurston's place within literature in terms of a confluence of oppressive forces: "The codification of Blackness and femaleness by whites and males is contained in the terms 'thinking like a woman' and 'acting like a nigger,' both based on the premise that there are typically negative Black and female ways of acting and thinking. Therefore, the most pejorative concept in the white male world view would be thinking and acting like a 'nigger woman.' This is useful for understanding literary criticism of Hurston's works, which often attacks her personally for simply conducting herself as what she was: a Black woman."[7] By insisting on her right to be a "Black woman," free from prescribed roles, Hurston was perhaps as immediately intimidating to black men as to white. Because she was a black woman without independent resources, her white patrons undoubtedly experienced a more secure relationship based on dominance. Hurston necessarily tolerated the situation, although it did little to earn public praise for her literary accomplishments when she struggled to tell her own story rather than the one whites constructed for her to tell. Within this arena of sexual and racial conflict, Hurston's literary reputation suffered.

Over the years, critics have commented variously on the central theme of *Their Eyes Were Watching God*. Washington argues that the novel's most powerful theme "is Janie's search for identity, an identity which finally begins to take shape as she throws off the false images which have been thrust upon her because she is both black and woman in a society where neither is allowed to exist naturally and freely."[8] Hurston expresses this theme, Washington maintains, through the images of the horizon and the pear tree, the former symbolizing Janie's personal, individual quest, the latter, her search for fulfillment through union with another.[9] Ann Rayson argues similarly that Hurston chooses "becoming" rather than "being" as the principal focus of her fiction, suggesting a parallel with Ellison's protagonist, who says, "the end is the beginning."[10] While Rayson's comment reveals her sensitivity to Hurston's choice of narrative strategy, she does not examine that sense of circularity or the reasons underlying Hurston's choice. This question of creating form through narrative technique, which serves as the basis for Janie's deconstruction of the effects of power, provides the focus for my discussion of *Their Eyes Were Watching God* and offers one way of relating this work to those of other feminist writers.

The puzzle of the novel's structure is inseparable from considerations of its theme. Despite Larry Neal's contention that "Zora Neale Hurston was not an especially philosophical person,"[11] Hurston employs a narrative strategy that is culturally, philosophically, and aesthetically complex. This complexity reveals itself through Hurston's decision to re-tell the story rather than to tell it. Barbara Christian makes an important observation about this choice, which the scope of her book does not permit her to develop: "*Their Eyes Were Watching God* is a story within a story. Janie Stark tells the story of her childhood, her life, and her loves to her best friend, Phoebe [*sic*], and to the community to which she has just returned. This aspect of the novel is critical to its substance, for Janie Stark is not an individual in a vacuum; she is an intrinsic part of a community, and she brings her life and its richness, joys, and sorrows back to it. As it has helped to form her, so she also helps to form it."[12] Lillie Howard, however, finds fault with Hurston's method and maintains that "the story is rather awkwardly told by both the heroine, Janie Crawford, and an omniscient narrator, and is revealed, for the most part, in a flashback to Janie's best friend, Phoeby Watson. The narrative is awkward in some places because much of what Janie tells Phoeby, Phoeby must already know, partly because she is Janie's best friend, and partly because Phoeby was a part of Eatonville just as Janie was."[13] It is neither through accident nor uncalculated device that Janie's story is re-told rather than told. Why does Hurston choose to do this when, as Howard correctly observes, Phoeby—the audience for the fiction within the fiction—surely knows much of the story she is being told? The value of the approach as strategy exists in what Hurston accomplishes through its use; here as well rests much of the novel's significance for feminist readers today.

Hurston's artistic method displays a keen awareness of the performative quality of fiction as it emerges from the tradition of oral narrative, as well as a clever consciousness of the storyteller/writer's role in constructing the history of a people through language. Her brilliant use of dialect, specifying pride and ownership, lends credibility to the novel's claim as a work for the black community. It is a testament to the power and beauty of blackness. Hurston is culturally and artistically at ease with the narrative convention of re-telling the tale, just as her character Janie has grown used to an audience: "Phoeby's hungry listening helped Janie to tell her story."[14] On this point, Bethel comments that "In presenting Janie's story as a narrative related by herself to her best Black woman friend, Phoebe, Hurston is able to draw upon the rich oral legacy of Black female storytelling and mythmaking that has its roots in Afro-American culture."[15] But this is not an end in itself. Hurston's aim is textuality—the process of producing a text through the transformation of other texts—and through this textuality, a form of feminist self-definition. By transforming Janie's orality—Hurston's intertexts—into textuality, the writer creates both herself as a writer and her own story, while Janie creates her life through language. Creator and character fuse in Hurston's description of Janie's motivation for relating the story that follows: "that oldest human longing—self revelation" (p. 18). All the events of the novel's one long evening find their center in the act of telling the tale.

To understand the effects of the novel's frame, the embodiment of Hurston's narrative strategy, it is useful to suspend consideration of that device for the moment in order first to examine the story Janie tells. The frame consists only of the first chapter and the final three pages of the novel's twentieth and last chapter. Since the story within the story comprises much of the novel, it always commands the greatest critical attention. Here Hurston offers the tale of Janie Crawford's development from puberty to womanhood as a model of black female development. The story begins in the home of her grandmother, moves to the homes of her two husbands, Logan Killicks and then Joe Starks, and concludes with the death of her third husband and lover Vergible "Tea Cake" Woods. Janie orders the story in such a way that she chronicles her progress from dependence to independence, while Hurston gives us the story of Janie's development from silent "object" to speaking "subject."

At the beginning of the story within the story, Janie receives her sense of definition from others. She is woman as object under the control of a racist, patriarchal culture. Failing to recognize herself as the one black child in a photograph, she begins her story without name or color: " 'Dey all useter call me Alphabet 'cause so many people had done named me different names' " (p. 21). Initially she reconciles herself to the received wisdom, the history of black women's place in the prevailing power structure as imparted by Nanny, her grandmother: " 'Honey, de white man is de ruler of everything as fur as Ah been able tuh find out. Maybe it's some place way off in de ocean where de black man is in power, but we don't know nothin' but what we see. So de white man throw down de load and tell de nigger man tuh pick it up. He pick it up because he have to, but he don't tote it. He hand it to his womenfolks. De nigger woman is de mule uh de world so fur as Ah can see. Ah been prayin' fuh it tuh be different wid you. Lawd, lawd, lawd' " (p. 29). Nanny projects a stereotypical identity (wife) and a secure future (house and land) for Janie based upon what she knows, which is limited by the historical constraints of what she has seen of the white man's power over blacks and the black man's relationship to the black woman. Thus, she explains to Janie: " 'Ah was born back due in slavery so it wasn't for me to fulfill my dreams of whut a woman oughta be and to do. Dat's one of de hold-backs of slavery' "(p. 31).

Nanny arranges Janie's marriage to Logan Killicks and his sixty acres of land, thereby "desecrating" Janie's vision from the pear tree of idyllic union. Bethel explains Nanny's behavior as a protective measure: "She is attempting to adjust Janie to the prevailing sexual and racial milieu, and her protective-ness emerges as violence directed against Janie. Nanny attempts to explain to Janie the historical and social forces that make her innocent actions so serious. . . ."[16] Bethel sees in this cross-generational relationship the pattern of black women's victimization by oppressive racial and sexual forces. "In this sense," she concludes, "Janie and her grandmother illustrate the tragic continuity of Black female oppression in white/male America."[17] While it is true that the oppression continues, it is also evident that Hurston makes Janie differ from Nanny in some important ways. Part of what the character learns is to place her grandmother's words in perspective—to understand how Nanny's recounting of experience shaped what Janie was later able to see. In this respect, Hurston stages a break with the oppressor's culture and points to the sexual and racial liberation of women.

The grandmother's gift of a life different from her own permits Janie to pursue dreams and visions beyond those that Nanny, " 'a cracked plate' " (p. 37) damaged by slavery, could have projected. Janie creates her own future, the way to her individual happiness, at the same time that Hurston constructs a new legacy through the tale Janie tells. The story Janie tells Phoeby and the narrative the reader receives are vastly different from the shaping and socializing story Nanny tells Janie. In a sense, Nanny is the unreconstructed past, and Janie her fulfillment through a newly constructed present. Although the grandmother's narrative power has been repressed into further silence, Nanny still envisions the story she longed to tell: " 'Ah wanted to preach a great sermon about colored women sittin' on high, but they wasn't no pulpit for me' " (pp. 31–32); but silence distorts this story to the point where the horizon of women's potential is constricted to the private sphere of domestic life. Through Janie, Hurston exposes the crack in the plate and preaches the liberating and defiant sermon that Nanny was never able to deliver and that black women, indeed all women, have been waiting to hear. Janie's story can be read as a new (hi)story constructed out of love and passed from one black woman to another.

The process of Janie's freedom from oppressive roles entails several steps and engenders predictable male opposition. Logan Killicks expresses his complaint about Janie's independence in racial terms: " 'You think youse white folks by de way you act' " (p. 51). Joe Starks brings Janie closer to racial/cultural autonomy by escaping the control of white hegemony. His desire to be a "big voice" in a place beyond the authority of white men suggests change, chance, and the far horizon to Janie, although from the outset she realizes that Starks does not completely embody her vision: "He did not represent sun-up and pollen and blooming trees" (p. 50). From the day she rides off with him in a hired rig, sitting in a seat "like some high, ruling chair" (p.54), Janie confronts the delimiting structures of language: "Her old thoughts were going to come in handy now, but new words would have to be made and said to fit them" (pp. 54–55). Hers is a new life beyond the limits of the imagined, demanding the creation of a new story for its expression.

Their Eyes Were Watching God is a novel about orality—of speakers and modes of speech: Joe's "big voice" wields power modeled on white culture; the grandmother speaks the language of slavery time; the store porch hosts "mule-talkers" and "big picture talkers"; and each town has its complement of gossips. Here, as everywhere, language produces power and knowledge as well as constraint; it is the ability to interpret and to transform experience. The townspeople perceive the equation of word and law, how Joe's big voice commands obedience: " 'You kin feel a switch in his hand when he's talkin' to yuh' "(p. 78); " 'he's de wind and we'se de grass. We bend which ever way he blows' " (p. 78). Commenting on this effect, Howard makes the clever observation that "It is no mistake that he [Joe] often prefaces his remarks with 'I, god.' "[18] Just as the town chorus is alienated by Joe's power of speech, they also note Janie's silence. In this world of lively speakers, Janie lives a speechless existence. At the town's dedication ceremony, Joe speaks when Janie is asked to say a few words. Although he robs her of this opportunity, she sees and reflects upon her loss: "She had never thought of making a speech, and didn't know if she cared to make one at all. It must have been the way Joe spoke out without giving her a chance to say anything one way or another that took the bloom off of things" (pp. 69–70). Janie discovers the emptiness of class status, and especially of status by affiliation—the territory of women. In particular, she grows to understand the loneliness of silence, how orality is required for community. She loves the mule stories people tell on the store porch and creates her own tales in silence, but Joe restricts Janie's personal autonomy by prohibiting her participation in discourse. She can neither tell stories nor serve as a member of an audience—the folk community required for the telling.

Through the novel, Hurston also exposes phallocentrism and instructs her readers in the terms of discourse. By means of their oral skills, the porch speakers demonstrate the powerful effects of logocentrism: "They are the center of the world." As in white patriarchal culture, language serves as a locus for social control through its centrality within an order of meaning. Robert Hemenway and Roger Abrahams both comment on the importance of "negotiating respect" through verbal skill in the black community. In "Are You a Flying Lark or a Setting Dove?" Hemenway remarks that "negotiating for respect is not a static process dependent upon the institutions or instrumentalities offered to a woman by society—marriage, the home, the church—but a dynamic response to events growing out of a woman's capacity for self-expression."[19] Phallocentrism is so fundamentally pervasive that it is difficult to conceive of one's self, actions, and meaning outside of its system of control. To attempt to escape its constraints, Janie must use power in order to have power. By transforming her characteristic silence into speech, she stands a chance of establishing a different relationship with Joe, that is, a relationship based on acknowledging difference and accommodating change. Eventually she tires of his endless verbal disputes designed to bring about submission. Her silence in the external world reflects her internal repression until the hollow image of Joe Starks crashes from the shelf in her mind, and she discovers her emotional silence: "She had a host of thoughts she had never expressed to him, and numerous emotions she had never let Jody know about. Things packed up and put away in parts of her heart where he could never find them. She was saving up feelings for some man she had never seen" (p. 112).

Crossing the Double-Cross

The three places in the text where Janie speaks publicly are marked in the novel. When Joe implements Janie's idea by freeing a persecuted mule—the analogue of black slaves, and especially of black women ("de mule uh de world")—Janie praises him. She gives a speech in which she compares Joe with Abraham Lincoln. The townspeople note her skill: " 'Yo' wife is uh born orator, Starks. Us never knowed dat befo'. She put jus' de right words tuh our thoughts' " (p. 92). In the second instance, Hurston herself, through the omniscient narrative voice, underscores Janie's incursion into orality: "Janie did what she had never done before, that is, thrust herself into the conversation" (pp. 116–17). This time, instead of presenting an oblique defense of women through the suffering mule, Janie, like Freeman's Sarah Penn and Alice Walker's Celie, gets "too moufy" and preaches her sermon on women (the one Nanny never could deliver) to the men on the porch: " 'Sometimes God gits familiar wid us womenfolks too and talks His inside business. He told me how surprised He was 'bout y'all turning out so smart after Him makin' yuh different; and how surprised y'all is goin' tuh be if you ever find out you don't know half as much 'bout us as you think you do. It's so easy to make yo'self out God Almighty when you ain't got nothin' tuh strain against but women and chickens' " (p. 117). The final instance of Janie's mastery that ultimately establishes her power occurs when, in retaliation for Joe's verbal abuse, she humiliates him in front of his male friends (pp. 122–23). She seizes his authority—language—and leaves him speechless.

No unquestioning user of language, Hurston creates her character as a critic of phallocentrism who speaks her defiance. As such, Janie positions herself in a different relation to discourse, moving beyond the exercise of language as a means of establishing power over others or of fixing absolute meaning, to "a practice of language" that Stephen Heath describes as "wild, on the body, unauthorised."[20] Out of pity when Joe is on his death bed, Janie contemplates "what had happened in the making of a voice out of a man" (p. 134). Hélène Cixous's analysis of the politics of language clarifies what Hurston is doing through her character: "No political reflection can dispense with reflection on language, with work on language. For as soon as we exist, we are born into language and language speaks (to) us, dictates its law, a law of death: it lays down its familial model, lays down its conjugal model, and even at the moment of uttering a sentence, admitting a notion of 'being,' a question of being, an ontology, we are already seized by a certain kind of masculine desire, the desire that mobilizes philosophical discourse."[21] Constructing another course for black women, Hurston directs Janie's language toward the discovery of a discourse of emotion, a language she learns through her relationship with Tea Cake who fulfills the bee and blossom imagery of the novel's opening. He demands a union of speech and feeling, and she asks that he speak "with no false pretense" (p. 165). He is the master linguist of "otherness"; as

Orality and Textuality

Janie tells Phoeby in the story within the story, " 'So in the beginnin' new thoughts had tuh be thought and new words said. After Ah got used tuh dat, we gits 'long jus' fine. He done taught me de maiden language all over' " (p. 173). This "maiden" language defies the social construction of difference and permits new perspectives to emerge from narrative action. For example, Janie rejects being "classed off" (p. 169), separated from other black people through her imprisonment in Joe's house and store as "his showpiece, his property."[22] To a degree, she frees herself from his story, another constriction of her horizon, and shares her perception with Phoeby: " 'And Ah'd sit dere wid de walls creepin' up on me and squeezin' all de life outa me' " (p. 169). Janie rejects the "race after property and titles" in favor of "uh love game" (p. 171). Recognizing that the exclusion of others is the repression of differences within one's self, she merges her life with the life of the black community, telling big stories, listening to them, working along with the other women, and rejecting Mrs. Turner's politics of color—a pecking order that privileges white features over black.

By freeing herself from the oppressor's language and by learning a new integration of words and feeling, Janie develops her critique of color, class, and sex.[23] The narrator, Janie of the re-telling, speaks of the repression inherent in Nanny's "mis-love": "Nanny had taken the biggest thing God ever made, the horizon—for no matter how far a person can go the horizon is still way beyond you—and pinched it in to such a little bit of a thing that she could tie it about her granddaughter's neck tight enough to choke her. She hated the old woman who had twisted her so in the name of love" (p. 138). But this recognition becomes Janie's own and is modified by her interpretation of Nanny's circumstance—one can only dream the next dream, and until it is reached, its true value is unknown. Janie explains:

> "She was borned in slavery time when folks, dat is black folks, didn't sit down anytime dey felt lak it. So sittin' on porches lak de white madam looked lak uh mighty fine thing tuh her. Dat's whut she wanted for me—don't keer whut it cost. Git up on uh high chair and sit dere. She didn't have time tuh think whut tuh do after you got up on de stool uh do nothin'. De object wuz tuh git dere. So Ah got up on de high stool lak she told me, but Phoeby, Ah done nearly languished tuh death up dere. Ah felt like de world wuz cryin' extry and Ah ain't read de common news yet" (p. 172).

To a degree Hurston validates Nanny's dream for Janie through Phoeby who, less affluent than her friend, lends sympathy to the grandmother's way of thinking. At the same time, Hurston demonstrates how Nanny's values are the effects produced by the oppressed having internalized the oppressor's consciousness.

Crossing the Double-Cross

Robert Hemenway, commenting on Janie's effort to come to terms with Nanny's vision, maintains that "the vertical metaphor in this speech represents Hurston's entire system of thought, her social and racial philosophy. People erred because they wanted to be *above* others, an impulse which eventually led to denying the humanity of those below. Whites had institutionalized such thinking, and black people were vulnerable to the philosophy because being on high like white folks seemed to represent security and power."[24] In other words, if you haven't had it, power and status look good; so goes the hierarchical dream of the phallocentric economy. Reflecting her commitment to an essential relationship between experience and knowledge, Janie mitigates Tea Cake's regret over his decision not to stay when the hurricane was imminent: " 'When yuh don't know, yuh just don't know' " (p. 240). She prefers not to trust the projections that, like Nanny's dream for Janie, reproduce the oppressor's logic. In a remarkable way, Hurston wages an early battle on behalf of oppressed people and anticipates black feminist writers such as Audre Lorde. Citing Paulo Freire's *The Pedagogy of the Oppressed*, Lorde proclaims: "The true focus of revolutionary change is never merely the oppressive situations which we seek to escape, but that piece of the oppressor which is planted deep within each of us, and which knows only the oppressor's tactics, the oppressors' relationships."[25] Hurston's effort to supplant the language and logic of this consciousness relates her to radical feminist writers today.

According to Hurston's defiant (deviant) narrative logic, only the Janie of the narrative frame, the one who returns to Eatonville, is capable of telling the story. The voiceless existence of the less experienced Janie prevented narration, except as the story might be presented through a third-person limited or omniscient narrator. This strategy, however, would have diminished the power of Janie's having come to speak, one of the highest forms of achievement and artistry in the folk community. Thus, Janie's story cannot be told and can only be re-told. Surely it is more than my illusion as a white feminist critic that Hurston presents us with a novel of the black woman's struggle to construct a language that destroys the conditions of her historic silence and creates the stories that articulate and make memorable a new (hi)story. Janie can return with an understanding she and Hurston share of the liberating force of language within the black community.

One of Janie's greatest lessons about language centers on its power to deconstruct and to construct, to kill or to give life. When she is on trial for Tea Cake's murder, she recognizes this potential in the black members of the audience: "They were there with their tongues cocked and loaded, the only real weapon left to weak folks. The only killing tool they are allowed to use in the presence of white folks" (p. 275). This passage recalls the frame's opening segment in which Hurston describes the townspeople sitting on their porches at night: "They became lords of sounds and lesser things. They passed nations through their mouths. They sat in judgment" (p. 10). Adopting the traditional means of defense against gossip, Janie selects Phoeby, a trusted member of the community network, to whom she can provide an account of her behavior.[26] In addition to this pragmatic motive for narration, Janie uses language to give life and memory to feeling. Following the death of the mule, for example, it is memorialized in story by the porch talkers, just as the life of the black woman in slavery is fixed in Nanny's discourse when contrasted with Janie. Thus, according to the conventions of their discursive fields, Janie's story enters oral tradition while Hurston's novel passes into literary tradition. Through her character's discovery, the writer gives us a story of how language outwits time and exclusively patriarchal determinations of meaning, and the reader finds new significance in the frame's opening commentary comparing men, "whose dreams [are] mocked to death by Time," and women: "Now, women forget all those things they don't want to remember, and remember everything they don't want to forget. The dream is the truth. Then they act and do things accordingly" (p. 9).

Although the novel's work is conducted primarily through Janie's story, much of its significance rests in and in relationship to the narrative frame. The importance of the frame is that it permits Hurston to tell her story through a re-constituted subject. Hurston holds to this even at the expense of creating anomalies in Janie's story—the places where Phoeby is mentioned in the third person, dialogues between Phoeby and Janie in which Phoeby is presumably a participant in the telling, since Janie addresses her remarks to her friend. The story we receive is not constituted until Janie returns, changed. She arrives as the witness to a new epistemology: "you got tuh *go* there tuh *know* there" (p. 285). Through Janie's story, Hurston presents an alternative conception of power as it operates in black female discourse. Rather than replicating verbal power as oppression, its form among whites and blacks imitating whites, Hurston espouses a form of narrative authority indigenous to black tribal tradition. As Ruth Borker notes of the Buhaya of Tanzania, "The key cultural concept for thinking about speech is that of 'knowing.' "[27] Janie operates according to a system whereby you don't say what you don't know, and you can't know something until you experience it; or, as Jacques Derrida puts it, "the logocentrist or logocentric impulse is rocked by historical events, rocked by things that happen."[28] Having gone there, you are changed, and the story you have to tell is a different story. The interpretations of the phallocentric hegemony are called into question rather than assumed. This move wrests the control of meaning from a sexist, racist culture and locates the potential for change within the individual.

Besides the significance of how the story is changed by the fact that Janie has gone and returned, it is additionally important that Janie returns as a "speaking subject" to bring her story to the people. At this point, the changed

Janie, Janie the storyteller, fuses with the author. Hurston designates the end of Janie's story with the novel's only authentic silence—one that is elected rather than imposed, and is as natural as the sounds that mark the ending: "There was a finished silence after that so that for the first time they could hear the wind picking at the pine trees" (p. 285). With the full resonance of the parallel, *Their Eyes Were Watching God* might well be understood as a "Portrait of the Artist as a Black Woman."

Through the overarching and elusive meaning of her title, Hurston confronts the dilemma of the phallocentric ground of determinate meaning. At the most critical moments in the novel, Janie and others scrutinize the heavens for a sign of God's intention. Like their African ancestors (and the Puritan interpreters), they are seeking a way through nature to unlock and interpret the meaning of events. They act out the reader's effort to interpret the text. In the novel's opening frame, we encounter the Watcher, an Everyman waiting for the ship of dreams to come in and trying to outwit Death who was "there before there was a where or a when or a then" (p. 129). Following Janie's sensual awakening, she desires validation for her dreams: "She was seeking confirmation of the voice and vision, and everywhere she found and acknowledged answers. A personal answer for all other creations except herself. She felt an answer seeking her, but where? When? How?" (p. 24). Only once does there seem to be a sign—the arrival of Tea Cake, which Janie invests with referential power taking us back to the blossoming pear tree and the bee: "He looked like the love thoughts of women. He could be a bee to a blossom—a pear tree blossom in the spring. He seemed to be crushing scent out of the world with his footsteps. Crushing aromatic herbs with every step he took. Spices hung about him. He was a glance from God" (p. 161).

While Janie accepts Tea Cake as a sign, his presence cannot resolve the problem of interpretation—the signification of events. When the hurricane is imminent, people consider God's purpose: "They sat in company with the others in other shanties, their eyes straining against crude walls and their souls asking if He meant to measure their puny might against His. They seemed to be staring at the dark, but their eyes were watching God" (p. 236). The only answer given is the storm itself, suggesting that the people's question, as related by the narrator, contained its answer, that this was indeed a contest of force. The hurricane and Tea Cake's love for Janie ultimately contribute to his death, so that on a symbolic level, it would seem that what was once responsible for his presence is in the end responsible for his absence. Through the compelling imagery of the frame, Hurston refuses this simple dichotomy by rejecting the bipolar logic of absence: "Tea Cake, with the sun for a shawl. Of course he wasn't dead. He could never be dead until she herself had finished feeling and thinking. The kiss of his memory made pictures of love and light against the wall. Here was peace. She pulled in her horizon like a great fishnet. Pulled it from around the waist of the world and draped it over her shoulder. So much of life in its meshes! She called in her soul to come and see" (p. 286). The effect Derrida describes in approaching Sollers' *Numbers* expands our sense of Hurston's accomplishment here: "The text is out of sight when it compels the horizon itself to enter the frame of its own scene, so as to 'learn to embrace with increased grandeur the horizon of the present time.' "[29] Through Janie's exemplary insistence on a different (black and female) determination of meaning and value, and through her own narrative art as the teller within the tale, Hurston resists the binary opposition of phallocentrism as it inhabits Western metaphysics, just as she seeks to revise its attendant notion of interpretation. The present, as an unexperienced future, cannot unlock the meaning of what is to come. It has no predictive or determinative value.

In place of this practice, Hurston offers a particular concept of presence—the presence of a present—through Janie's re-telling. The only present is its illusion in narration, occasioned by and filling in for absence. Bringing the past into the present, Hurston gives both dimensions a particular reconstructed value, and propels the past, itself a former present, toward a future that exists only as an anticipated possibility for black women.[30] Thus, these elements of time remain fluid, each containing traces of the other. As storytellers, as speaking subjects, Janie and Hurston don't escape phallocentrism. Rather, they stage a critique from what Derrida calls "a certain inside of logocentrism. But it is an inside that is divided enough and tormented enough and obsessed enough by the other, by contradictions, by heterogeneity, for us to be able to say things about it without being simply 'outside of it.' And we say them within the grammar, within the language of logocentrism while allowing the alterity or the difference which obsesses this inside to show through."[31] By extricating herself from cultural control, Janie/Hurston creates culture. Through the re-telling of Janie's story, orality becomes textuality. Textuality is produced by Janie's learned orality, her participation in the oral tradition of the culture. She learns to be one of the people; thus, this is a story of her acculturation into black womanhood and her artistic entitlement to language. By chronicling Janie's development, Hurston transforms the status of narrative from the temporality characteristic of oral tradition to the more enduring textuality required to outwit time's effect on memory. In doing so, she presents feminist readers with a map of a woman's personal resistance to patriarchy, and feminist writers—in particular Alice Walker—with the intertext for later feminist works.

CHAPTER 4

A WORLD
OF WOMEN

MARILYNNE ROBINSON'S
HOUSEKEEPING

You can have a men's novel with no women in it except possibly the landlady or the horse, but you can't have a women's novel with no men in it.

 —Margaret Atwood, "Women's Novels"

If we continue to speak the same language to each other, we will reproduce the same story. Begin the same stories all over again. . . . Words will pass through our bodies, above our heads, disappear, make us disappear.

 —Luce Irigaray, "When Our Lips Speak Together"

The unstated assumptions shaping traditional criticism determine its reluctance to consider "first novels," a category of postponement we have specifically designated. In a move that retards change and restricts the encroachment of outsiders, critics prefer to await the accumulation of a more substantial corpus that in itself might justify our attention. Occasionally we make rare exceptions for the singular work that enters the world bearing obvious marks of its influences and its relationship to the "great tradition." The kinship of deconstruction with post-modernism, and its theoretical potential for reading anything, open the field of possibility for approaching contemporary feminist texts. In her first novel, *Housekeeping*, it is Marilynne Robinson's fate to tell a different story from most contemporary writers. Her very departure from the conventional demands our attention, in spite of the norms governing critical practice in the past. She presents a world almost exclusively populated by women, where experience filters through female consciousness and reflects the actions of women. This is not a world of Amazons or utopian androgynes—those presented by writers such as Ursula Le Guin, Joanna Russ, or Monique Wittig. It is not the milieu of Ernest Hemingway, Jack Kerouac, or Norman Mailer in reverse. If there are any resemblances, they are to the circumstances of women's lives as presented by writers such as Freeman and Jewett, or to the motive that directs Hurston and Walker to portray life within the black community.

Robinson's small-town America is familiar in setting, event, and character, with the striking exception that men rarely figure in it. Some readers find this disturbing and strange; they ask why an author would choose to situate her fiction in such a world. It is as though reader and writer reenact the script of Adrienne Rich's poem, "Natural Resources":

Could you imagine a world of women only,
the interviewer asked. *Can you imagine*

a world where women are absent. (He believed
he was joking.) Yet I have to imagine

at one and the same moment, both. Because
I live in both. *Can you imagine,*

the interviewer asked, *a world of men?*
(He thought he was joking.) *If so, then,*

a world where men are absent?
Absently, wearily, I answered: Yes.[1]

In the choice to imagine such a world, Robinson defies the nature of fiction noted in the epigraph taken from Margaret Atwood. Instead, she elects the "unnatural"—to characterize women's experience in its own right, thereby subverting the oppositional view of seeing and understanding women only or principally in relation to men. The politics of sexual relationship are for the most part enacted off-stage, though the characters' world is not without its own version of the effects of male power, particularly as embodied in social institutions. In this choice lies Robinson's single most significant strategy for the construction of a work endowed with striking originality and artistic force.

Robinson strips things to the reality of a female essence—to matters of caregiving and "housekeeping." She handles these dangerously clichéd and stereotypical terms in a startlingly new way—one that challenges us to revise our previous understandings. The novel centers around the lives of a woman, two of her daughters—Sylvia and Helen—and Helen's two female children. The text's opening sentences announce the primacy of these relationships and establish Helen's absence: "My name is Ruth. I grew up with my younger sister, Lucille, under the care of my grandmother, Mrs. Sylvia Foster, and when she died, of her sisters-in-law, Misses Lily and Nona Foster, and when they fled, of her daughter, Mrs. Sylvia Fisher."[2] The Foster family history is marked with mysterious disappearances, life filled with losses. Husbands and fathers are gone virtually before the narrative begins, before the lives of their wives and children really develop. Sylvia Foster's husband, Ruth's grandfather, is entombed in the lake outside of Fingerbone, the victim of an accident that occurred when the train he was riding slid off the bridge into the water below. His body is never recovered. The women remain to cope with the demands of everyday life, awaiting "the resurrection of the ordinary" (p. 18) out of the pall of mourning, the confusion of change. All three of Sylvia Foster's daughters leave her—Molly to be a missionary in the Orient, Helen and Sylvie to Seattle and beyond. Helen's husband deserts her and the two children; Ruth tells us she has no memory of him. Then Helen repeats the family pattern of mysterious disappearance: she borrows a neighbor's car, goes home for the first time in more than seven years, arranges her children on her mother's front porch, and sails off a cliff "into the blackest depths of the lake" (p. 22). By the end of the first chapter, the grandmother also dies, though naturally and peacefully of age.

In these early moves, Robinson kills the biological mothers in order to come to terms with "mothering." She then presents us with a surrogate mother who refuses to keep house—in fact, ultimately sets it on fire—so that we can understand the meaning of female identity and of "housekeeping." Without men, women lose identity as it is normally constructed—secondarily, by affiliation and difference. Of necessity, they then confront loss and individual identity on their own terms, and the texture of life changes. Following the death of Edmund Foster, for example, Sylvia and her three daughters enter a period of "almost perfect serenity," which the narrator elaborates as follows:

"My grandfather had sometimes spoken of disappointment. With him gone they were cut free from the troublesome possibility of success, recognition, advancement. They had no reason to look forward, nothing to regret. Their lives spun off the tilting world like thread off a spindle, breakfast time, suppertime, lilac time, apple time" (p. 13). These changes at the opening are important because they enable Robinson to create the life situation of women as it is often experienced. She goes beyond woman's affiliative existence as wife and mother, exemplified in the grandmother's obituary, with only her husband's photograph and none of her own funeral details; her life is rewritten and reprinted as the spectacular tragedy of her husband's death (p. 40). Robinson's construction of a world without men, or more accurately always with men only in the margins, permits her to explore the idea of "woman" and gender roles in essentially female terms.

In *Housekeeping*, Robinson explodes the prevailing cultural mythos of motherhood and the nuclear family. Instead she offers a rare, momentary glimpse into the lives of women whose circumstances, both literal and metaphorical, seem strange despite their statistical frequency in our society. Without men and without mothers, the definitional status of women and family life changes radically. In her exploration of the question, the author is careful not to reduce women's diversity to a monolithic view. In other words, she resists the impulse to substitute a new model that merely replicates the reductive inadequacies of the old. Among the cast of adult characters, only Sylvie, the itinerant drifter with no children of her own, is able to "mother," to make a home, and to live out an autonomous female identity. The narrator's mother is distracted and quiet, lost in the shadows of her daughter's memory. Ruth tells us that her grandmother tends them "with scrupulous care and little confidence, as if her offerings of dimes and chocolate-chip cookies might keep us, our spirits, here in her kitchen, though she knew they might not" (p. 25). This dread is underscored by the disappearance of Sylvia Foster's own daughters, and her mother's archetypal story of a woman who, like Sylvie later in the novel, sees the ghosts of black, starving children from her window at night. The narrator summarizes: "Sometimes it seemed to me my grandmother saw our black souls dancing in the moonless cold and offered us deep-dish apple pie as a gesture of well-meaning and despair" (p. 26). Through Sylvie's wistful, marginal character, Robinson calls into question the cultural construction of housekeeping and mothering.

Sylvie keeps house in a most unorthodox way, rather like her choice "not to act married, though she had a marriage of sufficient legal standing to have changed her name" (p. 43). At home she creates an equilibrium of exterior and interior, relating to the outside more than the inside; housekeeping becomes a tending to and a nurturing of the exterior world, an opening up of the inside to the outside. The house is its setting in the environment: "She preferred it sunk in the very element it was meant to exclude. We had crickets in the pantry, squirrels in the eaves, sparrows in the attic" (p. 99). One night Lucille turns on the kitchen light and casts the naked reality of Sylvie's housekeeping into relief against the softening edges of darkness. She exposes the chaos of the kitchen —chipped and yellowing paint, heaped up dishes and pans, unhinged cupboard doors: "A great shadow of soot loomed up the wall and across the ceiling above the stove, and the stove pipe and the cupboard tops were thickly felted with dust. Most disspiriting, perhaps, was the curtain on Lucille's side of the table, which had been half consumed by fire once when a birthday cake had been set too close to it. Sylvie had beaten out the flames with a back issue of *Good Housekeeping*, but she had never replaced the curtain" (p. 101). This is not "good housekeeping" by popular standards. Sylvie never throws out a can or a newspaper, preferring to store them in the parlor since no one ever comes to call. Ruth surmises that Sylvie kept these things "because she considered accumulation to be the essence of housekeeping, and because she considered the hoarding of worthless things to be proof of a particularly scrupulous thrift" (p. 180). We see that Sylvie is not completely unaware of what is expected, because when the legal system threatens to separate Ruth from her, she keeps house in the conventional way.

For Ruthie, Sylvie succeeds as a mother in the most elemental way that others have not—she stays. We sense the importance of this gift because Sylvie is an inveterate drifter who feels the tug of every train that comes through the town of Fingerbone. Sylvie is "love": an elusive essence, drifting away—there and not there, always about not to be. She is that which can only be desired but never possessed.

We are led to believe that there are in fact strong family resemblances among these women. The grandmother, careful "not to startle the strangeness away" (p. 19), raises her daughters in a way that accommodates or fosters difference. As wistful and distracted as Sylvie, Helen in an early scene stands in her apartment door, "smiled at the floor, and twined her hair" (p. 21) as she listens to her neighbor Bernice. Helen and Sylvie fuse in Ruthie's memory as she creates the "substantial restitution" (p. 42) she anticipated before her aunt's arrival: "As I watched Sylvie, she reminded me of my mother more and more. There was such similarity, in fact, in the structure of cheek and chin, and the texture of hair, that Sylvie began to blur the memory of my mother, and then to displace it. Soon it was Sylvie who would look up startled, regarding me from a vantage of memory in which she had no place" (p. 53). Ruthie struggles against her adolescent sense of invisibility in the effort to create herself: "I often seemed invisible—incompletely and minimally existent, in fact. It seemed to me that I made no impact on the world, and that in exchange I was privileged to watch it unawares" (pp. 105–6). In more widely divergent efforts, Ruth and Lucille define themselves referentially in relation to the mothers they create.

Lucille, like the townswomen in the novel with whom she comes to identify, makes an issue of her sister's resemblance to Sylvie. Eventually Ruth senses "that Lucille's loyalties were with the other world," as Lucille engages in a "tense and passionate campaign to naturalize herself" to the life of the well-groomed girls in her class (p. 95). Sylvie inevitably fails to meet Lucille's more conventional expectations for mothering. Her aunt bears no resemblance to Rosette Brown's mother, who travels the countryside securing ballet and baton lessons, sews her daughter's costumes and embroiders dish towels for Rosette's hope chest. Ruth is, however, comforted by the very behavior that disturbs Lucille: "I was reassured by her sleeping on the lawn, and now and then in the car, and by her interest in all newspapers, irrespective of their dates, and by her pork-and-bean sandwiches. It seemed to me that if she could remain transient here, she would not have to leave" (p. 103). In ways paralleling their reactions to Sylvie, the sisters construct their dead mother differently, projecting their individual desires in their divergent memories: "Lucille's mother was orderly, vigorous, and sensible, a widow (more than I ever knew or she could prove) who was killed in an accident. *My* mother presided over a life so strictly simple and circumscribed that it could not have made any significant demands on her attention. She tended us with gentle indifference that made me feel she would have liked to have been even more alone—she was the abandoner, and not the one abandoned" (p. 109). Finally, Lucille also abandons what remains of her "family" to take up residence, appropriately, with the home economics teacher, and Ruth becomes almost indistinguishable from Sylvie, who resembles the girl's construction of Helen. Lucille is the woman coopted by the other side, and, as such, our sentiments as feminist readers are structured against her. Her weakness inspires her conformity to conventional gender roles for women. Still, to challenge the reader's more superficial response, Robinson plays the perfect mother, refusing to abandon Lucille, and her departure remains a real loss for the characters of the novel, who forgive and regret and search. Through this special relationship of unfailing love, the author mitigates our judgment, calls exclusion into question, and carefully guards Lucille's right to pursue her own way, even though this "other" way is really the way of the world at large, of sameness rather than difference. This stands in counterpoint to another effect of Robinson's position: how humanly, tragically, we continue to love (desire) what abandons and rejects us. These things the reader, as site of all the novel's texts, feels more deeply than any of the characters.

Much of the effect of Robinson's originality issues from her decision to inhabit women's other world. She establishes Ruthie and Sylvie's point of view as the norm: for a fictive moment the "other" becomes the "One." There is no utopic role reversal where women seize male power in the sociosexual economy. We see how Robinson's perspective differs when the sheriff, symbol of law and social order, enters this otherwise female space. His mission is carefully identified. Ruthie explains that it was not her truancy or the "theft" of a rowboat: "It was that we returned to Fingerbone in a freight car. Sylvie was an unredeemed transient, and she was making a transient of me" (p. 177). Ruth and Sylvie have only the personal power residing in them as women—the power to withhold, to create a break in the sexual economy by resisting and living as fugitive (feminist) transients. In a sense, one of the text's ultimate purposes is to explicate difference as represented in Sylvie's transiency—a way of life Fingerbone children are taught to fear so that their souls remain captives of ordinary society. Sylvie whispers: " 'It's not the worst thing, Ruthie, drifting. You'll see. You'll see' " (p. 210). Robinson demonstrates that transiency is an exercise of female autonomy, a necessary outcome of woman's refusal to participate in the socially imposed economy of gender roles.

Exploding our fear of difference through the figure of the drifter epitomized by Sylvie, Robinson symbolizes a relationship to society that can be occupied by anyone. These transients elicit a moral reaction from the well-socialized citizens, "since morality is a check upon the strongest temptations" (p. 178). The drifters, terrifying "because they were not very different from us" (p. 178), embody everyone's human potential to cut loose from and to be cast out of society; they are the difference within. They possess obscure and powerful stories awaiting discovery: "Like the dead, we could consider their histories complete, and we wondered only what had brought them to transiency, to drifting, since their lives as drifters were like pacings and broodings and skirmishings among ghosts who cannot pay their way across the Styx. However long a postscript to however short a life, it was still no part of the story. We imagined that if they spoke to us they would astonish us with tales of disaster and disgrace and bitter sorrow, that would fly into the hills and stay there in the dark earth and in the cries of birds. For in the case of such pure sorrow, who can distnguish mine from thine?" (p. 179) In this passage, the text speaks of itself—its purpose and effect.

Robinson extends her questioning of women's existence to self-conscious narration. The text's action is as much vertical as horizontal, built by layering and accretion—a piling up of stories analogous to Sylvie's housekeeping and her discursive practices. The mood of the piece is that of a vision just beyond consciousness, of figures seen below the surface of the water with blurred vision, recalling Rich's exploration in "Diving into the Wreck."[3] Perhaps it derives from the way the elements merge in Fingerbone—earth and sky are watery substances, indistinct from the lake itself: "A narrow pond would form in the orchard, water clear as air covering grass and black leaves and fallen branches, all around it black leaves and drenched grass and fallen branches, and on it, slight as an image in an eye, sky, clouds, trees, our hovering faces and our cold hands" (p. 5). Or perhaps it is that Sylvie's character verges in and out of the conscious present, mixing with those blurred elements: "Sylvie always walked with her head down, to one side, with an abstracted and considering expression, as if someone were speaking to her in a soft voice. But she would have glanced up sometimes at the snow, which was the color of heavy clouds, and the sky, which was the color of melting snow, and all the slick black planks and sticks and stumps that erupted as the snow sank away" (pp. 48–49). Then again, it might be the text's own pentimento effect, the archaeological work of sifting through the levels of consciousness, through the legacy of history in an effort to comprehend the present or to anticipate the future. Describing how Sollers' *Numbers* opens the beyond of a whole, Derrida also applies the figure of layered images to reading the contemporary text: "The act of reading is thus analogous to those X rays that uncover, concealed beneath the epidermis of one painting, a second painting: painted by the same painter or by another, it makes little difference, who would himself, for lack of materials or in search of some new effect, have used the substance of an old canvas or preserved the fragment of a first sketch. And beneath *that*, etc."[4] The textual thickness of *Housekeeping* is captured in Ruth's description of the chest her grandfather painted: "Each of these designs had been thought better of and painted out, but over the years the white paint absorbed them, floated them up just beneath the surface. I was always reminded of pictures, images, in places where images never were, in marble, in the blue net of veins at my wrists, in the pearled walls of seashells" (p. 90). Perhaps, for Robinson's text, this undecidedness over originary images produces the narrative's speculative alternatives—explanations which ask more than they answer, affirming only the absence of certainty, as in this list of possibilities I have just proposed.

These meditations on interpretation are some of the narrative's most beautiful passages. They disclose the text's consciousness of its own construction: "Say that my mother was as tall as a man, and that she sometimes set me on her shoulders, so that I could splash my hands in the cold leaves above our heads. Say that my grandmother sang in her throat while she sat on her bed and we laced up her big black shoes. Such details are merely accidental. Who could know but us?" (p. 116). Robinson's approach to meaning within fiction suggests how we might compose meaning in life. Our own strategies of interpretation, attribution, and assertion parallel those of the narrator and the author, with whom we share problems of deepest personal and philosophical import: what was, what is, what matters, and why. In pursuit of such complexities, Robinson seems implicitly to challenge the tradition of the novel of manners, and particularly manners as windows to morals, to value. Hers is the feminist's most pressing axiological concern—what is valued and why?

This preoccupation with value gives rise to the text's function as memory. It is reinforced by the lake, which serves as a repository—a Walden-like pond that is the center of town life, a kind of continuum. Nothing is lost to it, not even the grandfather whose body remains captured there, frozen in time like an event in a history book. The house too is "a reliquary, like a brain" (p. 209), containing vestiges of a family life that has come to an end. To secure the value of its contents, its permanence in memory, Sylvie and Ruthie burn the house before leaving so that its "relics" won't be "pawed and sorted and parceled out": "Imagine the blank light of Judgment falling on you suddenly. It would be like that. For even things lost in a house abide, like forgotten sorrows and incipient dreams, and many household things are of purely sentimental value, like the dim coil of thick hair, saved from my grandmother's girlhood, which was kept in a hatbox on top of the wardrobe, along with my mother's gray purse. In the equal light of disinterested scrutiny such things are not themselves. They are transformed into pure object, and are horrible, and must be burned" (p. 209). In this ceremonial cremation, the materiality of objects is destroyed, while their place in memory is affirmed. Then, in a final gesture to the permanence of family relationships, one that stands in strict contrast to Kerouac's male fantasy of life on the road, Sylvie takes Ruth with her into transience.

Like the clever feminist psychoanalyst, Robinson examines the development of female identity through the narratives she creates for her characters to tell. To investigate character is to examine the narrative impulse. The characters converge as their stories duplicate and recall one another—stories of strange, fleeting encounters with women whose only context is the road they travel together and the impermanence of their relationship in the moment of speaking. Robinson reveals them to us through their stories:

> You may have noticed that people in bus stations, if they know you also are alone, will glance at you sidelong, with a look that is both piercing and intimate, and if you let them sit beside you, they will tell you long lies about numerous children who are all gone now, and mothers who were beautiful and cruel, and in every case they will tell you that they were abandoned, disappointed, or betrayed—that they should not be alone, that only remarkable events, of the kind one reads in books, could have made their condition so extreme. And that is why, even if the things they say are true, they have the quick eyes and active hands and the passion for meticulous elaboration of people who know they are lying. Because, once alone, it is impossible to believe that one could ever have been otherwise (p. 157).

In this passage, the author obviously speaks of her own narrative, its truth and untruth, her characters' tales of lost children, "beautiful and cruel" mothers, and abandonment.

Through her narration of *Housekeeping*, Ruthie becomes herself (which is more like Sylvie). Ruth's difference is that she tells a long, elaborate narrative that Sylvie could not have told. Related in Ruth's own voice, the discourse of identity is the novel's text, and like identity itself, the stories comprising the novel are challenged. Perhaps, recalling the tale of the boy who discovered the train wreck, this story is not a matter of belief or disbelief; it simply is: "This boy was an ingenious liar, a lonely boy with a boundless desire to ingratiate himself. His story was neither believed nor disbelieved" (p. 8). The boy's story is merely the boy's story, but it is also all we have. These fictions, the novel as a whole, are constructed out of loneliness, in the effort to bridge alienation and belonging. They are chronicles of desire and human affection, not designed to engage "people of reasonableness and solidity" (p. 104), people such as those reasonable men I mentioned in chapter one. In a continuation of the passage above, Robinson explains:

> Loneliness is an absolute discovery. When one looks from inside at a lighted window, or looks from above at the lake, one sees the image of oneself in a lighted room, the image of oneself among trees and sky—the deception is obvious, but flattering all the same. When one looks from the darkness into the light, however, one sees all the difference between here and there, this and that. Perhaps all unsheltered people are angry in their hearts, and would like to break the roof, spine, and ribs, and smash all the windows and flood the floor and spindle the curtains and bloat the couch (pp. 157–58).

Through narrative alone the dead are restored, resurrected from their reliquaries—lake, house, and memory. A similar metaphoric logic, as shown in the previous chapter, permits Janie to carry Tea Cake with her after his death. Impelled by the essence of loss and the desire for restitution, language returns the dead from the depths of "the undifferentiated past" (p. 41); it stands in for absence. Thus, Ruth imagines the train leaping, caboose first, back out of the water to restore her grandfather. In one of narrative's tricks, the restitution completes itself: "Say that this resurrection was general enough to include my grandmother, and Helen, my mother. Say that Helen lifted our hair from our napes with her cold hands and gave us strawberries from her purse. Say that my grandmother pecked our brows with her whiskery lips, and then all of them went down the road to our house, my grandfather youngish and high-pocketed, just outside their conversation, like a difficult memory, or a ghost. Then Lucille and I could run off to the woods, leaving them to talk of old times, and make sandwiches for lunch and show each other snapshots" (pp. 96–97). Only through the narrative record of memory are the dead at once dead and alive. Similarly, their construction and deconstruction in discourse are simultaneous.

Extending this paradox, Ruth, in her narrative on mutability and its subversion, enacts Robinson's exploration of the margins—that shadowy territory between objects, institutions, characters, and codes. Here the author questions the difference inherent in conventional oppositions such as presence/absence,

Crossing the Double-Cross

permanence/impermanence, and affirmation/negation. These sets of terms reinforce one another. For example, Ruth stays with Sylvie because she believes her aunt possesses something she has lost. Ruthie's description of her belief applies as well to Robinson's narrative impulse: "It seemed to me that what perished need not also be lost. At Sylvie's house, my grandmother's house, so much of what I remembered I could hold in my hand—like a china cup, or a windfall apple, sour and cold from its affinity with deep earth, with only a trace of the perfume of its blossoming. Sylvie, I knew, felt the life of perished things" (p. 124). As long as darkness is separated from light, requiring our attention to "relic, remnant, margin, residue, memento, bequest, memory, thought, track, or trace" (p. 116), Derrida's observation is applicable —we track not the thing itself but tracks.[5]

The novel's cast of lost women play out the drama—mother, grandmother, sister, the woman in the train window, those unfortunate women populating the stories accumulated in the text, as well as the functions of mothering and female identity. Unlike Rich and her persona in "Diving into the Wreck," but through their intertextual relationship, Robinson provides character and reader with a book of mythic discourses in which women do figure. They capture and inhabit Ruthie's imagination. Though "memories are by their nature fragmented, isolated, and arbitrary" (p. 53), they are even more compelling than "presence" because they are elusive, absent. My point is illustrated by the strangely familiar woman Ruth sees in the window as the train sails across the bridge: "So she was gone. Yet I remember her neither less nor differently than I remember others I have known better, and indeed I dream of her, and the dream is very like the event itself, except that in the dream the bridge pilings do not tremble so perilously under the weight of the train" (p. 55). Looking out the window of the lighted train as it speeds by, this woman only appears to see the children running alongside, trying to catch up. Instead of seeing them, she self-referentially regards her own image in the glass. She becomes an archetype of the lost mother, the essential woman—a key to the kind of female existence that I want to call feminist: never to be discovered except in the self as it becomes the self (Ruth becomes more like Sylvie, inhabiting her dream, but she also grows to resemble her mother). Responding to or creating the prototypical quality of the figure in the window, Ruth repeats it several times. She tests the notion of identity as static and monolithic. In her reflection on the relationship between mother and daughter, self and other, Ruth comments:

> It would be terrible to stand outside in the dark and watch a woman in a lighted room studying her face in a window, and to throw a stone at her, shattering the glass, and then to watch the window knit itself up again and the bright bits of lip and throat and hair piece themselves seamlessly again into that unknown, indifferent woman. . . . And here we find our great affinity with water, for like reflections on water our thoughts will suffer

no changing shock, no permanent displacement. . . . I think it must have been my mother's plan to rupture this bright surface, to sail beneath it into very blackness, but here she was, wherever my eyes fell, and behind my eyes, whole and in fragments, a thousand images of one gesture, never dispelled but rising always, inevitably, like a drowned woman (pp. 162–63).

In another context, she similarly remarks: "Then there is the matter of my mother's abandonment of me. Again, this is the common experience. They walk ahead of us, and walk too fast, and forget us, they are so lost in thoughts of their own, and soon or late they disappear. The only mystery is that we expect it to be otherwise" (p. 215). Like Ruth's memory, or the lake and the house, the text as a repository becomes an "other" collective unconscious or tribal history of women as a class. Reinforcing this purpose, Robinson rewrites Ruthie's lost aunt Molly as a female apostle, a "fisher of men," and the characters struggle in their own ways to exemplify Margaret Atwood's maxim in *Surfacing*: "This above all, to refuse to be a victim."[6]

In an important sense, Ruth's narrative displaces loss or absence, as centered in her self-development and in her relationship with her mother. Earlier, we were warned that "to cease to hope would be the final betrayal" (p. 158), and indeed that posture is never abandoned. Discourse and identity are both driven by the difference between desire and possession, as this self-reflexive observation suggests: "For need can blossom into all the compensations it requires. To crave and to have are as like as a thing and its shadows. . . . For to wish for a hand on one's hair is all but to feel it. So whatever we may lose, very craving gives it back to us again. Though we dream and hardly know it, longing, like an angel, fosters us, smooths our hair, and brings us wild strawberries" (pp. 152–53). Discourse materializes the mother because Ruth creates her by writing her: "Every memory is turned over and over again, every word, however chance, written in the heart in the hope that memory will fulfill itself, and become flesh, and that the wanderers will find a way home, and the perished, whose lack we always feel, will step through the door finally and stroke our hair with dreaming, habitual fondness, not having meant to keep us waiting long" (p. 195). The author shows us what it means for the text to inscribe itself within its readers.

Robinson's double gesture in the final pages—the negation of certainty and the affirmation of possibility—compels characters and reader alike to unending constructions and deconstructions of what might be. Language plays a crucial role in the production of meaning and value. It writes the heart's memory and must itself be discovered and salvaged. Thus the narrator remarks on her discovery: "It had never occurred to me that words, too, must be salvaged, though when I thought about it, it seemed obvious. It was absurd to think that things were held in place, are held in place, by a web of words"

(p. 200). Discourse is constructed as it deconstructs, assembles as it dissembles. Robinson commits herself and her narrator to dissolving common distinctions between fact and interpretation, truth and lies. Near the conclusion of her story, Ruth takes a position similar to Virginia Woolf's: "All this is fact. Fact explains nothing. On the contrary, it is fact that requires explanation" (p. 217). Therefore, in the novel's concluding pages, it is not whether the old house is there or not there, whether Lucille lives in it or sits in a Boston restaurant, or whether she even thinks of Ruth and Sylvie that matters. Rather, through the affect invoked by the play of Ruthie's imagined possibilities, all of these things are true and not true, the only reality being the fact of how the narrative's own discourse is interpreted. These possibilities are written here— a fact that in itself requires explanation.

Tradition, as a guide to interpretation, does not easily accommodate or unlock Robinson's *Housekeeping*. The novel, both exploration and celebration, is firmly grounded in the mystery of "ordinary life," which, pursued to its extreme, is far from ordinary. Simone de Beauvoir complicates the matter through her apparently contrary view of woman: "One is not born, but rather becomes, a woman."[7] While I will discuss this apparent conflict at greater length in the following chapters, it is important to recognize it here as a dilemma within feminist writing—the paradox of attempting to write one's self as woman on one's own terms. It is as though Robinson sets out to discover the nature of woman distinct from her existence as a male invention or as a function of her role in patriarchally defined institutions—until the force of Beauvoir's assertion interposes itself, where the social code prescribes a different view of mothering and female identity. Theory, as Culler remarks in *On Deconstruction*, makes the familiar strange: "The works we allude to as 'theory' are those that have had the power to make strange the familiar and to make readers conceive of their own thinking, behavior, and institutions in new ways."[8] Through the women in *Housekeeping*, Robinson composes both feminist theory and fiction; by making the strange familiar, the reverse effect occurs as well. She maps a shadowy territory between difference and sameness, preparing us for an existence predicated on hope and defined only by uncertainty.

CHAPTER 5

CROSSING THE
DOUBLE-CROSS

THE CONCEPT OF
"DIFFERENCE" AND
FEMINIST LITERARY
CRITICISM

The perenniality of the sexes and the perenniality of slaves and masters proceed from the same belief, and as there are no slaves without masters, there are no women without men.

—Monique Wittig, "The Category of Sex"

For the master's tools will never dismantle the master's house. *They may allow us temporarily to beat him at his own game, but they will never enable us to bring about genuine change. And this fact is only threatening to those women who still define the master's house as their only source of support.*

—Audre Lorde, *Sister Outsider*

The writers whose works we have discussed thus far, in spite of significant variations in period, genre, and race, display certain similarities in their concerns, motives, and strategies. Each presents characters illustrative of the tensions that accompany being a woman. Their characters attempt to invent existences independent of male constructions of them. As these writers strive to envision such constructions through their characters, they engage the sexual politic and create themselves as feminists. In the context of these assumptions, I want to explore this relationship further in the next four chapters with respect to differing constructions of "woman" and "feminism" within literary theory.

For the past decade, American feminist literary criticism has been struggling at the crossroad of theory and praxis. Most literary critics, regardless of their persuasion, have, at least until recently, practiced highly individualized versions of eclectic criticism—a phenomenon not unusual within the arts and humanities. Like these other critics, feminists tend to be schooled in the tradition of rhetorical argument rather than in the rigorous application or development of any particular methodology or critical paradigm. Nonetheless, because we claim to see things differently, feminist critics have been called upon to articulate our own theoretical posture. In addition to this challenge on the theoretical level, we are continually asked to define "feminism" (that is, to agree on a definition of it) so that it might at least be understood in relation to what is called "feminist criticism." Because this second and not unreasonable challenge goes unmet, the invitation to articulate a feminist critical theory remains doubly difficult.

On the whole, the tradition of feminist criticism has not evidenced a dynamic progression toward definition or theoretical clarity. In her 1975 *Signs* review of literary criticism, Elaine Showalter characterized "literary criticism concerned with women" as having "gone well beyond sexual politics" and as being "still more coherent as an ideology than as a methodology."[1] She advocated the study of women writers within the context of their "sub-culture," an advantageous approach "because it provides a coherent framework for studying the development of writers in a separable tradition, without either denying their participation in a larger cultural system or involving questionable assumptions of innately feminine modes of perception and creativity."[2] In several deft strokes, we were steered away from examining the presumed political coherence of feminist criticism and directed toward proposed methodology: there is no purpose in recapitulating the politics of sexuality (which threaten to divide us); there is no benefit in struggling with epistemological difference (shades of biology as destiny).

In the same year, Annette Kolodny noted that "feminist criticism must continue, for some time, to be avowedly 'political'—in the largest sense of

71

that term," by which she meant that the critic as reader should not divorce herself from transformed attitudes and ideology.[3] She urged feminist critics to cultivate dual commitments, to one another as colleagues and to the methodological rigor of the established literary-critical community. The positive result of this dual allegiance manifests itself in Kolodny's own work, while the negative effect was displayed in her conclusion the next year in *Signs* that feminist criticism reveals at once "a kind of critical stasis," and is "more like a set of interchangeable strategies than any coherent school or shared goal orientation."[4] In this version, feminist criticism is strategy (method) without shared orientation (theory or politics). She left unexplored the critical relationship between method and orientation. These and other early statements express a contradiction within feminist criticism that can be read in its practice over the years and they continue to pose a significant problem in its development today, even though feminist critics recognize diversity as strength at the same time.

In her 1978 lecture entitled "Towards a Feminist Poetics," Elaine Showalter develops her earlier position to the point where she attempts to account for problems with theory-construction from a feminist perspective. Her movement toward theory consists of identifying two varieties of feminist criticism: 1) *"woman as reader,"* which she exemplifies in terms of women reading male texts, situated theoretically with respect to "Marxist sociology and aesthetics,"[5] and 2) *"woman as writer,"* or *"gynocritics,"* which she describes as "more self-contained and experimental," the ground for a uniquely feminist criticism. Beyond this limited beginning point and her exhortation to pursue its development, she acknowledges once again "the current theoretical impasse in feminist criticism."[6] In what seems a confusion of categories, feminist criticism as semiotic and ideological critique is termed "male-oriented" and is cut off from the "woman as writer" variety of criticism.

As recently as the Winter 1981 issue of *Critical Inquiry*, feminist critics continue to note the absence of a distinctly feminist methodology. The volume is, in fact, interesting for what it lacks, suggested by Annette Kolodny's final footnote to her essay on "The Panther Captivity": "This is not to suggest that feminist literary criticism can generate no new methods or analytical procedures; indeed, I think this is already beginning to happen. Nonetheless, the emphasis of most work to date—at least in the United States—has been on refining and correcting the tools and methods already available."[7] The refrain is a troublesome one—reiterated year after year, with comments on critical stasis as its counterpoint.

Just as historic, disciplinary reasons determine why literary critics generally are ill-prepared to articulate theory and to justify methodology, there are fundamental philosophical and political pitfalls that feminists detect in the recurring challenge to define themselves and to broadcast that definition to the literary-critical establishment. Having perceived the restrictive politics of groups in the world at large, American feminists are suspicious of definition— the basis of exclusionary practice. Instead, having been constrained and divided by definitions imposed upon us by others, we tend to value autonomy and individual development. Definitions, whether formulated by feminists or not, threaten to divide us. Feminist criticism, as the academy's manifestation of the women's movement, shares the historically rooted fragmentation of Marxists, reform feminists, radical feminists, and lesbians, in addition to further diversification resulting from compelling racial loyalties and variations in critical practices. The gulfs between these segments, always viewed as essentially destructive, have narrowed and broadened over the years in different circumstances. Finally, it is as though we have reached a tacit agreement to conceal our disagreements, or to confine them for the most part to the pages of feminist journals. By refusing to define ourselves publicly, feminists protect the notion of consensus, making group identity at once possible, problematic, and misleading. This ambiguity makes it difficult for theorists to reflect our contributions to the field, and even more difficult for us to come to feminist terms with developments in critical theory.

The recent interest of some members of the "interpretive" community in deconstruction, and particularly in the concept of difference, is a case in point. Many feminist critics harbor a legitimate fear that deconstruction, which is currently commanding the attention of some of our best women scholars, may represent another alluring backroad leading away from the principle challenges to define feminism and feminist criticism. Is Showalter correct in asserting that this current theoretical preoccupation requires such "a long apprenticeship to the male theoretician, whether he be Althusser, Barthes, Macherey or Lacan . . . [that] (t)he temporal and intellectual investment one makes in such a process increases resistance to questioning it, and to seeing its historical and ideological boundaries"?[8] The new method is seductive on a number of levels: it has been valorized by a larger community of scholars; it incorporates enough of the fundamental concern with gender that has emerged from the women's movement to appeal to many of us, at least initially; and, furthermore, aside from its frequently obscure politics, it affords some startlingly original readings of literary texts.[9]

Certainly, I agree with Showalter's more general observation that "feminist criticism cannot go around forever in men's ill-fitting hand-me-downs, the Annie Hall of English studies. . . ."[10] At the same time, I don't think that feminist criticism can refuse theory out of an antitheoretical bias that in some instances borders on anti-intellectualism; nor can it reject deconstruction because the apprenticeship is long and the payoff uncertain. Neither can we expect to import deconstruction-as-is to do the work of feminism. If we fail to expose the veiled politics of deconstructive criticism, or at a minimum, to shape its practice in ways that are compatible with feminist objectives, inevitably we will have spent another decade on the path to a theoretical and methodological dead end. Before we commit ourselves to this attractive yet uncertain project, feminist critics need to explore the potential value of the deconstructive method and to discover what interests it serves.

I believe that the blurred and falsely dichotomized positions of Showalter's poetics produces her judgment against deconstruction. Jane Gallop offers a more provocative view when she claims that the Derridean notion of phallocentrism "declares the inextricable collusion of phallocentrism with logocentrism . . . and unites feminism and deconstructive, 'grammatological' philosophy in their opposition to a common enemy."[11] In this chapter, I want to examine some points of divergence and convergence between deconstruction and feminist criticism through an exploration of the relationship between concepts of sexual difference and the deconstructive approach to difference and "differance."

Patriarchal power requires differentiation as its corollary. The fact that men and women are not physically identical provides the ground upon which discourse produces its historic justification for male dominance. There are actually few undeniable facts of difference: reproductive organs, orgasmic potential, secondary sexual features, and morphological structure, for example. None of these features in themselves—the presence of a vagina and ovaries, for example—determines woman's inability to preside over the economic, political, and cultural institutions of society; possessing no inherent meaning, these features are "read" or interpreted in the same way as texts, within a system of sociopolitical values. Thus, Beauvoir concludes that "the facts of biology take on the values that the existent bestows upon them."[12] Similarly, Kate Millett describes the means by which male dominance justifies itself, reminiscent of fallacious arguments basing white supremacy on the allegedly inferior mental capacity of blacks: "Male supremacy, like other political creeds, does not finally reside in physical strength but in the acceptance of a value system which is not biological."[13] Monique Wittig's assessment is even more comprehensive: "The fundamental difference, any fundamental difference (including sexual difference) between categories of individuals, any difference constituting concepts of opposition, is a difference belonging to a political, economic, ideological order."[14] Furthermore, we have come to see this as a difference within, which we then externalize as a difference between individuals, sexes, races, belief systems, and so forth. In response to this awareness, some feminists have concerned themselves with the social construction of sexual difference—a problem quite distinct from the physical variations noted above.[15]

The concept of sexual difference gained prominence in contemporary femi-

The Concept of "Difference"

nist theory with Simone de Beauvoir's *The Second Sex*, first published in the French edition in 1949 and then issued in English in 1953, although difference was a problematic concept long before that for writers such as Virginia Woolf, as I shall show in the next chapter. A principle and overriding assumption of Beauvoir's work involves the view of woman as "Other" in contrast to the Absolute, transcendent male. No one, she observes, volunteers to serve as the Other: "The Other is posed as such by the One in defining himself as the One."[16] Citing Lévinas's essay *Temps et l'Autre*, in which he designates the feminine as the full flowering of Otherness, Beauvoir challenges the author's intended objectivity and substitutes the strikingly contemporary view that "his description . . . is in fact an assertion of masculine privilege."[17] In *The Second Sex*, Beauvoir asks a lasting question: "does the word *woman*, then, have no specific content?"[18] Later she responds with the provocative answer that figured in the previous chapter: "One is not born, but rather becomes, a woman."[19] Woman, defined by negation, opposition, limitation, and lack, is appropriated in the service of the male prerogative to define itself, although Beauvoir's unspecified other version of woman as her own, not man's invention, echoes in the space. Through her elaboration, Beauvoir suggests an engaging interrelationship that captivates feminist theorists and elaborates the conceptual structure for debate through the late seventies and into the eighties.

As a result of the current interest in post-structuralist approaches to literary texts, the concept of difference has assumed added importance and become a major preoccupation of critics speaking for and against deconstruction. American feminist critics, subject to the same continental influences as their male colleagues and reinforced by certain preoccupations within their own tradition, are exploring the theoretical and methodological value of the concept of difference in works such as the Barnard conference proceedings of 1979, published as an anthology entitled *The Future of Difference* (1980), and in issues of journals such as *Critical Inquiry*, *New Literary History*, and *Diacritics*. While the general influence of continental thought has become more pronounced, the specific reservations voiced by French feminists have been insufficiently addressed as American feminist criticism meets deconstruction.

Since at least 1979, feminist intellectuals in France have been issuing cautionary statements concerning the uses of the concept of "difference" in intellectual and political work. In an article entitled "The Question of Difference," Colette Guillaumin presents a carefully conceived but largely unacknowledged exploration of the dangers inherent in approaching the concept of difference.[20] Her opening remarks provide a useful overview of her position:

> The notion of difference, whose success among us is now prodigious—
> among us, as well as elsewhere—is both a heterogeneous and ambiguous
> notion. The one because of the other.

It is heterogeneous because it masks on the one hand anatomico-physiological givens, and on the other hand socio-mental phenomena. This permits a double-cross, conscious or not, and the use of the notion on one level or another depending upon the moment or the needs. It is ambiguous in that it is typically a manifestation of false consciousness (and politically disastrous) and *at the same time* the mask of a real *repressed* consciousness.

Its very ambiguity assures its success. . . .[21]

Because the term expresses various conditions ranging from the more obvious debates over the nature and effects of sexual difference, to the deconstructive critic's notion of repressed otherness, to deconstructive strategy, it lends itself to misrepresentation through its ambiguity or multivalence. According to Guillaumin, difference is: 1) "an *empirical reality*" that "manifests itself on a day-to-day basis in a material fashion"; 2) "a *logical form*, that is, a certain form of reasoning, a way of understanding what happens in and around us"; and 3) "a *political attitude* in that it presents itself as a demand, a project . . . which has consequences for our lives." In short, the concept's very multivalence gives it the potential for creating what Guillaumin regards as "a sort of superficial consensus."[22] This danger—the all-too-easy consensus—of which we have been wary in other contexts (feminism versus humanism or racism or classism), should compel us to unravel, or better, to cross the terms of the "double-cross" in order to avoid an unwittingly naive replication of the operations feminism is attempting to undo.

The decidability of the actual effects of sexual difference as "empirical reality" depends upon the as yet and perhaps ever incomplete accumulation of sociobiological evidence and our ability to separate one from the other, cause from effect. But for the most part differences are not given; they are effects, produced by constituting terms in opposition, by designating one term "natural" and another "unnatural," as Guillaumin demonstrates with respect to woman, and as I shall discuss again later with respect to the literary canon. The project is further complicated by the socioeconomic realities of women's oppression, which are so fundamental and ubiquitous that they too masquerade as natural facts, despite the essential undecidability of this relationship between nature and culture. Audre Lorde notes the parallel ways in which racism and heterosexism similarly depend on privileging one aspect as "natural" in order to establish dominance.[23] In her extension of the nature/culture debate, Guillaumin observes, women's "status as a tool used for maintenance is so deeply rooted in everyday life, in facts, and therefore in people's mentality, that there is no wondering, much less any questioning, and no unease whatever when faced with the fact that women keep in material working order their possessor and the other properties and dependents of this possessor (and moreover all the social marginals: the sick, the elderly, the infirm, and orphans) either in the framework of private appropriation (marriage) or in the framework of collective appropriation (family, religious life, prostitution)."[24] The social effect of women's appropriation "is the production of a discourse of Nature"[25] in which this appropriation, both collective (by the class of men) and private (by an individual man) presents itself as inescapably *literal* rather than metaphoric or symbolic.

We are plagued by ambiguity at every turn. Like Audre Lorde, Mirtha Quintanales exposes the double-cross at work with respect to racism: "But I think we need to keep in mind that in this country, in this world, racism is used *both* to create false differences among us *and* to mask very very significant ones—cultural, economic, political."[26] In terms of sexual difference, confusion results from the socialization of the biological. There is the undeniability of physical differences, Guillaumin's empirical reality of difference. To ignore or to deny this is to argue foolishly, but it seems equally foolish to argue about it at all. The interpretation of any such differences, particularly the act of constituting them as social differences, constructs an ideological order of sexual (heterosexual, racial, or class) opposition and oppression. As Terry Eagleton explains, this is ideology fulfilling its role: "It is one of the functions of ideology to 'naturalize' social reality, to make it seem as innocent and unchangeable as Nature itself. Ideology seeks to convert culture into Nature, and the 'natural' sign is one of its weapons."[27] As Nature, cultural ideology assumes greater powers of determinacy and is less subject to scrutiny, because, as Barbara Johnson reminds us, we do not know what we do not know.

By such means, social reality as "natural fact" joins the ranks of the inevitable and the dangerous. Monique Wittig advances a similar argument in "The Category of Sex": "The ideology of sexual difference functions as censorship in our culture by masking, on the ground of nature, the social opposition between men and women. Masculine/feminine, male/female are categories which serve to conceal the fact that social differences always belong to an economic, political, ideological world."[28] She maintains that oppression creates sex ("one is not born . . . a woman"), rather than the contrary, a sociocultural operation that most of the writers I have presented thus far have sought to expose. This assumption is so fundamental that we are blind to its operation— it is us: "The primacy of difference so constitutes our thought that it prevents turning inward on itself in order to question itself, no matter how necessary that may be to apprehend the bases of that which precisely constitutes it."[29] The pervasiveness of the effects of difference leads radical French feminists to equate its opposition with feminism itself: "*Feminism. Or: women's liberation movement. Or: an attack on the social roots of difference.*"[30]

The real issue for Wittig, however, is not one of *difference* per se but of *opposition* and domination—the form that difference takes in our phallocentric economy. Within the present system of dualistic thought, one cannot constitute difference without opposition and conflict, without a winner and a loser, without one term occupying a position of privilege over the other. Thus, the status of the term itself contributes to the politicization of its interpretation by feminists.

The social dominance resulting from the ambiguity and extension of the natural, from having constituted it oppositionally within a power hierarchy, produces the following false "lessons" summarized by Wittig:

—that there are before all thinking, all society, "sexes" (two categories of individuals born) with a constitutive difference, a difference that has ontological consequences (the metaphysical approach),

—that there are before all thinking, all social order, "sexes" with a "natural" or "biological" or "hormonal" or "gentic" difference that has sociological consequences (the scientific approach),

—that there is before all thinking, all social order, a "natural division of labor in the family," a "division of labor [that] was originally nothing *but* the division of labor in the sexual act" (the Marxist approach).[31]

Basically Wittig is arguing that the category of sex is a category of domination rather than an *a priori* category that derives from or resides in nature "before all society." It is a political category existing in the service of a heterosexual economy to insure the reproduction and maintenance of the society through the domination of women—or, from the standpoint of race and class respectively, to ensure white dominance and black subordination, and the perpetration of capitalism's exploitation (construction) of the poor. We are entrapped within a phallocentric culture that constitutes women in terms of men's repressed, displaced power and desire in order to establish their difference within a fundamental opposition between the sexes, and, further, to insure the supremacy of men. As Féral puts it: "The woman's mark lies precisely in this marginality, but it is a marginality internal to the system, integrated in it, indispensable."[32] Sex, then, becomes the category outside of which woman cannot be conceived, and woman becomes the category without which man cannot exist.

Against this background, the question we need to explore is whether or not the concept of difference, as it is understood in deconstructive criticism, helps us to undo the paired opposition of male/female that has been the object of feminist literary criticism and, more specifically, of feminism. We must consider, for example, whether deconstructive strategy, in presenting the "female" as one term in a theoretical binary opposition, conceals women's socioeconomic situation and renders the female within feminism, or feminism itself, politically neutral. Does such a representation of the opposition—the alternative to Difference is Sameness—mask the political relationship at the heart of the opposition of terms? Philip Lewis asks a similar question of the structuralist enterprise as a whole: "Does structuralist poetics not surreptitiously protect or resurrect the truth of a subjectivist humanism that would retain the individual subject's domination over an object that is, originally and finally, that subjecting master's own creation?"[33] If we answer these queries affirmatively, the end result may be a premature de-privileging of woman as the political or feminist force within feminist criticism itself. Similarly, it would certainly close the case for deconstruction as a viable method for critics speaking from/for the margin—the position the "center" requires in order to secure its place as the Center.

Feminist deconstructors argue another view: that the concept of difference empowers claims that women's work has been misrepresented and disregarded. Additionally, they maintain that deconstruction provides theoretical strategies with which feminists can construct a more comprehensive critique of the dominant culture. The kind of understandings resulting from the application of feminist and somewhat post-structuralist approaches to works by such diverse writers as Mary Wilkins Freeman, Tillie Olsen, and Alice Walker provides another form of support for this argument. To assess the usefulness of the concept of difference, I want to consider, first, how deconstruction approaches the play of difference/"differance," and then, what the effects of this representation are for women.

The deconstructive critic claims as a goal the undoing of the fundamental hierarchy of meaning within which binary oppositions structure western metaphysics. Deconstruction attempts to show how the text's own system of logic betrays itself as it constructs itself, revealing what it wishes to conceal, mask, or repress in the service of a dominant ideology. While it is somewhat reductive to characterize deconstructive critics as a group, I hope to limit my capriciousness by focusing primarily on Derrida's discussion of the binary opposition of difference/sameness, and particularly on the issue of its recuperation or "reinscription" into the dominant discourse, a point touched on in the consideration of Freeman's work. Derrida creates a whole, fluid lexicon of (non)terms and (non)concepts for confronting various textual paradoxes. While "differance" and "supplement" are discussed here, I could just as well have considered "trace," "dissemination," or "double writing," to suggest only a few of the other possibilities his work offers.

Beginning with an understanding of the "difference" between the opposed terms, the deconstructor considers their play in relation to or as "differance." Derrida explains his neologism ("difference" with an "a") as follows: "On the one hand, it indicates difference as distinction, inequality, or discernibility; on the other, it expresses the interposition of delay, the interval of a *spacing* and *temporalizing* that puts off until 'later' what is presently denied, the possible

Crossing the Double-Cross

that is presently impossible."[34] By means of "differance" the deconstructive critic seeks to temporalize or negate the stasis of "difference" as a structure of paired opposites inscribed and reinscribed forever in a fixed power relationship within a closed system. Through "differance," determinate meaning is endlessly deferred, pushed away from the present moment. Returning to the concerns of feminism, we see that woman as the Other is frozen or at best deferred as a term within the pair of opposites, the imbalance of which the critic then demonstrates.

Having exposed this imbalance, deconstruction confronts what appears to be a logical impasse dictating two possibilities with respect to the relationship between *same* and *other*: 1) the reinscription of the historic relationship of difference; 2) the reduction of the other to the same, by negating its otherwise irrepressible difference, its alterity. In the commitment to (non)terms and (non)strategies promoting undecidability, deconstruction attempts to slip through this impasse. It is easy to see theoretically how "differance," by problematizing difference, changes the inevitable reinscription of terms into difference-with-a-difference. The "logic of the supplement" (addition and/or substitution) functions similarly with respect to how it makes identity problematic by refusing closure. As Barbara Johnson explains Derrida's term: "The logic of the supplement wrenches apart the neatness of the metaphysical binary oppositions. Instead of 'A is opposed to B' we have 'B is both added to A and replaces A.' A and B are no longer opposed, nor are they equivalent. Indeed, they are no longer even equivalent to themselves. They are their own difference from themselves."[35] This tricky move undermines the illusion of singular identity that the system of dominance and subordination requires for its operation. What woman is—as woman is added to man and replaces man—we cannot know, just as we no longer know the "meaning" or "identity" of man.

Philip Lewis offers the following explanation of the dilemma:

> The philosophic project—to bespeak the other without compromising its alterity—would indeed fall out beyond the field of deconstructive activity. No doubt deconstruction beckons toward this project since its unsparing devastations of the *same* weaken the defenses that screen out or repress the conditioning function of the *other*. But because its discovery of the *other* transpires in the dimension of the *same*, in a discourse that knows its incapacity to approach concretely the *other* it spies from a distance, to treat the *other* as anything more than an abstract condition, deconstruction could not reckon directly with the *other* without itself being different. To approach the *other* requires a further step toward a discourse *of* the *other*.[36]

By an extension of this logic, some feminist critics represent woman as nonrepresentation: "the blank page" (Gubar) or "the other woman" (Irigaray)

—an unnameable, undefinable something. Through gaps in the framework of structuration, opened strategically, we can glimpse or perhaps only approach the alterity of the other. Lewis characterizes these forays as "adventurous writing that seeks in some sense to exceed the logic of identity, and precisely not by 'identifying' the *other* in the manner of deconstructive analysis, but rather by fabricating embodiments or inscriptions of the *other*, by factoring heterogeneity into the text."[37] This heterogeneity, as we will see exemplified in the works of Olsen and Wittig, signals the need for the Derridean "double discourse," as well as other duplicitous moves designed to defer reappropriation.

While I do not claim in this fairly positive view any specific feminist accomplishments for deconstruction, I do want to suggest its promise. This potential is not, however, without its difficulties. From a feminist perspective, one basic problem with "difference" issues from the sense that, regardless of its specific form or content, regardless of "differance," it fixes women within the same oppositional economy that, at least on the level of gender, has oppressed us through exclusion and misrepresentation. Though "differance" changes our understanding of difference through reinscription, it cannot promise to free women from their oppositional, secondary relationship to men. As Derrida himself acknowledges in *Positions*, "we are not dealing with the peaceful coexistence of a *vis-à-vis*, but rather with a violent hierarchy. One of the two terms governs the other (axiologically, logically, etc.), or has the upper hand. . . . The hierarchy of dual oppositions always reestablishes itself."[38] Thus, we seem to perpetuate (albeit through negation) the image of woman in opposition to man. Although she is defined only in relation to male terms of self-definition and desire—not her own, this definition of woman's identity is always inadequate. Deconstruction as a method depends upon the positing of those categories in order that they can be "undone" textually but not literally, a distinction some would not grant me. In a similar sense, which initially sounds perverse, feminism might also depend upon or be inextricably related to the domination of women within the phallocentric economy. A consideration of this perversity, whether of my statement and/or of feminism's dependence on oppression or opposition, may disclose some points of relationship and nonrelationship between feminist and deconstructive projects.

Derrida's examination of Nietzsche's apparent misogyny and his not so evident feminism offers a way of reading deconstruction's approach to feminism. Derrida asserts: "Feminism is nothing but the operation of a woman who aspires to be like a man. And in order to resemble the masculine dogmatic philosopher this woman lays claim—just as much claim as he—to truth, science and objectivity in all their castrated delusions of virility. Feminism too seeks to castrate. It wants a castrated woman. Gone the style."[39] Having followed Derrida to his "point," I can feel the inevitability (yes, even the predictability) with which his logic turns on me, just as it does on him. It is requisite that the post-structuralist project stall (in all of the word's meanings: by deception, evasion, and delay) foreclosure and frustrate determination, while it is feminism's strength (as it differs from those outside it) and its weakness (as it differs within itself) to attempt to prefigure liberation for all women and to describe our "otherness" in "other," that is feminist, terms. These "truth claims" Derrida reads as feminism's delusions, its masculinism.

Assuming this difference between deconstruction and feminism for the moment, I will return to the perplexing question of whether or not feminist critics can afford to play the difference game of deconstructive criticism. By saying that women are made (as Beauvoir does) and that oppression creates the category of sex (as Wittig maintains), feminism sets the scene for deconstructive moves. In ways paralleling Foucault's attempt to write the hi(s)tory of madness, for example, feminist deconstructive critics can and have shown how women, defined by the dominant culture as other and condemned to silence, have been relegated to the privatized and policed world of the family. The value of deconstruction to feminism rests in the power of its sociocultural critique of difference—a critique that exposes, among other things, the domination structuring relationships between man and woman, white and black, heterosexual and homosexual, rich and poor—actualities we cannot afford to conceal or to elevate to the level of immaterial abstraction. As Guillaumin astutely observes, the critique of difference points to a fixed center, the concealed or not so concealed referent for a standard of judgment: difference "is quite simply the statement of the *effects* of a power relationship. There's a great realism hidden in the word 'difference': the knowledge that there exists a source of evaluation, a point of reference, an *origin of the definition*. And if there is an origin of the definition, it means precisely that this definition is *not* 'free.' The definition is seen for what it is: a fact of dependence and a fact of domination."[40] Within our self-confirming, phallocentric system, the ideology of difference creates the social effects of difference, which then, as I suggested earlier, are used to confirm the "natural" cause or origin of difference, blinding us to the ideological sources of oppression.

An important function of deconstruction's critique of the discourse of difference is the revolutionary role it can play in the consciousness of the "other": it provides a specific way of seeing relationships between men and women as well as a means of threatening the efficacy of the dominant discourse to maintain the social institutions that oppress women. While women have been created to fulfill male definitions of themselves, a perverse power of "otherness"—an inherent psychic disloyalty or double-vision—has always characterized certain members of oppressed classes. For example, this double action is clearly a fundamental aspect in the characterization of Freeman's Sarah Penn and Walker's Celie, and further demonstrates itself in the proprietor's greatest fear: that one day disloyalty will overwhelm the loyalty he commands by means of language, law, money, confinement, and violence. Or, the oppressed woman might finally succeed in her effort to exorcize the oppressor's image of herself that lodges within her. By revealing how the discourse of dominance writes its own undoing in the discourse of subordination, deconstruction can be used to cross the double-cross of difference by fostering women's "disloyalty to civilization" as it is embodied textually in discourse and structurally in relationships and social institutions. Furthermore, this critique applies equally well to other forms of oppression based on differences in race, class, and sexual orientation that feminism must address if it is to create the liberation for all women that it desires.

The women's movement and, within the academy, feminist literary criticism signal a momentary triumph of disloyalty. There is a sense in which deconstruction and feminism reinforce one another in the method of exposing the aporia, the point at which phallocentrism is blind to itself, particularly the ways in which it conceals its own self-centeredness and its politics of exclusion. But feminist concerns are not necessarily shared by deconstructive critics who have not, on the whole, produced many readings that address the power relationships expressive of sexual, heterosexual, racial, and class oppressions. In this respect, most French and American male deconstructors evidence no more interest in women's texts than their predecessors or colleagues of other critical persuasions.

The greatest limitation of deconstruction is that thus far it has not been able to bridge the theoretical and the political, to move beyond discourse to political action or amelioration. The posture of deconstruction is problematic because, in its resistance to closure and definition, it finesses questions of truth and decidability, resists ideological commitment, and therefore appears unable and unwilling to support a specific program of sociopolitical change. In *Criticism and Social Change*, Frank Lentricchia offers his analysis of the position taken by American deconstructors (that irresistible monolithic category), particularly as represented in the ideas of Paul de Man; in the name of the radical intellectual, Lentricchia recapitulates the invisibility of women on the left and writes the need for feminist criticism and black power. The experiences of the sixties and seventies taught revolutionaries an important lesson concerning the irrepressibility of dialectical opposition—how the privileged term tends to right itself with a vengeance and grow stronger through cooptation, only another word for the recuperation of the opposition. Lewis elaborates upon this view: "Insofar as it [deconstruction] exposes such instances of recuperation as structurally determined, it shows the folly of any attempt to overcome or escape them once and for all. Consequently, the only possibility that a deconstructive critique can presume to open up is that of thwarting them with a *tactical resistance*."[41] The tactics of this resistance are philosophical and linguistic unravellings, but the translation of these textual moves into action in the world is left to the solution of others. The deconstructor's dilemma, as Lewis sees it, is "to avoid the destructive step of deconstructing deconstruction"[42]—a problem whose solution feminism also should hold in high regard. Once the double-cross of difference has been undone, its unending cycle of recuperation in any approximation of the previous, apparently ubiquitous, binary threatens the foundations of both the feminist and the deconstructive enterprises. Theoretically, the successful deconstruction displaces the original opposition. Despite overturning and reinscription, the same is never the same, and, by extension, the other is never the same other; rather, each is seen as a fiction of the discourse that constitutes it as such. For the feminist, however, a certain danger lurks in the way "differance" infinitely defers determinacy and endlessly perpetuates women's state of oppression. The conflict, the pressure within feminism, asks that both theory and practice ameliorate the material conditions of women's lives. Deconstruction needs to struggle to become more like feminism in terms of specifying its political goals. Through its critique of meaning, it needs to declare what matters and how cultural transformation can be achieved.[43]

Similarly, to further its own project, feminism needs to struggle to become more like deconstruction by sharpening its own critique and, while articulating its method, resist the monolithic specification of its own ideology to the extent that it requires a simplification of the difference within in order to represent itself to the world outside. These moves parallel, in a sense, Jane Gallop's motive in *The Daughter's Seduction*: to make feminism and psychoanalysis more genuinely interactive in the interest—speaking almost simplistically—of politicizing psychoanalysis and of shaking feminism loose from its acceptance of a singular, traditional concept of identity. There is a way in which feminism and deconstruction threaten one another in their respective insistences on political transformation and radical reconceptualization.

If the dominant social group constitutes women as different ("other"), and women learn to perceive the oppressive force of this exclusion from sameness, the groundwork for revolution within the social order has been constructed. Gallop offers the view that "this problem of dealing with difference without constituting an opposition may just be what feminism is all about."[44] Although opposition depends upon difference, difference does not need opposition if we could presuppose the absence of a hierarchy that designates one term as the norm. Encouraging us to re-value difference, Audre Lorde asks us to turn it from a cause for suspicion and separation into a force for social change: "Within the interdependence of mutual (nondominant) differences lies that security which enables us to descend into the chaos of knowledge and return with true visions of our future, along with the concomitant power to effect those changes which can bring that future into being. Difference is that raw and powerful connection from which our personal power is forged."[45] Achieving a social order founded upon difference without opposition sounds easier, more gradual and peaceful, than it has proved to be. Commenting on Derrida's insistence on a phase of reversal in power relations, Culler remarks: "Affirmations of equality will not disrupt the hierarchy. Only if it includes an inversion or reversal does a deconstruction have a chance of dislocating the hierarchical structure."[46] It is not sufficient to disrupt the hierarchy, if by that we mean that people simply exchange positions in the order. What feminism and deconstruction call for is the displacement of hierarchicization as an ordering principle. Reversal exposes the structure of relationships, revealing them rather than concealing them within the assumptions of correctness or naturalness that discourse masks. Furthermore, it is just this condition—when difference asserts itself against sameness—that marks a shift in the *episteme* or, on a smaller scale, in the paradigm. So, perhaps in this way, deconstruction challenges feminist politics.

The feminist notion of a social order free from hierarchy and exclusion is always viewed as utopic, and this charge, usually pejorative, suggests grounds for dismissal. By its very nature, feminist criticism, based as it is in feminism, must remain a utopic enterprise. In the words of the Editorial Collective of *Questions féministes*, "utopias, like cries, are vital to us: they are our words as oppressed persons, our sociological imagination."[47] With respect to this need for utopic resolution, there is an interesting parallel between Lewis's description of the deconstructive condition and the chapter's epigraph from Audre Lorde. Lewis notes that, like the feminist project, "the deconstructive process always knows that it is, itself, impaired by the critique it effectuates insofar as its use of language is at issue, just as it knows that it can never reach that utopic point where analysis would yield a definitive constitutive premise, rooting the inquirer's language outside the hold of reflexion."[48] But unlike the deconstructive position (or is it really?) feminism does not want to concede that it has been captured forever within a system of discourse that perpetually fixes woman as "other," or that there is no point beyond what we presently "know" (or think we "know"), no discourse through which alterity can be represented outside of a system of domination. Elaborating on this view, Catherine Clément describes the goal of feminist activity as follows: "To change the imaginary in order then to be able to act on the real, to change the very forms of language which by its structure and history has been subject to a law that is patrilinear, therefore masculine. Reflection on feminist action, therefore, calls into question and into play the transformational powers of language, its capacity to motivate change in both ideology and economy."[49]

If deconstruction does not want to accept a utopic or transformative motive, must it not lend credence to views accusing it of dependence on hierarchical oppositions, as well as to those alleging its nihilism or at least its textual captivity? For example, the predictable frustration of the social visionary shapes Terry Eagleton's scathing assessment of deconstruction: "One advantage of the dogma that we are the prisoners of our own discourse, unable to advance reasonably certain truth claims because such claims are merely relative to our language, is that it allows you to drive a coach and horses through everybody else's beliefs while not saddling you with the inconvenience of having to adopt any yourself. It is, in effect, an invulnerable position, and the fact that it is also purely empty is simply the price one has to pay for this."[50] Derrida (and the same might have been said of Foucault), while he may be without Beliefs, is certainly not without motives and dreams (suspect though they are) of social revolution.

Feminism appears to want for itself the very definitive and predictable future that deconstruction proscribes in order to protect its own future work. By appearing to know—or to think it knows—what it wants, feminism seems to substitute gynocentrism for phallocentrism. This move constitutes only the phase of reversal that exposes but preserves a hierarchical structure of domination. Obviously, this position is not an end in itself, but a means requiring us to envision another end. It is then the difficult, utopic dream of nonoppositional difference, the unspecifiable something, that feminism wants.

Derrida, my metaphor for deconstructive criticism, limits feminism's meaning for deconstruction by reducing the feminist to a woman wanting to be like a man who simply repeats the traditional order in reverse. Although feminism is a movement marked by contradiction, it appears to those outside to be shaped by a more unified, monolithic vision than we ever suggest to ourselves. So within feminism we can say what is wrong more easily than we can agree upon what is right or what liberation for all women means. In this respect there is no feminism. There is only «feminism(s)», the content of which is still vigorously debated and has not been decided. It would seem that men's fear or the extension of their own monological vision leads them to believe that feminism is—or, more correctly, that «feminism(s)» wants to be—a gynocentrism that has as its goal the reversal of their own phallocentrism.

Derrida takes care to comment that his remarks about women are neither feminist nor antifeminist (to the French the term itself is troublesome, tainted). He urges that "re-active feminism," against which he speaks (for Nietzsche), not be permitted to occupy or chart the whole terrain for women. Discussing women's history in the name of Emma Goldman as "maverick feminist," he suggests a path which some other «feminism(s)» might take:

> Your "maverick feminist" showed herself ready to break with the most authorized, the most dogmatic form of consensus, one that claims (and

this is the most serious aspect of it) to speak out in the name of revolution and history. Perhaps she was thinking of a completely other history: a history of paradoxical laws and non-dialectical discontinuities, a history of absolutely heterogeneous pockets, irreducible particularities, of un-heard of and incalculable sexual differences; a history of women who have—centuries ago—"gone further" by stepping back with their lone dance, or who are today inventing sexual idioms at a distance from the main forum of feminist activity with a kind of reserve that does not necessarily prevent them from subscribing to the movement and even, occasionally, from becoming a militant for it.[51]

But what does it matter how Derrida speaks of feminism? Are we not once again, now by this new master of deconstruction, simply condemned to an-other epoch of silence—one in which we cannot speak "woman" but cannot *not* speak, and cannot join with other feminists while we must? Still, there is something in Derrida's caution worth translating to other purposes—a call for the possibilities of openings rather than the risks of foreclosures. We will need to speak of *** in place of "woman"—that something the meaning or non-meaning of which our phallocentric structure will not allow us to say. And this unimaginable, imaginary something, this understanding of ***, this «femi-nism(s)»—the effects of freedom/utopia itself—are not so different from what appears to be deconstruction's utopic projection as it asserts its motion toward the unthinkable, unknowable point(s) beyond the system it deconstructs. In this sense, can we not say that both Derridean deconstruction and feminism share a utopic and political motive to "go beyond" and to move toward the expression of the inexpressible, the unknowable?

CHAPTER 6

DECONSTRUCTING THE SEXUAL POLITIC

VIRGINIA WOOLF AND TILLIE OLSEN

Or do I fabricate with words, loving them as I do?

—Virginia Woolf, *A Writer's Diary*

*"Tell me a riddle, Grandma. (*I know no riddles.*)"*

—Tillie Olsen, "Tell Me a Riddle"

"Liberty is the right not to lie."

—Olsen citing Camus

n this chapter and the next, I will consider works that explore the movement between deconstruction and reconstruction more consciously than most of those discussed in my earlier chapters. Because their work is more consciously political, Woolf, Olsen, Walker, and Wittig, in particular, present alternative strategies for working in the fluid space of feminist critique (a deconstruction of sorts) and creation. An examination of their writing will prepare us to return again, explicitly and with greater specificity, to the questions of feminist theory and literary criticism.

While Virginia Woolf's *A Room of One's Own* (1929) and *Three Guineas* (1938) and Tillie Olsen's *Silences* (1978) are among the most frequently cited texts of twentieth-century feminism, they have received in print less attention than they deserve as works making simultaneous contributions to critical and feminist theory.[1] Both writers as feminists read culture's texts in the way that feminists read literary texts, "if . . . by 'feminist,'" as Peggy Kamuf explains, "one understands a way of reading texts that points to the masks of truth with which phallocentrism hides its fictions."[2] Certainly their value has been assumed, and Woolf's work has been considered more broadly than Olsen's, but the scope of their contributions has been artificially delimited by the uses we have made of them. This kind of treatment results from the primary identification of their authors as fiction writers, a persistent bias against the genre of intellectual prose, and our historic inability to treat such works with the level of sophistication evidenced in critical considerations of poetry and fiction. For the most part, we read their feminism through content, as I did in chapter one, at the expense of other kinds of considerations. Furthermore, the essentially interactive relationship between Woolf and Olsen also goes unremarked; their work, taken together, suggests that Woolf's texts function as the type validated (though changed) by Olsen's antitype, and the latter subverts the construction of this kind of closed system of meaning. These texts establish a dynamic connectedness in which Olsen is foreshadowed by and requires Woolf, just as Woolf requires Olsen for the fulfillment of her own meaning.

Woolf's essays are essentially contemporary and feminist in method as well as content. Jane Marcus observes in her introduction to *New Feminist Essays on Virginia Woolf*: "As a literary critic, Virginia Woolf is the mother of us all, in precisely the personal and political ways that Gertrude Stein meant when she claimed this kinship with Susan B. Anthony."[3] A unique combination of both fact and fiction, *A Room of One's Own* displays the full range of Woolf's talent as essayist and novelist in the presentation of a theoretical work that stands as an apt catalog of, and an initial response to, the principle issues of contemporary feminist literary criticism.[4] Furthermore, Woolf demonstrates a dual awareness, also noted by deconstructive critics today, of how telling the "truth" constantly affirms the fictions or "lies" the text produces as it weaves its fabric.

Crossing the Double-Cross

Woolf was an obsessive reader. In *A Room of One's Own*, she commented that "great poets do not die; they are continuing presences."[5] Developing this observation, Beverly Ann Schlack discusses the author's use of quotation in her fiction and summarizes her findings as follows: "Her use of literary allusion is at once idiosyncratic and ideally suited to many of her preoccupations: the immanence of the past in the present moment; that universality which transcends purely personal truths; the permanence within change and the unity within diversity; the symbiotic interplay of life and literature; the search for a remedy for the modern sense of discontinuity and fragmentation."[6] In his discussion of Woolf's fiction, Avrom Fleishman shares Schlack's interest in the author's use of sources, which he sees as the means to relate her to contemporaries such as Pound, Eliot, Yeats, and Joyce, and to their shared participation in literary modernism through an "encyclopedic style: the network of allusion that stands as the dominant mode in modern British literature."[7] Fleishman provides an illuminating demonstration that explores the similarities between Woolf and her contemporaries—a critical strategy that implicitly argues for her place in the great tradition according to its own rules of analogy. But the tradition in which he chooses to situate her, and the terms upon which he argues, are the basis of Woolf's personal quarrel with the past and present. In essence, Schlack and Fleishman deny Woolf's difference by constructing generalizations that fail to articulate her special relationship to her literary Fathers, to phallocentric discourse, and to the exercise of her own creativity.

Jane Marcus gives us an alternative view within which Woolf's feminism can be more fully appreciated. In "Thinking Back through Our Mothers," Marcus describes the revolutionary value Woolf finds in writing as "a conspiracy against the state, an act of aggression against the powerful, the wilful breaking of a treaty of silence the oppressed had made with their masters to ensure survival."[8] Through the act of writing, Woolf exercises the power that has historically been reserved for educated men. She acknowledges its subversive potential in ways that Tillie Olsen later makes more explicit and complete.

In the three works under discussion, both Woolf and Olsen quote other writers' material so extensively that its use attains the level of strategy. Comparing Woolf's motive to Walter Benjamin's, Marcus gives the following account of what is achieved: "By quotation she sought to rob history of its power over women. The quotations she used in *A Room of One's Own*, *Three Guineas* and *The Pargiters*, the scholarly footnotes in which documentation is a form of possession of the truth and exorcism of evil, are the intellectual pacifist outsider's only weapon against lies and injustice."[9] Through Woolf's own criticism of Kipling, Marcus depicts her as consciously playing the role of "raider on received history": " 'All notebook literature,' she wrote in "Mr Kipling's Notebook," 'produces the same effect of fatigue and obstacle, as if there dropped across the path of the mind some block of alien matter which must be removed or assimilated before one can go on with the true process of reading. The more vivid the note the greater the obstruction.' "[10] Marcus prepares us to see another aspect of quotation: as obstructing rather than facilitating forces within Woolf's work. The accumulation of cultural artifacts in the form of quotations and notes becomes a verbal assemblage representative of the obstacles to women's creativity posed by the collective cultural tradition; the author's use of these references also points toward a particular understanding of women's writing.

Woolf's two major essays suggest the ways in which intertextual forces play out the feminist critical and artistic drama. From the relatively more self-contained *A Room of One's Own*, Woolf moves in *Three Guineas* to a text with more explicit lineage, requiring over forty pages of apparatus in the form of 123 discursive notes and references. Between the publication of these two books nine years elapsed, during which time Woolf refined her already complex understanding of the interrelated problems she set out in the opening of *A Room of One's Own*: "The title women and fiction might mean, and you may have meant it to mean, women and what they are like; or it might mean women and the fiction that they write; or it might mean women and the fiction that is written about them; or it might mean that somehow all three are inextricably mixed together and you want me to consider them in that light" (p. 3). The last view is, in Woolf's mind, the most interesting approach to her topic, and it is on this ground that a relationship between her two works, and between Woolf and contemporary feminist critics, can be established.

Woolf provides an insightful discussion of many of the major problems of contemporary feminist criticism, subsuming them under the question of the conditions necessary for women's artistic production: economic freedom, leisure, education, tradition, freedom of mind, and self-confidence. She takes up some of the same topics that Olsen considers later—the childless woman writer, the "state of mind . . . most propitious for creative work" (p. 58); the "narrowness of life" imposed on women (p. 71); the silence of women without the benefit of an inherited tradition; and the enabling circumstances of class privilege. These concerns substantially contradict the impression Showalter gives of the "coy" writer: "Woolf plays with her audience, refusing to be entirely serious, denying any earnest or subversive intention."[11] From the beginning of *A Room of One's Own*, however, Woolf wisely asserts that her lecture will be inconclusive because the issues she raises are indeterminate. Although this is a reasonable position for a lecturer or a writer to take, she pushes it further—moving from the problem of conclusiveness to the question of truth. Since her subject, sex, is by definition controversial, she maintains that "one cannot tell the truth" (p. 4). The speaker can only explore the matter, and in doing so, reveal her biases. Through the acknowledgment of her own limitations, Woolf immediately makes the question of "truth" problematic: "Fiction here is likely to contain more truth than fact. Therefore I propose, making use of all the liberties and licences of a novelist, to tell you the story. . . . Lies will flow from my lips, but there may perhaps be some truth mixed up with them; it is for you to seek out this truth and to decide whether any part of it is worth keeping" (p. 4). Here we confront the text's dual nature—it is always both truth and fiction, asserting and questioning—and the method of this writer/speaker who professes to tell lies when asked to speak "the truth." Similarly, in *The Pargiters*, Woolf insists, "I prefer, where truth is important, to write fiction."[12] According to the narrator of *A Room of One's Own*, almost everyone tells lies—history, male writers, women not culturally free to tell the truth, and Woolf herself. With the awareness of the powerless, Woolf declares her own inability to "tell the truth" and confers the burden of interpretation on her readers.

When the narrator relates the incident of being chased from the college lawn, men's turf, she reinforces her point with the revelatory episode of viewing the Manx cat, "a cat without a tail," crossing the lawn. Through her identification with the cat, she considers her own lack: "Certainly, as I watched the Manx cat pause in the middle of the lawn as if it too questioned the universe, something seemed lacking, something seemed different. But what was lacking, what was different, I asked myself" (p. 11). She concludes her meditation by striking a phallic pun, "It is strange what a difference a tail makes" (p. 13). But ultimately this truth of the difference between the sexes goes unspoken: "For truth . . . those dots mark the spot where, in search of truth, I missed the turning up to Fernham" (p. 15). (A comment in her diary of 19 May 1933 reiterates Woolf's dilemma: "then . . . Three dots to signify I don't know what I mean."[13])

Having followed the twists and turns of road and mind, the narrator resituates her commentary.[14] Again, she reminds us of the relationship between fact and fiction: "Fiction must stick to facts, and the truer the facts the better the fiction—so we are told" (p. 16). This murky distinction grows even more complicated when the narrator pursues her investigation in the British Museum, where she discovers that what we know of women is received from male writers. In the significance lurking in her idle drawings, visual (and therefore more easily decipherable) rather than verbal manifestations of her unconscious working, she discovers her own anger. More surprisingly, she discovers the anger of the oppressor—the professor/patriarchal authority with his power, money, and influence—against the oppressed, woman. Constructing his superiority through " 'indisputable proofs' " (p. 40) of women's inferiority, Professor von X. offers a text of fact or "truth" that turns before our very eyes into a web of "lies": "If he had written dispassionately about women, had used indisputable proofs to establish his argument and had shown no trace of wishing that the result should be one thing rather than another, one would not have been angry either. One would have accepted the fact, as one accepts the fact that a pea is green or a canary yellow" (p. 34). But the professor cannot write dispassionately any more than Woolf herself can. Peggy Kamuf, in her elegant essay, "Penelope at Work: Interruptions in *A Room of One's Own*," argues that this scene exposes "the fault lines in Woolf's speculations about women's writing" and that these marks are "too easily overlooked whenever Woolf's text is taken as model for a feminist critical practice which, it often appears, is content to go on making nasty caricatures of angry Professor von X., the nameless author and authority of masculine privilege and feminine subjection. What such criticism seems unwilling to countenance is any notion of sexual differentiation as an historical production which, if it has produced a privileged masculine subject, cannot also be seen to originate in the subject it only produces."[15] While Kamuf's argument has wide-ranging and usefully unsettling implications, it glosses over one of Woolf's recurring insistences that even though one cannot tell the truth, the writer can own up to it by not pretending otherwise. As Woolf does in the opening of *A Room of One's Own*, the writer can attempt to "lay bare the ideas, prejudices" (p. 4) underlying his or her point of view.

Woolf unveils the specular logic of the sexual politic. Féral explains this process of specularization, which we will examine more fully in chapters 7 and 8: "Having become the virtual other side of the mirror, a pure, ungraspable reflection for herself and for him, [woman] reflects back to man the inverse image of what he knows himself to be, and of what he wants himself to be, reinforcing his very specularization, doubling this narcissistic investment of the penis/phallus that the discovery of another sexuality threatens."[16] Males constitute and protect their power by imposing powerlessness on the "others." Anticipating Féral, Woolf remarks that "women have served all these centuries as looking-glasses possessing the magic and delicious power of reflecting the figure of man at twice its natural size" (p. 35).

Society, from her point of view, enforces an insider/outsider distinction. The woman writer is both locked *in* her domestic sphere and locked *out* of church, library, and cultural tradition: "I thought how unpleasant it is to be locked out; and I thought how it is worse perhaps to be locked in"; she further considers the effects of "the safety and prosperity of the one sex and of the poverty and insecurity of the other and of the effect of tradition and of the lack of tradition upon the mind of a writer" (p. 24). Woolf assumes the intertextual nature of artistic creation—a point that is obvious to her as a woman writing in/outside of a tradition dominated by male voices. Through her persona she maintains that "books continue each other, in spite of our habit of judging them separately" (p. 84). She describes her own habit of writing through her kinswoman Mary Carmichael who, in *Life's Adventure*, creates a society of women who like women, where "Chloe liked Olivia perhaps for the first time in literature" (p. 86). In this imaginary novel, women are shown in relationship to women rather than men. Claiming that each sex has only partial knowledge of the other, Woolf poses the problem of what we would know of men if they were depicted only through the arbitrarily limited view of women: "Suppose, for instance, that men were only represented in literature as the lovers of women, and were never the friends of men, soldiers, thinkers, dreamers; how few parts in the plays of Shakespeare could be allotted to them; how literature would suffer!" (p. 87).

The woman writing about women undertakes a creative task almost beyond imagination. Through Mary Carmichael, Woolf describes its challenges as catching "those unrecorded gestures, those unsaid or half-said words, which form themselves, no more palpably than the shadows of moths on the ceiling, when women are alone, unlit by the capricious and coloured light of the other sex" (p. 88). The greatest peril, as Woolf understands it, is "to absorb the new into the old without disturbing the infinitely intricate and elaborate balance of the whole" (p. 89). But this absorption without disruption proves impossible, based as it is in an economy of the Same.

What then is woman, apart from her role as servant, lover, or mirror for man? And what is her text? Woolf cannot answer, and therefore cannot hope to speak "the truth" about women and fiction. She makes her position clear in "Professions for Women" (the original version of *Three Guineas*), where she asks: "What is a woman? I assure you, I do not know. I do not believe that you know. I do not believe that anybody can know until she has expressed herself in all the arts and professions open to human skill."[17] With revealing intuition, she tells us that, by pursuing the difference of/in women's writing, she fears she will stray "into trackless forests where I shall be lost and, very likely, devoured by wild beasts" (pp. 80–81). Foreshadowing the strategies I explore in the next chapter, where the body becomes the site of resistance, Woolf asserts her belief that "the book has somehow to be adapted to the body" (p. 81), and as such she enters the "dark continent" that is woman, "this organism that has been under the shadow of the rock these million years" (p. 88). Exploring the question through her imaginary woman writer, she reinforces the darkness within which woman is hidden: "For if Chloe likes Olivia and Mary Carmichael knows how to express it she will light a torch in that vast chamber where nobody has yet been. It is all half lights and profound shadows like those serpentine caves where one goes with a candle peering up and down, not knowing where one is stepping" (p. 88).

Woolf proceeds to spin her tale. Placing her persona in the company of three of the four Marys from the Child ballad, "Mary Hamilton" ("There was Mary Beaton, and Mary Seton, / And Mary Carmichael, and me"), she leaves unmentioned Mary Hamilton, the narrator of the ballad who is beheaded by the state for killing her illegitimate offspring.[18] Suggesting a relationship between herself and the mothers of great men, and the silent, anonymous women, the "mute and inglorious" Jane Austens of women's collective life, Woolf establishes her own narrator's place with Anon and the women whom she insists created the ballads and folksongs. The "I"/dentity of the narrator is explained parenthetically: "(call me Mary Beaton, Mary Seton, Mary Carmichael or by any name you please—it is not a matter of any importance)" (p. 5). Indeed, following the legendary meal at the women's college, we learn that the narrator is visiting Mary Seton (p. 18). Then Mary Beaton is described as the narrator's aunt and namesake (p. 37). And finally, it is revealed that the narrator is reading a work by Mary Carmichael (p. 84). The only one of the four who remains unnamed is Mary Hamilton, whose circumstances parallel those of "Shakespeare's sister." The invisible Mary, the speaker of the Child ballad, fulfills Woolf's expectation for women: "The truth is, I often like women. I like their unconventionality. I like their subtlety. I like their anonymity" (p. 115). By simultaneously concealing and revealing Mary Hamilton's identity, Woolf expresses her identification with this fourth Mary, and through her, imaginatively projects the consequences of her own subversive activity in *A Room of One's Own*.

The (non)identity of Woolf's female narrator contrasts with the presumably free, self-confident, and successful Mr. A of the essay's conclusion. His work bores the narrator, who reacts negatively to the oppressive force of his ego: "A shadow seemed to lie across the page. It was a straight dark bar, a shadow shaped something like the letter 'I.' . . . In the shadow of the letter 'I' all is shapeless as mist. Is that a tree? No, it is a woman. But . . . she has not a bone in her body, I thought, watching Phoebe, for that was her name, coming across the beach. Then Alan got up and the shadow of Alan at once obliterated Phoebe" (pp. 103–4). Even Alan's shadow possesses a more powerful materiality than Phoebe's amorphous body (without a "bone" in it). Nelly Furman uses the same passage to illustrate women's relationship to language and literature. Specifically, Furman explains how the narrative persona of *A Room of One's Own* functions in support of Woolf's position: "Mr. A's I represents a specific person designated by the initial of a name, that is to say, an individual psychological and historical being. Mr. A's I is a traditional, referential, first-person pronoun. The *I* assumed by the narrator of *A Room of One's Own* is divested of its usual meaning and function. It stands for a depersonalized identity, a pluralized *persona*; it is simply a functional agent of discourse—a speaking subject. The narrator's *I* and Mr. A's I convey different perceptions of the self and different experiences of life."[19] For this reason, according to Furman, Mr. A's I is situated in the context of centuries of tradition and education, whereas the narrator's *I* is different: "As a differentiated subject, as other, the narrator's *I* is inscribed in Woolf's text as a woman's voice in a patriarchal literary tradition."[20]

Having structured her essay according to principles of fiction—"life conflicts with something that is not life" (p. 74)—Woolf finally cannot sustain the tension required to keep these forces, men and women, separate in life or art; it is an effort that "interferes with the unity of the mind" (p. 100).[21] To explore this split, she creates the scene in which her narrator witnesses a man and a woman meeting and entering a taxi together; it is as though she merges the right and left brain in the figure of the taxi, giving us the illusion of moving from the unnatural (separation) to the natural (union). On the level of fiction, Woolf stages a sexual drama of illusory union. The imaginary merger, the containment in the taxi, frees Woolf to transgress the stalemate of opposition and separation. Showalter reads this and other similar moves as representing Woolf's choice of a "utopian" and "inhuman" androgyny over feminism: "Whatever else one may say of androgyny, it represents an escape from the confrontation with femaleness or maleness. Her ideal artist mystically transcends sex, or has none."[22] This observation, however, denies the complex strategy Woolf employs and obscures the place of this figure in relation to the writer's other preoccupations.

Woolf refuses to let Mary Beaton rest in the illusion of androgyny and thereby settle the questions of woman and women's writing. Commenting on Woolf's view of androgyny, Gayatri Spivak astutely offers the following corrective to interpreters of another often-cited instance of Mary Beaton's wisdom: "I would like to remind everyone who cites *A Room of One's Own* that 'one must be woman-manly or man-womanly' is said there in the voice of Mary Beaton, a persona. Woolf must break her off in mid-chapter and resume in her authorial voice. Who can disclaim that there is in her a longing for androgyny, that artificially fulfilled copula? But to reduce her great texts to *successful* articulations of that copula is, I believe, to make a mistake in reading."[23] To concentrate on one sex to the exclusion of the other, to thwart cooperation, is unnatural, is to repeat the perversity tradition demonstrates. The narrator describes her experience in terms of "unconsciously holding something back, and gradually the repression becomes an effort. But there may be some state of mind in which one could continue without effort because nothing is required to be held back" (p. 101). One is then at liberty, free to speak at will.

It is the union of difference within the mind, as much or more than that of one body with another, that preoccupies Woolf herself and that she sees as a precondition for creation. In contrast to Showalter, Jacobus reads Woolf's utopian move as "a harmonising gesture, a simultaneous enactment of desire and repression by which the split is closed with an essentially Utopian vision of undivided consciousness. The repressive male/female opposition which 'interferes with the unity of the mind' gives way to a mind paradoxically conceived of not as one, but as heterogeneous, open to the play of difference."[24] Even Mary Beaton harbors her uncertainties. Because identity is represented as fluid and changing, the split in consciousness can't be bridged with confidence. The terms are always shifting: "Again if one is a woman one is often surprised by a sudden splitting off of consciousness, say in walking down Whitehall, when from being the natural inheritor of that civilisation, she becomes, on the contrary, outside of it, alien, and critical" (p. 101). In this view, woman is neither always fully (a)part or separate from society in her role as other. Perhaps most importantly, such a conceptualization of the question permits Woolf, at least for the moment, to sustain a focus on the essential difference. As Barbara Johnson reminds us, "what is often most fundamentally disagreed upon is whether a disagreement arises out of the complexities of fact or out of the impulses of power. . . . The differences *between* entities (prose and poetry, man and woman, literature and theory, guilt and innocence) are shown to be based on a repression of differences *within* entities, ways in which an entity differs from itself."[25] By locating difference within the mind, rather than between identities, and by permitting Mary Beaton her own uncertainties, Woolf unsettles her persona's utopic resolution. The reader must ask if Woolf, through the deconstruction of Beaton's closing gesture, has escaped the power relationship constitutive of "the tyranny of sex" that incited the discourse in the first place.

Having constructed Mary Beaton as a persona, Woolf grants herself and her readers further rights of contradiction.[26] When Woolf (or is it another Mary?) takes up the piece again, she undermines the conclusiveness of the argument that had gone before: "You have been contradicting her [Mary Beaton] and making whatever additions and deductions seem good to you. That is all as it should be, for in a question like this truth is only to be had by laying together many varieties of error" (p. 109). In other words, the power of "truth" is situated only in the assemblage of fictions.

Ending is difficult for Woolf. She tells us in *A Writer's Diary* that the more one's vision encompasses, "the less it is able to sum up and make linear."[27] If we know anything about her writing, it is that she deliberately subverts the linearity of history by juxtaposing it to the circularity of the poetic imagination. There are no easy answers. Woolf undertakes the task of revising linear determination by complicating it through an understanding of woman that is nonexclusive, bridging the extraordinary and the ordinary woman. The majority of women, with their "infinitely obscure lives," are not represented in biography or history, "and the novels, without meaning to, inevitably lie" (p. 93). So not even fiction tells the truth. Woolf presents her one unqualified conclusion in the form of Judith Shakespeare, the consummate woman artist who never wrote a word. She, in her silent, fictive identity, is the (non)origin of the woman writer and her tradition, the foremother whose "truth" can only be materialized—"the dead poet who was Shakespeare's sister will put on the body" (p. 118)—through the writing of later women who will comprise the tradition within which Judith can/could speak.

The ending does not fail the text, nor does it disappoint the feminist reader.

Crossing the Double-Cross

Its carefully chosen (non)position is one Woolf shares with some contemporary feminist theorists. Hélène Cixous, for example, writes: "It is impossible to *define* a feminine practice of writing, and this is an impossibility that will remain, for this practice can never be theorized, enclosed, coded—which doesn't mean that it doesn't exist. But it will always surpass the discourse that regulates the phallocentric system; it does and will take place in areas other than those subordinated to philosophico-theoretical domination. It will be conceived of only by subjects who are breakers of automatisms, by peripheral figures that no authority can ever subjugate."[28] By means of her unsettling strategy, Woolf, the outsider, attempts to deconstruct past understandings of women and fiction, to create a new view of the subject, and to provide the potential for undoing what she has just constructed by asserting that this new truth is as well an assemblage of fiction.[29] Where then does the "truth" reside? Perhaps nowhere. As Adrienne Rich explains, "there is a danger run by all powerless people: that we forget we are lying, or that lying becomes a weapon we carry over into relationships with people who do not have power over us."[30] In Woolf's unwillingness to commit the arbitrary gesture of closing the gap between fact and fiction, truth and lie, of filling in the spaces of the ellipsis, she constructs a field within which women's creativity will be exercised. Further, as Rich concludes, at issue are "the possibilities of truth," not "the truth," which make conceivable "the possibility of life between us."[31] In that move, in her resistance to determinacy and closure, Woolf refuses to "fix" her conclusion and thereby creates, indeed demands, the future possibility of other voices and other conclusions. She develops this strategy deliberately and carefully, and through it she asks for Olsen, just as Judith Shakespeare demands Woolf.

Three Guineas stands in relationship to contemporary feminist cultural analysis as *A Room of One's Own* does with respect to feminist literary criticism. Lillian Robinson gives this description of the difference between the works: "Whereas *A Room of One's Own* is a book about money, sex, and culture, *Three Guineas* is a book about money, sex, and power."[32] The latter work revolves around the central problem of women's (the outsiders') relationship to culture as expressed in this question: Given the condition of women as created or perpetuated by men in power, how could or why should women presume to help men prevent the wars they insist on making? The problem is an exceedingly difficult one that continues to compel our attention. Because the issue of power is at the heart of Woolf's exploration, the work continues to provoke critical disapproval displaced in arguments concerning supposed problems of style, tone, or organization.

Critics such as Elaine Showalter, Herbert Marder, and Michael Rosenthal simplify the work's complexity and pass harshly reductive judgments on its author. Showalter sees the work as politically naive and marked by the limitation of Woolf's personal experience: *"Three Guineas* rings false. Its language, all too frequently, is empty sloganeering and cliché; the stylistic tricks . . . become irritating and hysterical."[33] Showalter wants to read the book in a particular way, as advocating "an almost total withdrawal from male society."[34] Her final judgment is that "Woolf's view of womanhood is as deadly as it is disembodied. The ultimate room of one's own is the grave."[35] (Showalter could have invested the word "hysterical" with new significance had she chosen to understand it as Kristeva does—the speech and writing of "outsiders to male-dominated discourse."[36]) Marder calls it a "neurotic" book but claims to be speaking metaphorically, although he goes on to call it "too shrill and self-indulgent to succeed, even as propaganda."[37] Referring to the work as a "moral tract," Rosenthal comments: "As a sustained piece of social criticism, *Three Guineas* is rather too simplistic to be totally convincing. Although it accurately depicts the massive injustice done women by centuries of sexist oppression, it loses some of its credibility in reducing all of civilization's ills to the villainy of the male. . . . The history of male domination is a singularly pernicious instance of a kind of exploitation that is all too peculiarly human, running throughout both sexes and all social classes at all times."[38] Rosenthal's humanistic levelling spreads social blame equally in order to obscure male privilege. I find the comments of these contemporary critics shocking at first, but on second thought I would not expect literary criticism, always blind to its own exercise of power, to appreciate such a devastating analysis of power either from one of its members or from an Outsider. While *Three Guineas* may have stylistic limitations worth noting, these critical indictments stem from a quarrel resulting from the critics' interpretations of the book's content, not its form or style—Showalter's anxiety that Woolf urges women to withdraw from men, Rosenthal's and Marder's fears that Woolf holds men responsible for all the ills of civilization.

Other perspectives on the work make these and similar critical judgments suspect. Carolyn Heilbrun's testimony concerning the way she modified her view of *Three Guineas* places the above remarks in another perspective: "For many years I was made uncomfortable by *Three Guineas*, preferring the 'nicer' *Room*, where Woolf never presses against the bounds of proper female behavior—where, it could seem, her art prevailed. I say this to my shame. What prevailed was not her art alone, but her fear (and mine) of arousing the patriarchy to disgust, of acting wholly apart from the 'script' assigned to women."[39] Heilbrun's candor is liberating and finds reinforcement in Brenda Silver's careful and revealing study of Woolf's preparation for writing *Three Guineas*: "All in all, twelve volumes of reading notes made between 1931 and the end of 1937, including three fat scrapbooks of cuttings and quotations, trace Woolf's preparation for the book that she 'wanted—how violently—how persistently, pressingly, compulsorily I can't say—to write.' "[40] Woolf's con-

I02

Crossing the Double-Cross

struction of the book and her accomplishments using that approach suggest the way in which *Three Guineas* is related to *A Room of One's Own* and to *Silences*.

Like the discussion of women and fiction in *A Room of One's Own*, the question of *Three Guineas*—how women can help men to prevent war—is an enterprise that from the outset "is doomed to failure."[41] This failure results from Woolf's refusal once again to espouse an absolute, unifying truth. She asks, as if in conversation with herself: "But is there no absolute point of view? Can we not find somewhere written up in letters of fire or gold. 'This is right. This wrong'?—a moral judgment which we must all, whatever our differences, accept?" (pp. 9–10). Despite her dream of unification, Woolf never accepts formulaic or predictable answers in her own writing or in anyone else's. She says, for example, of D. H. Lawrence's *Letters*: "And the repetition of one idea. I don't want that either. I don't want 'a philosophy' in the least: I don't believe in other people's reading of riddles."[42] Each time she arrives at a point of determination, she hesitates. When considering whether or not women's education will help them to achieve opinions independent of their fathers, she writes, "But . . . —here again, in those dots, doubts and hesitations assert themselves" (p. 58). Woolf stages a struggle with patriarchy or "fathers in general" as well as with her own and Antigone's father.[43] She recognizes the need to liberate thought from the "tyranny of sex": "They said that God was on their side, Nature was on their side, Law was on their side, and Property was on their side" (p. 65). Her indecision does not in the least represent a failure of nerve; rather, it results from the failure of patriarchal logic to serve woman's needs, the belief that no precise differentiation is possible between "pure fact" and "pure opinion" (p. 96), and the imaginative difficulty of constructing new solutions to problems seen differently.

Three Guineas is a meditation on the effects of difference, as well as a treatise on war or women's condition—or, more precisely, on the relationship between making war on other countries and oppressing women in one's own country. Woolf constructs a male correspondent who has sent her a letter, the selected contents of which are revealed through her answer to his invisible or unwritten letter. She also invents two other correspondents who are similarly (re)presented. Her discourse obscures and replaces theirs also. Even though Woolf begins her response by suggesting how she and her male correspondent are alike, the absent truth unspoken in the ellipsis of *A Room of One's Own* replicates itself here. That sign of uncertainty again marks the difference between man and woman, signifying in particular the unsignifiable difference "of the daughters of educated men" (p. 4): "But . . . those three dots mark a precipice, a gulf so deeply cut between us that for three years and more I have been sitting on my side of it wondering whether it is any use to try to speak across it" (p. 4). Because women experience culture's regulation of their bodies and minds differently, they develop an alternative conception of patriotism; they have different points of view. Addressing the male correspondent (and her readers), she writes: "It would seem to follow then as an indisputable fact that 'we'—meaning by 'we' a whole made up of body, brain and spirit, influenced by memory and tradition—must still differ in some essential respects from 'you,' whose body, brain and spirit have been so differently trained and so differently influenced by memory and tradition. Though we see the same world, we see it through different eyes. Any help we can give you must be different from that you can give yourselves, and perhaps the value of that help may lie in the fact of that difference" (p. 18). What then is this differing that is difference?

In the essay's second section, Woolf acts out the difference through two letters—the first a reactive attack impugning the fictitious female correspondent, the second a supportive endorsement acquitting her of telling lies and shirking her responsibility. The facts themselves are not really at issue, marshalled to the obvious extreme with notes, some of which are long, discursive explorations involving multiple sources; the problem Woolf struggles with is one of achieving a shared interpretation or reading of those evidentiary texts, of bridging the chasm . . . of difference between men and women. Woolf traces the rational structures of law and tradition to their aporia—the point of the double-cross, the logic of which she once again doubles back upon itself. For example, examining the history of how the church thwarted an early effort to establish a women's college, she writes: "But these facts, as facts so often do, prove double-faced; for though they establish the value of education, they also prove that education is by no means a positive value; it is not good in all circumstances, and good for all people; it is only good for some people and for some purposes. It is good if it produces a belief in the Church of England; bad if it produces a belief in the Church of Rome; it is good for one sex and for some professions, but bad for another sex and for another profession" (p. 26). Woolf repeatedly unveils those things that "have escaped the notice of the dominant sex owing largely it must be supposed to the hypnotic power of dominance" (p. 150). She returns unrelentingly to "facts," which, according to the rules of logic and persuasion, should produce predictable interpretations.

To unsettle the force of phallocentrism, Woolf steals the words of men and women, dislodging them from the unity of their original texts and locating them within the uncertainty of her own moral economy. She doesn't refuse unity; indeed, she wants the curriculum of the new college "not to segregate and specialize, but to combine" (p. 34). She understands that the replication of male structures for the use of females, as in the case of rebuilding the women's college, amounts to following "the old road to the old end" (p. 36), although no other more promising alternative presents itself. She is suspicious of the arbitrary perpetration of tradition, its own law, which (en)forces domination, ruling, killing, and acquisition. Likewise, she is wary of the mystical dreams of the poets, which, while they may guide us, cannot be allowed to seduce us from the material realities of dead bodies and burned houses. She underscores her dread of reappropriation, or recapitulation without change, by repeating the verse of "the same old song" that grimly recalls the prickly pear of Eliot's "The Hollow Men": " 'Here we go round the mulberry tree, the mulberry tree, the mulberry tree. . . .' " (p. 66). In this repetition Woolf perceives the consequences of women's failure to assert their unspecifiable difference. Describing such a reinscription as woman's real castration, Féral writes that to deny woman's difference "is to inscribe her in the law of the same; same sexuality, same discourse, same economy, same representation, same origin—with woman permitting the repetition of the same in disregard for difference, and with man using her to assure himself *of* and to reassure himself *about* the very structures which define him."[44] Under attack again in Woolf's text is the specular logic of patriarchy.

In writing *Three Guineas*, Woolf engages the problematics of revolutionary writing: she must employ the tools (language) and structure (syntax) of the tradition that she wishes to reform. With the notable exception of Peggy Kamuf, her critics do not always understand her position, and the necessary duplicity it entails is often regarded as one of Woolf's failures. Marder comments that "in *Three Guineas* she was trying to play the politics game herself, and at the same time to remain detached, to be both part of the battle and above it."[45] But it is more illuminating to view Woolf's choice of perspective as strategic. Roland Barthes provides further elaboration by suggesting in "The Utopia of Language" that the writer must stage a break with power at the same time that power is exercised in the act of writing. He describes the writer's essentially paradoxical position of borrowing what he or she wishes to destroy—a conundrum that preoccupies feminist theorists and post-structuralist critics today.[46] The irony runs even deeper for Woolf, who takes as her subject the very troublesome phenomenon of which Barthes remarks. Thus, Woolf materializes the domination of the fathers' discourse, the Law, over woman's attempt to speak: "We can hardly hear ourselves speak; it takes the words out of our mouths; it makes us say what we have not said. As we listen to the voices we seem to hear an infant crying in the night, the black night that now covers Europe, and with no language but a cry, Ay, ay, ay, ay. . . . But it is not a new cry, it is a very old cry" (p. 141).

Woolf constructs the imaginative possibility of a "new woman" in the educated man's daughter, the woman without a country, who "issues from the shadow of the private house, and stands on the bridge which lies between the old world and the new" (p. 16). In spite of the attraction unity offers, the writer withholds the reconciliatory gesture at the end of *Three Guineas*. Is it only that she personally does not like to "join" organizations or that she is not "politi-

105

Deconstructing the Sexual Politic

cal"? These questions suggest easy answers. Escaping the simple opposition, Jane Marcus points us in a better direction in her observation that "when one is both a radical and a feminist, one must build a counter-world to that of both the fathers and the mothers."[47] Certainly, Woolf has built her text, as she did the text of *A Room of One's Own*, to the union of the division she traces. The work develops structurally to this point; its symmetry, as a function of binary logic, demands it. Intellectually, Woolf longs for such an arrangement: "What a discovery that would be—a system that did not shut out."[48] Although she has the power, at least rhetorically if not literally, to unite men and women imaginatively (just like getting into a taxi), in *Three Guineas* she refuses poetic unity and elects instead to preserve difference. By then she has displaced the fiction of "two in a taxi" and substituted a more credible and complex conclusion reflective of the need to recognize the power of woman's position as outsider and the threat inherent in the phallocentric construction of difference.

In refusing to join, Woolf acts out women's position as the member who is not a member. She achieves this, with the difference being that she demonstrates the effects of the male economy on women just as she shows how she is both locked in it and out of it. Her radicalism requires that she demand change, not just a place in the profession as it is or a public voice to contribute to warmaking rhetoric. Berenice Carroll characterizes Woolf's stand as follows: "Certainly she did not mean . . . that women's position should remain unchanged; on the contrary she saw the oppression and constriction of women's lives as the foundation as well as the mirror of the whole corrupt and violent social system. But she saw too that that system could not be overthrown by imitating it."[49] Woolf's de(con)struction of the word "feminist" and her insistence on the Outsider's Society suggest their own internal consistency. In the text, she destroys the word because of its denigrating power against women, but at the same time she (re)constructs its meaning historically by designating the feminist struggle against "the tyranny of the patriarchal state" for "Justice and Equality and Liberty" as the forerunner of the antiwar movement (p. 102). She insists at every turn that women act out an impossible difference—their education shall be different, they shall help others in the professions, and, finally, they must re-member the old lessons of poverty, chastity, and derision in their struggle for " 'Freedom from unreal loyalties' " (p. 78).

She wants neither to become "man," merging her identity with his, nor to serve as his woman, the mirror he requires to maintain his identity. She describes male self-construction in terms linked inextricably to the domination of women: "Inevitably we look upon societies as conspiracies that sink the private brother, whom many of us have reason to respect, and inflate in his stead a monstrous male, loud of voice, hard of fist, childishly intent upon scoring the floor of the earth with chalk marks, within whose mystic boundaries human beings are penned, rigidly, separately, artificially; where, daubed red and gold, decorated like a savage with feathers he goes through mystic rites and enjoys the dubious pleasures of power and dominion while we, 'his' women, are locked in the private house without share in the many societies of which his society is composed" (p. 105).

To affirm her own contrary sense of the difference that is woman and to claim it for herself, Woolf deconstructs the sexual economy of phallocentrism —or, as she describes it, the ideology of inveterate anthropocentrism (p.146). She perceives the effects of male power in the structures of life and language. The most puzzling riddle she poses asks how women can participate in the phallocentric economy and not subscribe to its values. She therefore cautions women on the bridge of transition to note the cost of joining and to recognize the masters they are called upon to serve: "If you succeed in those professions the words 'For God and the Empire' will very likely be written, like the address on a dog-collar, round your neck. And if the words have meaning, as words perhaps should have meaning, you will have to accept that meaning and do what you can to enforce it" (p. 70). This woman on the threshold stands between two "evils": the patriarchal system of the past that seeks to entomb her in private houses, and the equally patriarchal professional system of the public world that wants to reappropriate her—the devil behind and the devil in front. Woolf's sense of a deconstructed history demonstrates how the father yielded in private, only to reconstitute his power publicly, socially, and politically. She therefore harbors few illusions concerning the terms of this opposition: "The one shuts us up like slaves in a harem; the other forces us to circle, like caterpillars head to tail, round and round the mulberry tree, the sacred tree, of property" (p. 74).

Through the affirmation of difference (in Kristeva's terms, that excess never fully absorbed by the symbolic), Féral suggests that woman will perhaps be allowed "to take control of her libidinal economy without lies and silence in order to articulate it in a new form of representation and specularization of the subject."[50] This, for Woolf, is the means of " 'protecting culture and intellectual liberty' " (p. 85), properties that can be bought and sold, prostituted or kept chaste like the female body. Freedom of body and mind are undifferentiated in Woolf's description of her desire that printed words speak for women: "They will speak your own mind, in your own words, at your own time, at your own length, at your own bidding" (p. 98). The inability of men and women to speak across the gap, with "(in)difference," threatens the concept of freedom. In a passage quoted in part by Olsen, Woolf remarks: "But it is so important to accustom ourselves to the duties of free speech, for without private there can be no public freedom, that we must try to uncover this fear and to face it. What then can be the nature of the fear that still makes concealment necessary between educated people and reduces our boasted freedom to a farce? . . . Again there are three dots; again they represent a gulf—of silence this time, of silence inspired by fear" (p. 120). By tracing the track back to the "archaic mother," the repressed voice, or what Woolf's narrator refers to as "thinking back through our mothers," woman will perhaps then, Féral says, "be able to take her place within artistic and political signifying systems."[51]

In her final gesture, the refusal to join, Woolf captures the unsolved riddle of woman and writing. In a sense, she cannot join because she is already a member, and she cannot join because she differs, is not one of the Same. Commenting on the texts of Kristeva and Irigaray, Féral makes an observation about their view of woman that serves as a useful summary of Woolf's strategy in *Three Guineas*: "More lucid than man, she nevertheless tends to safeguard the difference between the sexes and the abyss which separates them, all the while working to establish a new relationship between the two. This new arrangement will however entail not only a social upheaval, in that it aims at the forces of production and reproduction, but also and especially a symbolic upheaval, in that it opens onto the subversion of our logical structures of thought."[52] Although at the outset of her text, Woolf wonders whether or not it is possible to speak from (in)difference, she gives us *Three Guineas* as a meditation on this problem. In her decision to speak, she pre-settles the text's question and demonstrates her membership through participation in discourse.

Woolf, in writing *A Room of One's Own* and *Three Guineas*, was keenly aware of her place in the middle class and of the differences between her circumstances and those of working-class women. Having written an introduction to the collection of accounts by the Co-operative Working Women, published as *Life as We Have Known It*, she understood the difference between "first hand" narratives and descriptions written by "the educated class . . . through pro-proletarian spectacles" (p. 177). So, in a note to *Three Guineas* she comments: "Meanwhile it would be interesting to know what the true born working man or woman thinks of the playboys and playgirls of the educated class who adopt the working-class cause without sacrificing middle-class capital, or sharing working-class experience" (p. 177). Woolf's ability to recognize this unromanticized difference in the lives of working women, as well as her personal courage in speaking out against domination, earned her Tillie Olsen's acknowledged and enduring respect.[53]

Olsen herself realizes the way in which she lives out Woolf's texts (Olsen's pre-texts) in her struggle for the economic independence required for creative activity. She explains these circumstances as follows: "The habits of a lifetime when everything else had to come before writing are not easily broken, even when circumstances now often make it possible for writing to be first; habits of years—response to others, distractibility, responsibility for daily matters—stay with you, mark you, become you. The cost of 'discontinuity' (that pattern still imposed on women) is such a weight of things unsaid, an accumulation of material so great, that everything starts up something else in me; what should take weeks, takes me sometimes months to write; what should take months, takes years."[54] Olsen creates a nurturing *"essential angel"* (p. 34) who maintains everyday life, a counterpart to Woolf's repressive "angel in the house." Olsen is Woolf's "ordinary woman" become the "extraordinary woman."

Other concerns link Woolf and Olsen. In a fine argument for Olsen's place within a "socialist feminist" tradition, Deborah Rosenfelt locates Olsen at the intersection of the "literary tradition of women writers," as established by Ellen Moers and Elaine Showalter, and the writers of the radical (predominantly Marxist) literary tradition outlined by Walter Rideout and Daniel Aaron: "At the intersections of these larger traditions is a line of women writers, associated with the American Left, who unite a class consciousness and a feminist consciousness in their lives and creative work, who are concerned with the material circumstances of people's lives, who articulate the experiences and grievances of women and of other oppressed groups—workers, national minorities, the colonized and the exploited—and who speak out of a defining commitment to social change."[55] Out of this dedication to developing an art "based on the lives of 'despised people,' "[56] Olsen draws upon the tradition represented in *A Room of One's Own* and *Three Guineas* (originally entitled "On Being Despised"). Olsen assumes Woolf as she begins her discussion of women's historic silence: "I will not repeat what is in Virginia Woolf's *A Room of One's Own*, but talk of this last century and a half in which women have begun to have voice in literature" (p. 16). She then proceeds to show that "in this so much more favorable century" (p. 25), still only one woman writer for every twelve men is accorded literary recognition. Through her "first hand" analysis of gender, race, and class, Olsen re-presents Woolf's discovery of the oppressive force of phallocentrism as "the shaping power and inequality of circumstance" (p. vii).

Tillie Olsen's *Silences* is as much about breaking silences as it is about their causes. It is as though the word contains its own subversion; by speaking about the obstacles to creativity, Olsen creates a text that undercuts the very problem it takes as its subject. In retrospect, we see how Olsen's text, writing the affective, concrete dimension of otherness, prepares us to feel the significance of recent theoretical considerations of writing and oppression. Extending Woolf's observations in *A Room of One's Own*, Olsen observes that "the acceptance of these age-old constrictive definitions of woman at a time when they are less true than ever to the realities of most women's lives—and need not be true at all—remains a complex problem for women writing in our time" (p. 43). We read simultaneously the pain of creative and political silencing and the public acknowledgment of silence. Olsen writes the specificity of silence: "These pressures toward censorship, self-censorship; toward accepting, abiding by entrenched attitudes, thus falsifying one's own reality, range, vision, truth, voice, are extreme for women writers (indeed have much to do with the fear, the sense of powerlessness that pervades certain of our books). . . . Not to be able to come to one's truth or not to use it in one's writing, even in telling the truth having to 'tell it slant,' . . . results in loss to literature and the comprehensions we seek in it" (p. 44). Both the beauty and the power of Olsen's work reside in her uncompromising desire to express herself, and, through this desire, to confront the question of how one writes silence. Her epigraph addresses the dilemma:

> For our silenced people, century after century their beings consumed in the hard, everyday essential work of maintaining human life. Their art, which still they made—as their other contributions—anonymous; refused respect, recognition; lost.

> For those of us (few yet in number, for the way is punishing), their kin and descendants who begin to emerge into more flowered and rewarded use of our selves in ways denied to them;—and by our achievement bearing witness to what was (and still is) being lost, silenced.

Olsen is at once the exemplar of the silenced and the liberated, the powerless and the powerful, assuming power while always verging on powerlessness.

Silences is a strange text, a witness to so much more than Olsen's painful struggle to write. We remember its eloquence perhaps more than its persistent threat to disappear, undone by the silences it takes for its subject. Our memory of the work tends to center on the essays (118 pages) of Part 1: "Silences in Literature," "One Out of Twelve: Writers Who Are Women in Our Century," and "Rebecca Harding Davis." Part 2 (140 pages) contains the elaborating notes, and Part 3 (28 pages) consists of a brief comment on class and creativity and the re-presentation of several works. The book is what it can be—fragments, scraps, lectures, and essays with no continuous argument or apparent unifying design. Rosenfelt calls it "a sustained prose poem,"[57] and Erika Duncan describes it as "half a non-fiction essay, half a long prose poem, a collaging of words of other writers on the subject with her own."[58] As a critic approaching the text, I re-enact Woolf's response to the collected memories of the Co-operative Working Women; she begins by saying: "This book is not a book. Turning the pages, I began to ask myself what is this book then, if it is not a book? What quality has it? What ideas does it suggest? What old arguments and memories does it rouse in me?"[59] Playing out the interpretive drama, Woolf arrives at a position that resists decision—a passage Olsen also cites: "Whether that is literature or not literature I do not presume to say, but that it explains much and reveals much is certain."[60] Because Olsen, a writer of considerable talent, refuses to impose coherence as a way of achieving the conventional unicentered voice one expects in a book, the interpretive dilemma grows more complex, and it matters little whether Olsen won't or can't

Crossing the Double-Cross

order her words. The book recalls its own progression from silence (the circumstance of social hatred's repressive force), to speech (the unwritten talks that become the essays), to writing—the open, polyvocal text of multiple origins. In constructing this new text, Olsen privileges the other side of silence, that unspoken, unknown (non)center of woman's experience. Through actual borrowings of other writers' words, she allows many voices to speak her text, to traverse her territory. By means of a polyvocal chorus she questions silence and allows others to participate in the same process; she unites men and women, making the move that Woolf refused earlier in *Three Guineas*. She then calls upon the reader to write the text—no longer her text, but occasioned by it and by the voices speaking through it.

Quotation in Olsen's work serves a strategic function related to her preoccupation with the whole person and her view of herself "as writer, as insatiable reader, as feminist-humanist, as woman" (p. 118). Part 2 of *Silences*, entitled "Acerbs, Asides, Amulets, Exhumations, Sources, Deepenings, Roundings, Expansions," is the notebook and sourcebook with commentary of a writer/reader/feminist-humanist/woman. She explains this longest section as follows: "Much of this aftersection is the words of others—some of them unknown or little known, others of them great and famous. Each quotation, as each reference to lives, is selectively chosen for maximum significance; to become—or to become again—current; to occur and recur; to aim" (p. 119). These words refer "back" to the essays of Part 1, but they also "aim," exhuming texts and pointing toward a future unmarked by the "unnatural" silences of difference, restoring the words to us, her readers who are, as Roland Barthes remarks, "the space on which all the quotations that make up a writing are inscribed without any of them being lost; a text's unity lies not in its origin but in its destination."[61]

If we can say that the text has a sex—specifically the sex of the writer—then the transversals Olsen permits in the form of quotations create the play of male and female, the difference within her work, within herself, and within us as readers. In addition to staging almost forty appearances by Virginia Woolf, Olsen quotes many men and women directly: the men—Dreiser, Wilde, Artaud, Baudelaire, Emerson, Gardner, Thackeray, Gide, Hughes, West, Carroll, De Quincy, Borges, Auden, Whitman, Goncourt, Renard, Leopardi, Crane, Anderson, Babel, Chekhov, Hawthorne, Hardy, Hopkins, Rimbaud, Balzac, Conrad, Fitzgerald, Mailer, James, Mann, Kafka, Rilke, Du Bois, Blake, Camus, Herbert; and the women—Mansfield, Richardson, Austen, C. Bronte, Shreiner, Nin, Plath, Jewett, Calisher, Wollstonecraft, Lessing, Tsetsaeyva, Davis, Dickinson, Porter, De Ford, Smedley, Ozick, Hardwick, Shange, Beauvoir, Alta, M. Walker, Colette, Rich, Duras, L. Robinson, Toklas, Bogan, Sexton, Atwood, Cather, and numerous others. Because of her sensitivity to the "marginal," Olsen resists exclusion: "No one has as yet written *A Room of One's Own* for writers, other than women, still marginal in literature. Nor do any bibliographies exist for writers whose origins and circumstances are marginal. Class remains the greatest unexamined factor" (p. 146). In Part 2, it seems as though she allows others to re-write the essays of Part 1 in their own voices. She does not want to "write like a man," which she views as being "akin to 'passing': the attempt to escape inferior status, penalties, injustices, by concealing one's color, class, origin. Identifying oneself as of the dominant" (p. 248). Instead, she urges women "to validate our different sense of reality, to help raise one's own truths, voice, against the prevalent" (p. 264). Important in this effort "to tell the truth" is writing the experience of the body—the "knowledge of one's body that comes only through free use of it" (p. 254); "the problem of finding one's own truth through the primacy accorded sexuality by our times" (pp. 254–55); "the unworked through, unassessed relationship between the body difference and the actual power relationship permeating associations between the sexes" (p. 255); and finally, "telling the truth about one's body: a necessary, freeing subject for the woman writer" (p. 255). As though in response to the direction she suggests above, Olsen constructs the interplay between the voice of the Father (society, tradition, master) and the voice of the mother (repression, silence, slave), and between these quoted texts and her own text of Part 1.

Cixous's very particular understanding of bisexuality clarifies the political and aesthetic potential inherent in Olsen's strategy: "And it's this being 'neither out nor in,' being 'beyond the outside/inside opposition' that permits the play of 'bisexuality.' Female sexuality is always at some point bisexual. Bisexual doesn't mean, as many people think, that she can make love with both a man and a woman, it doesn't mean she has two partners, even if it can at times mean this. Bisexuality on an unconscious level is the possibility of extending into the other, of being in such a relation with the other that *I* move into the other without destroying the other: that I will look for the other where s/he is without trying to bring everything back to myself."[62] Thus, Olsen lets the "other" *be* the "other," the "not me" in relationship to the "me." She refuses to take sides against the "not me" by subsuming its text within her own, by reducing it to closure. Crossing the gender boundaries of discourse, she performs an act that creates a text unlike those of her male contemporaries.

When Simone de Beauvoir confronts the question of sexual difference in *The Second Sex*, she asks who it is that can undo the opposition between men and women. She rejects the "angel," as knowing nothing of human fact, and the hermaphrodite as being neither whole man nor complete woman; instead, she settles on the right of "certain women" to redefine the territory afresh after discarding such notions about women as inferiority, stupidity, and presumed equality.[63] Beauvoir's belief resides implicitly in the fact that women know men better than men know women—although she avoids stating it so explicitly. Thirty years later, Cixous echoes and extends this view: "To man it is much more difficult to let oneself be traversed by the other; writing is the passage, entrance, exit, sojourn in me of the other that I am and am not."[64] Rather than exclusion, it is the inclusion of the other that can bring about change. Derrida is responding to the same point when he theoretically rejects monological/monosexual discourse. Instead, he says, "I have felt the necessity for a chorus, a choreographic text with polysexual signatures. I felt this every time that a legitimacy of the neuter, the apparently least suspect sexual neutrality of 'phallocentric or gynocentric' mastery, threatened to immobilize (in silence), colonize, stop or unilateralize in a subtle and sublime manner what remains no doubt irreducibly dissymmetrical."[65] In choosing her own approach to textuality, Olsen as woman exemplifies the position Woolf asked men to adopt: "The future of fiction depends very much upon what extent men can be educated to stand free speech in women."[66] By using quotation so extensively that the words of others outnumber her own, Olsen, the perfect ventriloquist, establishes a feminist position that is permeable to the free speech of others. She mitigates the unicenteredness of phallocentric discourse and subverts the concept of textual ownership to forge a new "heterotextuality." Unicenteredness is further denied in her refusal to conclude; instead, she allows the voices of Rebecca Harding Davis, the (re)presented Lowell mill girl poet, and Baudelaire to speak her book's conclusion.

This difference has its own wisdom and marks the author's resistance to phallocentrism. Her text fulfills Cixous's definition of the "feminine textual body": "A feminine textual body is recognized by the fact that it is always endless, without ending: there is no closure, it doesn't stop, and it's this that very often makes the feminine text difficult to read. For we've learned to read books that basically pose the word 'end.' But this one doesn't finish, a feminine text goes on and on and at a certain moment the volume comes to an end but the writing continues and for the reader this means being thrust into the void. These are texts that work on the beginning but not on the origin."[67] This is a difference that recalls our reluctance to approach *Silences* on its own terms. Cixous's point is further clarified by suggesting the way in which Olsen exemplifies Féral's description of woman as "the guarantor of the heterogeneity which dislocates unity and of the pleasure which accompanies it. She is that which is neither power nor structure, nor system but its support; she is the otherness which permits the establishment of unity."[68] The pages' blank spaces, open invitations to the reader to participate in the text's creation, to break the silences by inscribing themselves, further reinforce Olsen's remarkable accomplishment.

The effects of these strategies suggest an important difference between Woolf and Olsen. Woolf marks the truth and traces the opening at the very point of conclusion—reminding us that she had asserted the same position at the beginning, perhaps mistaken by the reader as a rhetorical convention of authorial false modesty. She refuses to join the society, but the form of her text's production belies the authority of her decision. However, like Olsen, she does refuse the illusory and artificial closing of the system that would simply reestablish the oppositions of phallocentrism she has worked to deconstruct. She participates in the system and its flaws in order to exhibit them, just long enough to display them without allowing herself to be entrapped. Her fictions save her, or is it her facts? Olsen takes the next step and lays open the entire system: through direct quotation she permits the controlled presence of phallocentric utterances within her own discourse. In this move, she subverts both her own authorial control and the monological and monosexual contexts in which the quotations were once situated. Just as Janie's story in *Their Eyes Were Watching God* is given back to the community, and Celie's final letter in *The Color Purple* is addressed to everyone, Olsen seizes and wields the power of language in order to return it to the people; she never flirts with what might have become "lies" issuing from the assertion of her own author(ity).

CHAPTER 7

DEFIANCE

THE BODY (OF) WRITING/
THE WRITING (OF) BODY

*It's no accident: women take after birds and robbers just as robbers take after women and birds. They (*illes*) go by, fly the coop, take pleasure in jumbling the order of space, in disorienting it, in changing around the furniture, dislocating things and values, breaking them all up, emptying structures, and turning propriety upside down.*

—Hélène Cixous, "The Laugh of the Medusa"

(and whoever believes that one tracks down some thing?*— one tracks down tracks)*

—Jacques Derrida, "Differance"

n her unmasking of patriarchal fictions, Woolf equates the protection of cultural institutions with the safeguarding of the female body. Olsen similarly regards the female body as a necessary subject for the woman who desires "to tell the truth" in writing. The body is the site where the political and the aesthetic interpret the material. Male control of women's bodies has always been the cornerstone of patriarchy. Women often play out their resistance to this authority in sexual terms; as the appropriated objects of men, we seek to disturb the system of patriarchal control through acts of sexual defiance. Historically, this resistance or disruption through the assertion of sexual autonomy has assumed many forms, including chastity, celibacy, nonmonogamy, and lesbianism. By such means we attempt, in Collette Guillaumin's terms, to "regain . . . the possession of our *materiality*" on behalf of the entire class of women.[1]

In *The Second Sex*, Simone de Beauvoir cites a proposition advanced by Sartre and Merleau-Ponty that " 'sexuality is coextensive with existence.' " She continues by explaining how the statement "can be understood in two very different ways; it can mean that every experience of the existent has a sexual significance, or that every sexual phenomenon has an existential import."[2] In either case, however, control or the illusion of control over one's sexual expression is analogous to control over one's existence—a desire more complex for women as an appropriated class, and even further complicated for the multiply oppressed lesbian, black, and Third World women. In contrast with men, women are sex; they do not possess it, rather they are possessed as sex. Guillaumin explains, "ideologically men have the free use of their sexual organ, and practically women do not have the use of themselves—they are directly objects."[3] This assertion has two important aspects: women do not have sex, they are sex, defined for the use of men; women are nothing but sexual objects unless defined otherwise by men. Guillaumin claims an additional effect of women's status: "When one is materially appropriated, one is mentally dispossessed of oneself."[4] This notion gives rise to the image of the writer as "madwoman," or woman not in possession of herself.

The feminist critic's project—to write the story of woman's deviance itself—admits the same criticism Derrida makes of *Madness and Civilization*, in which Foucault attempts to write the archaeology of the silence that is madness itself, the unreason that reason imprisons in order to write itself. We would need to discover, according to Derrida, "the virgin [woman as her own] and unitary ground upon which the decisive act linking and separating madness and reason [women's silence and men's speech] obscurely took root."[5] Following this logic, we must discover the point at which men set themselves against women to control them and the logos and to consign women to silence. We would have to locate phallicization where it "erects" itself. Madeleine

Crossing the Double-Cross

Gagnon suggests the range of its power: "The phallus means everything that sets itself up as a mirror. Everything that erects itself as perfection. Everything that wants regimentation and representation. That which does not erase/efface but covets. That which lines things up in history museums. That which constantly pits itself against the power of immortality."[6] The origin of man (not humankind, not woman) as the phallus consists in his separation from and imprisoning of woman; seeking to protect his identity, he keeps woman the "other." But the location of such an origin for man and for woman—the point at which the literal body is distinct from the metaphorical body—is not recoverable.[7]

Here, in this constitution of woman's difference, the feminist critic encounters the classic Derridean double bind with respect to women's writing: to remain silent and to speak/write are to conform, to participate in, and not to depart from the controlling logos. To speak is to submit to the structure of phallocentrism. Representation itself, the symbolic order, is founded upon the repression of woman's desire, upon lack and castration. As Mary Jacobus puts it, femininity is "the repressed term by which discourse is made possible. The feminine takes its place with the absence, silence, or incoherence that discourse represses."[8] To refuse to speak is to reinscribe woman in silence, marginality and madness. Thus, woman as sign is the site of struggle between contradiction and repression. Derrida's critique of Foucault's intention in *Madness and Civilization* is easily extended: "The expression 'to say madness itself' is self-contradictory. To say madness without expelling it into objectivity is to let it say itself. But madness [woman] is what by its essence cannot be said: it is the 'absence of the work,' as Foucault profoundly says."[9] Through the extension of this schema, woman is the absence of speaking; the speaking subject is not woman. The speaking, thinking (*Cogito, sum*) identity is reserved for men.

What then is women's writing? Can there be such a thing? Nancy Miller and Peggy Kamuf debate this, among other questions, in a set of four articles, including their well-known *Diacritics* dialogue concerning the effective practice of feminist criticism. Their discussion revolves around the materiality of the text's signature, and specifically the female author as subject. The dialogue's pre-text, Kamuf's "Writing Like a Woman," interrogates the position: "Women's writing is writing signed by women."[10] Kamuf argues that the problem cannot be constructed in this simple, biologically deterministic reversal of patriarchal practice. She clinches her point by asserting that "man" as the central object of study is, in historical terms, a fairly recent and now outmoded epistemological invention; as such, the feminist critic who wishes to study "woman" is left without a ground to stand on except the oppositional logic she seeks to undo: "To put it yet another way: if feminist theory lets itself be guided by questions such as what is women's language, literature, style or experience from where does it get its faith in the form of these questions to get at truth, if not from the same central store that supplies humanism with its faith in the universal truth of man? And what if notions such as 'getting-at-the-truth-of-the-object' represented a principal means by which the power of power structures are sustained and even extended?"[11] Instead of focusing on texts signed by women, Kamuf would have feminist criticism address itself to all inscriptions of femininity.

Nancy Miller takes another view, some of the time. In her essay "Women's Autobiography in France," she maintains that "the historical truth of a woman writer's life lies in the reader's grasp of her intratext: the body of her writing and not the writing of her body."[12] Here, Miller sidesteps the problematic essentialist view with which Kamuf takes issue and that Showalter describes as "anatomy is textuality."[13] Yet in her dialogue essay, she disagrees with Peggy Kamuf's proposal to gloss woman as an archaic signifier. Here Miller argues that the signature, as indicative of the text's paternity/maternity, means everything to us, politically. Certainly Miller is entitled to her aporia with respect to the question of feminist criticism, which she professes from the outset presents an insoluble problem. And Kamuf, as Miller claims, adopts "the metalogically 'correct' position,"[14] but one that is only *metalogically* correct and is basically patrilineal in descent. While women's writing takes place within phallocentric discourse, it works ceaselessly and simultaneously to deconstruct it, or as Mary Jacobus explains, "to write what cannot be written."[15] Initially it seems, however, that critics are mixing two kinds of writing in these discussions: women's writing and feminist writing, and that most of the time we are really discussing feminist writing—writing that, as I have shown previously, constitutes a challenge to the boundaries of difference, writing that consciously attempts to traverse the limitations erected by phallocentric discourse. And for me it remains a question the extent to which all or some women, by virtue of their marginal relation to discourse, also unconsciously write as feminists.

That these questions are viewed as inherent contradictions—to write and not to write is to speak oneself, and woman's writing is feminist writing—are powerful effects of the Derridean metalogic. Certainly, there is a sense in which these terms do not contradict each other, so that to be a woman and to write can both constitute transgressions. As Alice Jardine explains: "woman must be released from her metaphysical bondage and it is writing, as the locus of the 'feminine operation,' that can and does subvert the history of that metaphysics. The attributes of writing are the attributes of 'woman'—that which disturbs the Subject, the Dialectic, and Truth is feminine in its essence."[16] At the same time, this writing always takes place within and by means of a circumscribing and repressive phallocentric discourse to which its very existence stands as a challenge. And feminist writing is never free from the traces of the oppressive discourse it seeks to undo. Mary Jacobus's concise description of how women's language works is instructive: "The transgression of literary boundaries—moments when structures are shaken, when language refuses to lie down meekly, or the marginal is brought into sudden focus, or intelligibility itself refused—reveal not only the conditions of possibility within which women's writing exists, but what it would be like to revolutionise them. In the same way, the moment of desire (the moment when the writer most clearly installs herself in her writing) becomes a refusal of mastery, an opting for openness and possibility, which can in itself make women's writing a challenge to the literary structures it must necessarily inhabit."[17] And these "women writers," whom I earlier claimed as feminist writers, are after all mad; nonconforming violators of reason, of the logos, they are also mad (angry) about the specific oppressions that have written women's historic condition. On the level of this double gesture, the feminist as writer, character, and even reader converge.

Captive in the structure of patriarchal metaphysics, the feminist critic occupies the same discursive space and shares the dilemma of writer/character. As Jill Johnston remarks in *Lesbian Nation*, "identity is what you can say you are according to what they say you can be."[18] Woman first breaks through this encapsulated and circumscribed self, in order to deconstruct the identity received from patriarchal culture, and at the same time to engage the process of constructing a self. This struggle with identity is an imperfect one. She is not really looking for new identities, separations from the discourse within the discourse that proscribes such autonomous definings of the illusorily autonomous self. Rather, she tracks down the tracks—silence, anger, defiance, destruction—of woman's escape that is never really complete, not a presence because never present. She searches for the traces of woman's resistance and of her apparently inescapable reinscription. Extending Mikhail Bakhtin's concept of the "dialogic imagination" to women's writing, Patricia Yaeger advances a provocative thesis: "Although the plots that women construct for their heroines continue to focus on, and therefore in a sense to privilege, the dominant sex/gender system, the language that women writers have begun to develop to subvert or deconstruct this system is at once traditional and feminocentric. Language is not a reductively patriarchal system but a somewhat flexible institution that not only reflects but may also address existing power structures, including those conditioned by gender."[19] This fluid, dynamic view of language (more appropriately languages) gives us a way of understanding the simultaneous traces of complicity and disruption in women's texts. Although the appropriated woman speaks without a voice of her own, the very act of writing, of speech, signals her defiance and requires that she transgress or (un)cross the double-cross of difference as constituted by phallocentrism.

She stages this defiance of mind and voice in her own body—the scene of

Defiance

her literal and metaphoric appropriation. As Kate Millett notes in *Sexual Politics*: "The notion of sexual resistance, the defense of integrity with frigidity, or the preservation of independence through chastity, are common themes in Victorian literature. Under the demands of a socially coercive or exploitative sexuality such as patriarchy had instituted, where sexual activity implied submitting to male will, 'chastity,' frigidity, or some form of resistance to sexuality took on something of the character of a 'political' response to the conditions of sexual politics."[20] Perhaps it is for similar reasons that so many of the better known women writers have defied sociosexual codes, and have been lesbian, single and/or childless. Tillie Olsen illustrates this point in her litany of distinguished women writers who remained childless: "Willa Cather, Ellen Glasgow, Gertrude Stein, Edith Wharton, Virginia Woolf, Elizabeth Bowen, Katherine Mansfield, Isak Dinesen, Katherine Anne Porter, Dorothy Richardson, Henry Handel Richardson, Susan Glaspell, Dorothy Parker, Lillian Hellman, Eudora Welty, Djuna Barnes, Anaïs Nin, Ivy Compton-Burnett, Zora Neale Hurston, Elizabeth Madox Roberts, Christina Stead, Carson McCullers, Flannery O'Connor, Jean Stafford, May Sarton, Josephine Herbst, Jessamyn West, Janet Frame, Lillian Smith, Iris Murdoch, Joyce Carol Oates, Hannah Green, Lorraine Hansberry."[21] Of course, not only are these writers childless, some of them—Welty, O'Connor, and Glasgow, for example—never married. Others among them are lesbians: Willa Cather, Gertrude Stein, Lillian Smith, and May Sarton. In any case, we could say that they all struggled to possess their own bodies in order to possess themselves as writers, as thinking/speaking subjects.

Another contradiction inhabits this proposition: while women may escape individual appropriation, we cannot escape collective appropriation. Nonetheless, our personal defiance threatens the social and symbolic order even though we are powerless to destroy it. As Guillaumin explains, women "escape the *institutions* which are an actualization of sexage [a neologism analogous to *esclavage* (slavery) and *servage* (serfdom)], and only the institutions. The relation of social appropriation of the whole class by the other class remains dominant, and collective appropriation is not overcome even if private appropriation does not take place."[22] This point is clearly exemplified in Kate Chopin's *The Awakening*, to which we will turn in a moment.

With respect to woman's self-definition, Myra Jehlen maintains that the only real power women characters have is to exercise the power of the imagination in the interior world of the psyche. (How the self-defining capacity and the interior imagination free themselves from phallocentric control is not clear.) The Anglo-American novel, she argues, grants women interior lives but suppresses their activity in the public sphere. On this basis, Jehlen characterizes women's writing as inherently political, because forbidden, and requiring as a "*pre*condition" for its existence that the women "confront the assumptions that render them a kind of fiction in themselves in that they are defined by others, as components of the language and thought of others. . . . . All women's writing would thus be congenitally defiant and universally characterized by the blasphemous argument it makes in coming into being. And this would mean that the autonomous individuality of a woman's story or poem is framed by engagement, the engagement of its denial of dependence."[23] The conclusion to which Jehlen proceeds, though speculatively, is that the novel is a form conceived by and placed in the service of patriarchy. As such, she says, "the possibility that an impotent feminine sensibility is a basic structure of the novel, representing one of the important ways that the novel embodies the basic structures of this society, would suggest more generally that the achievement of female autonomy must have radical implications not only politically but also for the very forms and categories of all our thinking."[24]

The force of Jehlen's speculation finds illustration in Kate Chopin's *The Awakening*. Edna Pontellier defies the codes of Creole society by removing herself from the physical (spatial) control of her husband, and by constituting herself as the subject of her own possession rather than as an object among the many material goods of Mr. Pontellier. Edna stamps on her wedding ring and breaks a vase, symbols of her sexual and domestic bondage, in the urge to destroy that accompanies her desire to create herself. As she abandons conventions, Edna appears mentally unbalanced from her husband's perspective of blindness and inadvertent insight: "He could see plainly that she was not herself. That is, he could not see that she was becoming herself and daily casting aside that fictitious self which we assume like a garment with which to appear before the world."[25] Similarly, Arobin characterizes Mademoiselle Reisz, the pianist, as "partially demented," whereas to Edna she seems "wonderfully sane" (p. 301). While Chopin grants Edna a momentary autonomy, she cannot permit her character to succeed in the terms of this world, to create an existence free from patriarchal dominance. Guillaumin elaborates this harsh reality: "When one is appropriated, or dominated, thinking means going against the vision of (and against) the social relationships imposed by the dominators. It does not mean ceasing to know what the relationships of appropriation harshly teach you."[26] Thus, author and character engage the double gesture, destroying as they create.

Chopin carefully develops the interrelationship between these two strains. Paula Treichler correctly notes the momentary fusion of body and consciousness, Edna's self-appropriation, as she learns to swim: "For a moment at least, Chopin creates a perfect verbal merging between the forces that act on Edna from outside her and the imperatives of her own self, between the abstractions of consciousness and the concrete language of her physical world."[27]

In addition to the more obvious strategies of presenting the sea's liberating potential and of linking death and freedom, Chopin fuses destruction and creation in the dual coloration of the sea that is at once the scene of Edna's symbolic liberation and the location of her death.[28] As a counterpoint to the lyric beauty of moon and water, Chopin creates the dark sea of solitude, desolation, and "hopeless resignation" (p. 229). It is seductive, luring the soul away from the body (p. 214), and dangerous: "The sea was quiet now, and swelled largely in broad billows that melted into one another and did not break except upon the beach in little foamy crests that coiled back like slow, white serpents" (p. 231). Emphasizing its significance, Chopin repeats the serpent metaphor in the novel's final scene. The sea, like the Creole society in which Edna finds herself immersed in the summer of her awakening, is not her "native element" (p. 231). For her it is an uncharted landscape, a wild zone, like the new self she is constructing: "As she swam she seemed to be reaching out for the unlimited in which to lose herself" (p. 232).

However, while she succeeds in removing herself from the control of social institutions such as marriage and motherhood, Edna's ultimate circumstance illustrates Guillaumin's view concerning the power of collective appropriation. Character and author create new fictions of the self, "pure invention," to replace the old—Edna's tale "of a woman who paddled away with her lover one night in a pirogue and never came back" (p. 285). Chopin's more politically realistic tale reveals the underside of her character's romantic fiction; the pirogue becomes a ship of death across the River Styx. Treichler, in her discussion of the novel's ending, comments that the self "undoes itself" in the act of asserting itself. She reads Edna's suicide as an "active passivity, a decision no longer to decide. For Edna," she continues, "this act translates many of the novel's metaphors into reality, and in turn parallels the critical fact about this story: that it is about a woman learning to perceive reality whose 'I' supplants the language of illusion."[29] But in these double gestures, reminiscent of those Freeman inscribes in her stories, Kate Chopin envisions Edna's inevitable reinscription at least as clearly as she acknowledges her character's freedom from cultural prescriptions, a freedom only conceivable through death.

The issue for women—writers, characters, and critics—is getting power, which is only attained by using it. What are the alternatives to marrying it, learning to live without it, or exploiting our powerlessness? To think of one's self alone, not in a specular relationship as the mirror to man's identity, is to enter the "dark continent" of woman; it is to begin a new process of self-definition, by attempting to refuse the role of Other to his Absolute One. Despite the prohibitions against transgression into this unbounded territory, *"the Dark Continent,"* according to Cixous, *"is neither dark nor unexplorable."*[30] Through defiance, women challenge the language and culture of patriarchy. Edna, for example, argues with Madame Ratignolle, the "motherwoman," about a woman's obligation to her children, saying she would give them the unessentials—money and her life—but never the essential, her self (which she is not in possession of anyway), and Chopin remarks, "the two women did not appear . . . to be talking the same language" (257). Similarly, the central character in Margaret Atwood's novel, *Surfacing*, cannot speak the language of her lover Joe: "It was the language again, I couldn't use it because it wasn't mine. He must have known what he meant but it was an imprecise word; the Eskimos had fifty-two words for snow because it was important to them, there ought to be as many for love."[31] For Atwood's character, language is inextricably bound up with existence. In her reflection on Americans, symbolic of the power politics of domination and destruction, she concludes, "if you look like them and talk like them and think like them then you are them, I was saying, you speak their language, a language is everything you do" (p. 148).

In *Surfacing*, Atwood creates a woman who refuses male domination and attempts female self-definition; in the process the writer challenges the form of fiction as described earlier by Jehlen. The work illustrates the flip side of Atwood's later, witty meditation on "Women's Novels": "Men's novels are about how to get power. Killing and so on, or winning and so on. So are women's novels, though the method is different. In men's novels, getting the woman or women goes along with getting the power. It's a perk, not a means. In women's novels you get the power by getting the man. The man is the power."[32] The heroine of *Surfacing* gets power by deconstructing received images and creating herself. She destroys the artifacts of her acculturation—a "wedding" ring, her old scrapbook full of disembodied images of women. She avoids man-made objects, paths, and docks, marked by civilization: "Anything that metal has touched, scarred; axe and machete cleared the trails, order is made with knives" (p. 215). After a ritual cleansing, the woman emerges re-(em)bodied; stripped of her clothes, she steps from the lake, "leaving my false body floated on the surface, a cloth decoy" (p. 206).[33]

Striving like her character to construct a "true vision; at the end, after the failure of logic" (p. 166), Atwood pushes her narrative to a mythic level. In a feminist re-vision of the *loup-garou* of Quebecois folklore, her character builds a lair of fresh needles, dry leaves, and dead branches. She forages for food and waits for her fur to grow. Pregnant with something that is hers, she begins a gestation designed to give birth to herself and her child. The gesture is credible in the moment, but like all fictions, destined for closure (a subject Atwood worries about later in "Happy Endings"). Reinscription lurks beyond the novel's (in)conclusion, as Atwood leaves her character poised in the decision to return—to Joe, to the civilization of the Americans—knowing that she cannot stay and live.

In *The Color Purple*, Alice Walker subverts social and aesthetic conventions through structure and language by her character's discursive gestures.

Employing the epistolary form of classical texts, the author challenges phallo-centrism with black language, style, and consciousness. Through the transformation of her character Celie, Walker extends the tradition of Hurston to create a new story for black women, spoken in their own idiom. Celie is ugly, abused, and pregnant twice before she is twenty by her presumed father, who gives the babies away and marries her off to Albert. Celie is a woman who doesn't know how to fight; in her own words, "all I know how to do is stay alive."[34] Despite the coaching she receives from her sister Nettie and Albert's sister Kate, Celie equates survival with compliance. She says of her own mother, "trying to believe his story kilt her" (p. 7). All of Walker's female characters have trouble with language, with other people's stories. Walker's use of black dialect reinforces this sense of distance. Celie's stepfather cautions Albert (whom Celie calls "Mr.———"), "she tells lies" (p. 10). When Shug Avery prepares Squeak to tell her "story" (a lie couched in the duplicitous discourse of Uncle Tom), Squeak worries "how I'm gonna tune up my mouth to say all that" (p. 82).

Celie's letters, first to God and later to her sister Nettie, chronicle a dispute between woman and god that produces a new kind of knowledge and power. Like her fictional ancestor Janie Crawford in Hurston's *Their Eyes Were Watching God*, Celie's act of defiance takes the form of talking back to her husband, and in removing her body and mind from his control. Walker similarly wrests language from white domination. Through her relationship with Shug Avery, Celie learns to express her anger and to experience sexual pleasure. When Nettie's letters correct Celie's misconceptions about her past, they also disrupt the phallocentric structure of Celie's life. She abandons god: "the God I been praying and writing to is a man. And act just like all other mens I know. Trifling, forgitful and low down. . . . If he ever listened to poor colored women the world would be a different place, I can tell you" (p. 164). Celie's god is the white man's god, the god of the Bible written in his own image—an image that confirms itself by the very nature of the letters Celie addresses to him. Through Shug, Celie learns to deconstruct phallocentric discourse: "Ain't no way to read the bible and not think God white. . . . When I found out I thought God was white, and a man, I lost interest" (p. 166). Shug dislocates god from the limitations of white phallocentric control, neuterizes god to "it," and locates "it" inside everyone and everything, pantheistically, as the source and recipient of human pleasure.

The Color Purple is a novel of letters sent and never received, or received by someone else and concealed or returned to the sender. In this sense, Walker relates the female body and the letter as effects of sexual difference. As long as Albert possesses Nettie's letters, he possesses Celie's body and mind. When he is caught in the act of repressing the logos, concealing the letter-as-truth, as signifier of Nettie's forbidden love for Celie, the direction of the novel and of

Celie's life within it changes. The invisible female signifier contains the challenge to phallocentrism. Nettie's first letter to Celie opens with sisterly advice: "You've got to fight and get away from Albert. He ain't no good" (p. 107). The system of sexual dominance entrapping Celie depends upon the repression, the concealment of woman's messages to her sister, to perpetuate itself. Albert produces his own self-reinforcing meaning at the cost of other meanings; by hiding Nettie's letters in his trunk, he forestalls the disruption that her discourse, if revealed, would create in his own logocentrism.

The force that conceals female discourse also perpetuates the sexual opposition between Celie and Albert. As long as the letters are concealed, the disruption (Celie's murderous defiance) is repressed. Through Shug's intervention in a gesture of black sisterhood, the letters are returned to Celie. When the power/knowledge of the letters is reinvested in its owner, Celie possesses herself. Her defiant curse on Albert displaces the opposition and ultimately transforms the discourse, making insight possible. The effect of her curse on Albert changes him, "womanizes" him: "Until you do right by me, everything you touch will crumble. . . . Every lick you hit me you will suffer twice" (p. 176). Celie's curse places Albert in her position. He is not castrated (he remains a "frog," Celie's image of male genitalia), but despite his difference, he becomes an ally (more like her) instead of an oppressor (other).

By reinvesting power in the female and disrupting sexual opposition, Walker projects a world of transformed relationships between men and women. The discovery of the letters discloses that Nettie's love is not confined to the texts; rather it exists inside Celie herself, a love Celie felt all the time the letters were concealed. Similarly, Nettie, who never received any of Celie's letters, continues to know Celie's love for her. In these moves, Walker negates the oppositional metaphor of insider/outsider. Celie's freedom from Albert's domination is coupled with his own freedom from the sociosexual economy. When Celie returns to town, she finds him changed: he helps her sew, an interest he had as a child that had been repressed; he searches for new knowledge through his shells. Because of their mutual love of Shug, Albert becomes the only one who understands Celie's feelings. Meditating on Shug's nature, Albert decides that he loves Shug because she is more like a man than a woman: "Shug act more manly than most men. I mean she upright, honest. Speak her mind and the devil take the hindmost, he say" (p. 228). Walker resists the reinscription of sexual opposition, as Celie and Albert explore the nature of woman:

> But Harpo [Albert's son] not like this, I tell him. You not like this. What Shug got is womanly it seem like to me. Specially since she and Sofia the ones got it.
> Sofia and Shug not like men, he say, but they not like women either.
> (p. 228)

By deconstructing "woman," Walker manages to construct women who are not "women" and men who are not "men."

At the end of the novel, Celie can once again address her letter to god, who is now redefined and embodied in, no longer outside or separate from, her world. She begins the final letter: "Dear God. Dear stars, dear trees, dear sky, dear peoples. Dear Everything. Dear God" (p. 242). In her conclusion, Walker demonstrates the play of the signifier beyond the text, generalized by the revision of god, sexual roles, and relationships. This final letter, written no longer to Nettie but to everyone, opens the significance of the novel as it closes this particular fiction.

While Walker specifically engages the material realities and sociopolitical concerns of black women, she also shares certain analytical perspectives with other feminists writing today. This relationship is most apparent in her attack on phallocentrism and in her desire to reconstruct black women's experience. Like Walker, Luce Irigaray, in "When Our Lips Speak Together," tries to write woman, to inscribe woman in a new relationship to herself, to others (through the lover who is indistinct from herself), and in so doing to write a new language. Irigaray's work assumes a more explicitly theoretical direction. She combines sexual play (the speaking of lips and labia) with linguistic and philosophical discourse on women—the lips are opened in sound and closed in silence that makes sound possible. The characteristics of this speech resemble the effects of Celie's last letter: multilocal—"you speak from everywhere at the same time";[35] polyvocal—"how could one dominate the other? Impose her voice, her tone, her meaning?" (p. 72); and improperly multiple—"we must invent so many different voices to speak all of 'us'" (p. 75). Irigaray is not creating woman as a truth (a replacement for man, his truth); rather, she situates woman in the silences, the gaps: "Of course, we were allowed—we had to?—display one truth even as we sensed but muffled, stifled another. Truth's other side—its complement? its remainder?—stayed hidden. Secret" (p. 73).

Irigaray subverts the verticality of meaning by attacking the hierarchy of the logos. Her insistence on the horizontal has both linguistic and political implications: "Stretching, reaching higher, you leave behind the limitless realm of your body. Don't make yourself erect, you abandon us. The sky isn't up there: it's between us" (pp. 75–76). In place of hierarchy and logocentrism, she offers a prescription to do without in order to engage possibilities: "Let's do without models, standards, and examples. Let's not give ourselves orders, commands, or prohibitions. May our only demand be a call to move and be moved, together. Let's not dictate, moralize, or war with each other. Let's not want to be right, or have the right to criticize each other. If you/I sit in judgment, our existence comes to a stop. . . . The lips never opened or closed upon one single truth" (p. 78). This refusal to locate a single truth, a controlling center, recalls Woolf's resistance in *A Room of One's Own* and *Three*

Guineas. Irigaray both aligns herself with and diverges from other French feminist writers in her desire to create woman and woman's writing, *l'écriture féminine*, in analogy with the female body.[36] I will examine another form of defiant alterity more carefully in the particular artistic elaborations Monique Wittig gives us that contradict and supplement Irigaray's views.

Wittig's three most recent books—*Les Guérillères, The Lesbian Body*, and *Lesbian Peoples: Material for a Dictionary*—can be viewed as a trilogy designed to establish the groundwork and amass the tools required to dismantle the institution of heterosexism. Hélène Wenzel argues persuasively for including Wittig's first novel, *The Oppoponax*, in this development as she suggests "a reading of Wittig's fictional work as an *oeuvre* that, in sequential order, documents the progression of this radical feminist ideology from resistance to feminine socialization in the quasi-utopic world of the children in *L'Opoponax*, to revolution against patriarchy in *Les Guérillères*, and to a recuperation of self, language, and history in *Le Corps lesbien* and *Brouillon pour un dictionnaire des amantes*."[37] In the three later works, Wittig much more explicitly presents the scene, structure, and words for a feminist discourse. Hers is a profoundly radical deconstruction of "woman" as the socially fabricated object of sexual oppression. For Wittig sex is a political category established in the service of a heterosexual economy to insure reproduction by means of the domination of women. Through her imaginative (de)constructions, Wittig does what the dominant ideology refuses to do: she turns it inward on itself by creating amazons who refuse to be women—that is, the sex possessed by men. Or as Wenzel puts it, in these "sex-segregated worlds" of the novels, "woman may provisionally create women who constitute themselves as speaking/naming subjects of discourse."[38] Wittig concentrates on lesbians as the runaway slaves of heterosexism, existing outside the boundaries of the binary opposition. In this process she valorizes lesbianism as a primary act of defiance and the lesbian body as the body analogous to the new text being written.

The progression represented in the order of texts is in itself instructive. *Les Guérillères* is at once lyric and epic, beautifully lush and brutally violent. In image and structure, the text celebrates "everything that recalls the O, the zero or the circle, the vulval ring,"[39] "the sign of the goddess" (p. 27); it simultaneously attacks the linearity of male sexuality and narration. Wittig frees her amazons from their imprisonment in the mirror of heterosexist specularity. These characters, named but remaining in a collective, create new, revisionary stories called "feminaries," repositories of women's wisdom. But even these new texts are limiting (perhaps they represent *l'écriture féminine*) and are eventually destroyed along with all of the other remnants of a dead culture. The women mock oppositional logic and ideology, resisting the simplistic gesture of reversal, refusing "to become prisoners of their own ideology" (p. 57).

Defiance

Wittig presents a vivid image of women in revolution who develop their critique of the dominant culture, forge individual strength and collective unity, and wage war: "They say, let those who call for a new language first learn violence. They say, let those who want to change the world first seize all the rifles. They say that they are starting from zero. They say that a new world is beginning" (p. 85). The women foster disruption, dissension, disturbance and general anarchy within the closed system of sexual ideology. Theirs is a revolt consciously designed to escape reappropriation or reinscription. They take in order to give away: "The women say, I refuse henceforward to speak this language, I refuse to mumble after them the words lack of penis lack of money lack of insignia lack of name. I refuse to pronounce the names of possession and nonpossession. They say, If I take over the world, let it be to dispossess myself of it immediately, let it be to forge new links between myself and the world" (p. 107). By experimentally altering the novel's form, Wittig tends to validate Jehlen's speculation about the requisites for women in the genre and suggests as well the limitations of her view when it is extended to encompass feminist writing today.[40] Wittig traces male appropriation to the origin of language so that the revolution staged in speaking and writing is the revolution to free the female body. The body (of) writing and the writing (of) body are identical.

The Lesbian Body deepens our understanding of what this revolution in language/body can mean. "The body of the text," as Wittig points out in the author's note, "subsumes all the words of the female body. . . . To recite one's own body, to recite the body of the other, is to recite the words of which the book is made up. The fascination for writing the never previously written and the fascination for the unattained body proceed from the same desire."[41] For Wittig, both the female body and female language are unattained, approached only politically and metaphorically, despite the author's specificity. In her desire to valorize the alterity of lesbian experience, Wittig graphically depicts the literal deconstruction and reconstruction of female identity through relationships between women. Wenzel explains: "No longer confined to the status of Other in relation to man, as have-not to have, or is-not to is, she is defined instead as lesbian, and mirrored in another who is also lesbian."[42] The narrative traces the lover's body with finger and tongue—the veins, arteries, skeletal structure, organs, skin. The brightness of "this dark continent" issues from the women themselves, marked by Sappho (which we will see later is no mark at all). Engaging in a simultaneous struggle with the female body and with language's exclusion of the female, Wittig deconstructs the language of identity. She represents "I" or *Je* as *J/e* to signify her break with the alien masculinity of language and to unsettle the phallocentrism of the speaking subject that masks the female: "*J/e* is the symbol of the lived, rending experience which is m/y writing, of this cutting in two which throughout literature is the exercise of a language which does not constitute m/e as a subject. *J/e* poses the ideological and historic question of feminine subjects" (pp. 10–11). This strategy graphically (re)presents and underscores, as Wenzel notes, "the implicit schizophrenic or split nature of any female who attempts to constitute herself as the subject of her own discourse."[43] Wittig crosses the unity of the subject to signal the difference within as she signals the difference between.

Lesbian Peoples: Material for a Dictionary glosses, redefines, and recontextualizes significant terms from Wittig's previous works. It is a response to the indictment and mandate she records in *Les Guérillères*: "You say there are no words to describe this time [before patriarchy], you say it does not exist. But remember. Make an effort to remember. Or, failing that, invent."[44] The dictionary materializes the language of the lesbian's newly created "Glorious Age." Through the redefinition of terms, Wittig sketches a struggle between the amazons, those who refuse to assume their destiny (lesbians who resist the notion of "feminine" essence), and the "mothers," akin to Kate Chopin's "mother-women." The amazons strive to reinstate the remembered harmony that existed before the break between themselves and the mothers. In a strategic move, Wittig gives analogous definitions to three significant terms—slave, wife, and woman. Since the material of the dictionary is designed to serve a new age, these three words are glossed as obsolete by the text's creators. The definition of "woman" summarizes the effect: "Obsolete since the beginning of the Glorious Age. Considered by many companion lovers as the most infamous description. This word once applied to beings fallen in an absolute state of servitude. Its meaning was 'one who belongs to another' [the definition given for "slave"]" (p. 165).[45]

Described as a rough draft produced collectively, the dictionary resists the urge to specify a lesbian origin: Sappho is represented as a blank page. For the creators, as Wenzel explains, "the collective, real authorship is a deliberate act to make women in the plural subjects of language."[46] Recalling the struggle to re-member language as well as the body, Wittig presents herself as a bearer of fables, one who recounts the changes undergone by words that are kept in a state of fluidity: "They constitute assemblies and together they read the dictionaries. They agree upon the words that they do not want to forgo. Then they decide, according to their groups, communities, islands, continents, on the possible tribute to be paid for the words. When that is decided, they pay it (or they do not pay it). Those who do so, call this pleasantly 'to write one's life with one's blood,' this, they say, is the least they can do" (p. 166). In this way, Wittig fuses the material that produces the body and that which produces the text, rendering neither separable from the re-visionary feminist construction of woman.

The works discussed here, spanning almost a century, represent the efforts of women to create themselves by defying inherited laws of separation through difference. The feminist writer is like the prisoner of Donzelot's account who protested through a hunger strike above all else his captivity within the mono-dimensional story of his judicial dossier.[47] At issue is the story of difference between the inscription of marginality and the narrative of sameness or partici-pation in discourse. Speaking of Donzelot's prisoner, whose position might be called "feminine," Mark Seltzer observes: "The subject, inhabiting a norma-tive scenario that defines his 'individuality' in the act of confiscating it as deviation, is produced at an exemplary crossing of knowledge, discourse, and power. Not surprisingly, his protest is situated at the place where these regula-tive technologies cross—the body."[48] The texts I have examined in this chapter (and elsewhere) reinforce Seltzer's point. They lend a supplemental, ironic value to the comment of Sydney Craw, the fictitious sexist critic in Marge Piercy's novel *Braided Lives*, who, in reviewing a volume of Jill Stuart's poetry, concludes: "Her poetry is uterine and devoid of thrust. Her volume is wet, menstruates and carries a purse in which it can't find anything."[49] In a sense, this chapter corroborates some common, simple generalizations: that the act of woman writing is an act of defiance, grounded in the body; that "woman" and writing are both political constructions; that feminist writing is a movement toward re-membered or re-bodied writing that materializes wom-an's specificity. As Jane Gallop reminds us in her response to *Writing and Sexual Difference*, on one level these are far from simple questions involving the body and the text, but on the other hand they are: "Not only is literature at the heart of sexual difference, but sexual difference is at the heart of literature as the absent original to which the translation must refer. I would accept the statement that literature is a translation of sexuality if I could add that we have no direct access to the original, that the best we ever have available is a good translation."[50] Finally, the direction of these writers' works suggests a struggle to liberate women and men from their oppositional positions in a hierarchical structure of sociosexual appropriation and domination. As women writers approach this liberation, they also point to a revolution in language and literature, the coming together of theory and practice, in which writers such as Walker and Wittig consciously subvert sociocultural conventions to embody feminist textual (re)presentations.

CHAPTER 8

IN/CONCLUSION

THE PROBLEM OF THEORY
AND THE PRACTICE
OF FEMINIST LITERARY
CRITICISM

this is the oppressor's language
yet I need it to talk to you

   —Adrienne Rich, "The Burning of Paper Instead of
   Children"

. . . *all Value is* rewritten *(* ⟶ *) as Theory.*

   —Roland Barthes, *Roland Barthes*

n this book I have been concerned with the politics of critical judgment—yours, mine, and the communities within which we write. The choices I have made revolve around the examination of a relationship between critical theory and feminist criticism. The conjunction linking the terms arbitrarily and fundamentally constructs their opposition or nonrelationship just as forcefully as it desires to conjoin them. Jane Gallop similarly questions the title of Abel's collection, *Writing and Sexual Difference*, and the subtitle of her own book, *The Daughter's Seduction: Feminism and Psychoanalysis*. Looking at feminism and deconstruction in this way, I want to make both terms problematic by describing a relationship for them that is simultaneously a scene of resistance and of possibility.

It makes sense to believe that if there is to be a feminist theory of criticism, it will differ from others currently vying for attention and loyalty. None of the last decade's commentaries on the nature of texts, interpretation, and models suggests that the situation could be otherwise, although some feminist critics frequently maintain that only aspects of their practice differ from the work of others. While it is tempting to take refuge in the notion that texts contain their own cues, which predict or determine the range of appropriate interpretive perspectives, it seems at the same time inevitable that assumptions shaping our judgments about literary value ultimately reside in the perceptions of critics and the models we use (or the models that use us). As challengers to existing practice, feminist critics invite counterchallenges that constantly confront us with demands to abandon our "marginal" work, to reconcile feminism with other current critical practices, or to replace extant literary critical theory with a new theoretical or paradigmatic base for criticism.

Parallel struggles or CONTRA/DICTIONS[1] are also at play within feminist criticism. There are those who reject theory as a masculinist enterprise irrelevant and perhaps even damaging to feminist goals. Others of us currently practice feminist criticism as though prevailing critical paradigms could be expanded, revised, or stretched a bit to accommodate feminist critics, texts, and analyses. As Elaine Showalter explains, "the feminist obsession with correcting, modifying, supplementing, revising, humanizing, or even attacking male critical theory keeps us dependent upon it and retards our progress in solving our own theoretical problems."[2] Still others insist on the need to construct themselves and their inquiry on their own terms. Some of us play each of these roles at different times and in different circumstances. Here, in/conclusion demands a return to the questions of my earlier chapters to consider how feminist criticism views theory and how these views differ from one another and from those of the masculinist tradition. With such an understanding, we can more clearly engage the uncertainties of the present and future. The situation of feminist criticism within the academy is analogous to culture's view of woman: she is man with a lack or a difference, nothing in her own right, a modification of or deviation from the "norm." Feminist criticism, as well as black and Marxist criticism, is "unnatural" (not normal) and "marginal" (deviant from the center, not significant). Regardless of the amount of personal consciousness-raising we undertake or of empirical data we amass, the structure of knowledge will remain unchanged until we create a revolution in the paradigm that controls what we can know about the things we have discovered, personally and intellectually. A painful truth lurks in Terry Eagleton's assessment concerning feminism's commitment to identifying the personal with the political: "That the personal is political is profoundly true, but there is an important sense in which the personal is also personal and the political political. Political struggle cannot be *reduced* to the personal, or vice versa. The women's movement rightly rejected certain rigid organizational forms and certain 'over-totalizing' political theories; but in doing so it often enough advanced the personal, the spontaneous and the experiential as though these provided an adequate political strategy, rejected 'theory' in ways almost indistinguishable from commonplace anti-intellectualism."[3] The "solution" to the dilemma of critical theory and feminist criticism, it would seem, rests in our ability to solve the problem of their relationship in such a way that it does not heighten oppositions within feminism and, thereby, diminish the power of the women's movement itself or compromise its goals by being unnecessarily restrictive and therefore exclusive. It is also important to admit that I assume both feminist criticism and critical theory have value; for this reason, what I say here may be suspect.

Most attempts at feminist critical theory fail to take into account the fact that the masculinist tradition is attempting to impose upon feminists a theoretical quandary of its own construction, belying the same unquestioned values that undergird the literary canon and dictate the limits of interpretation. Entrapped within the confines of the old paradigms, feminist critics inherit limited alternatives and predictable interpretations of the strategies we adopt. It is difficult to be patient enough to pursue the problem of theory in this power game of competing strategies. Within the prevailing model, we can play at feminist criticism as long as we are not too aggressive or accusatory. If we transgress these limits, two countercharges result (now I am speaking both personally and politically). First, we do not really have a theory. Such a view is comfortable for nonfeminists since by relegating feminist criticism to what they regard as an inferior or nonposition, they can easily dismiss us and write us out of recent history once again. If we fail to produce an original articulation of what we do—a fairly esoteric enterprise from the point of view of some—we will always be in a reactive position within the control of the phallocentric economy, rather than acting to transform it. Without a design or a direction of our own, we will have to accept this reactive posture in relation to what mainstream ("male-stream") criticism is doing and saying.

When we do attempt definition, we encounter the second countercharge: we recapitulate the phallocentric economy of texts or interpretive strategies. They are delighted; we are defused. As a recapitulation of the story of women's speech and women's silence from previous chapters, this second dilemma stems from the traditionalists' insistence that, if the model is inadequate, it is the feminist critic's responsibility to replace it with a new one before anyone is obliged to take us seriously. In the meantime, they go ahead without us. Since the alternatives afforded us are to accept or to replace, the interpretation of those options is fairly simple. When we challenge the presumptive authority of male hegemony, we are accused of having instituted a new hegemony, like the old except with a reversed gender hierarchy, and our opponents say that the very fact of our challenge suggests that we know "what is right" and they don't. So even if we haven't intended a hegemonic reversal of power relationships, the mere existence of our criticism demonstrates to some that we have.

Those are the most common alternatives and the subsequent interpretation of our actions in relation to those options. For the most part, the masculinist tradition negates and ignores us, but I believe that feminist writers and critics must continue to speak, even within paradigmatic constraints. We must contest the implicitly ideological limitations of critical tradition in our effort to negate the received images and interpretations of ourselves. The ethical force of feminism's argument makes nonfeminist liberals uncomfortable and leads feminists to believe, as suggested in chapter 1, that persuasion is the problem —but we must realize that our failure to persuade is only a problem if we wish to join the mainstream, or if we wish them to join us. A similar point can be made concerning the need for theory: if there is no need to explain oneself to oneself or to someone else, there is no need for theory. Because the motive of feminism, including feminist criticism, is political, it is automatically in the business of explaining itself to someone. Consequently, we need to explore theoretical alternatives more completely, and in terms of their importance to feminist projects. As a beginning, I want to consider the problem of what it means currently to have a theory and how theory functions.

In the concluding chapter of *Literary Theory*, Terry Eagleton presents a useful overview of how literary theories compete for dominance. Exploring the terms in which literary criticism, and attendantly, literary theory, might be defined, he rejects the definition of literary study by means of both *method* and *object* of study, as these approaches presume a stability that is not present in the respective terms.[4] He regards critics as "custodians of a discourse," operating according to the kinds of principles discussed earlier.[5] "Literary criticism," he maintains, "selects, processes, corrects and rewrites texts in accordance with certain institutionalized norms of the 'literary'—norms which are at any given time arguable, and always historically variable."[6]

Eagleton generalizes literature by substituting Foucault's designation—a field of "discursive practices"—for the privileged texts of the literary canon. (Foucault, it is worth remembering, was a structuralist and a Marxist who refused to be called either a structuralist or a Marxist.) Eagleton proposes to give a particular kind of attention to "such practices as forms of power and performance."[7] Replacing literary theory with a "theory of discourse," he then argues in favor of a *use* or strategy-based means of differentiating critical practice. He summarizes his rationale as follows:

> What you choose and reject theoretically, then, depends upon what you are practically trying to do. This has always been the case with literary criticism: it is simply that it is often very reluctant to realize the fact. In any academic study we select the objects and methods of procedure which we believe the most important, and our assessment of their importance is governed by frames of interest deeply rooted in our practical forms of social life. Radical critics are no different in this respect: it is just that they have a set of social priorities with which most people at present tend to disagree. This is why they are commonly dismissed as 'ideological', because 'ideology' is always a way of describing other people's interests rather than one's own.[8]

Accepting Eagleton's terms for the moment, one could argue that feminist criticism proceeds at present according to a set of non-institutionalized but nonetheless articulable standards of "literary" value, which it applies to a broad field of discursive practices, not limited to canonical texts. But the question arises as to whether or not feminist standards are actually distinct from other norms. Eagleton certainly thinks that feminist and socialist criticism are developing alternative theories and methods that "define the object of analysis differently, have different values, beliefs and goals, and thus offer different kinds of strategy for the realizing of these goals."[9] He argues that the feminist critic finds gender and sexuality such significant considerations "that any critical account which suppresses them is seriously defective."[10] We can say that feminist beliefs differ with respect to the understanding given to women and gender roles, and to the value placed on women's experience, as well as in their insights concerning conditions governing the production of women's texts. Feminist critics use criticism for a particular and distinct purpose: to undermine the sexist ideology of society's power/knowledge complex by exposing it in literature, literary criticism, and critical theory, as well as in the broader arena of discursive practice inclusive of media representations such as television, film, and the popular press. This is what I mean when I say that feminist criticism is political.

Eagleton's work deserves such a prolonged consideration because of the significance he grants to the feminist project. For the feminist critic, his view is initially reassuring, and agreement with his political analysis comes easily. It is encouraging because he attempts to link political and moral argument with the material realities of our existence in what can be read as his own hospitable revision of the feminist "personal as political." But at the same time, one wonders how different the effects of his analysis are from the work of Stanley Fish. Obviously, there are significant differences, although their schema for criticism assume curiously similar forms. Eagleton says that it all comes down to politics, to conflicting social ideologies, not literature or literary theory (themselves already political). Instead of arguing about conflicting interpretations and theories of literature, we should simply unveil and argue the political bases for differences in judgment: "There is no way of settling the question of which politics is preferable in literary critical terms. You simply have to argue about politics."[11]

While Eagleton provides a supplemental justification for what feminist critics do, he does not presume—and correctly so—to elaborate a particular feminist ideology. More troublesome is his refusal to suggest how these proposed political arguments among critics might be conducted and then used to elucidate literature. How will the economy of power within the literary establishment be altered so that the politics of the radical critic can be fairly argued and considered? Won't we simply recapitulate the sorts of arguments discussed in chapter 1, only now in terms of political "truth," the determining power for which will still be controlled by the reigning establishment? As Foucault observes, " 'truth' is to be understood as a system of ordered procedures for the production, regulation, distribution, circulation and operation of statements. 'Truth' is linked in a circular relation with systems of power which produce and sustain it, and to effects of power which it induces and which extend it."[12] This is the point at which the feminist critic loses heart. How will we be any more successful in arguing politics according to Eagleton's scheme than we are in arguing the assumptions underlying literary interpretation in Fish's scheme?[13] In fact, it would seem that we are enacting the same dispute, though perhaps with a different understanding of its significance, because we are engaging the same structure of authority within which it is to be conducted. In other words, this structure of authority seems to demand that we approach it in certain ways, in ways almost predetermined to failure. Since the prescriptions for settling disputes within criticism have always worked against feminists, we should have learned to be more suspicious of ourselves as we employ these same strategies and tactics to resolve problems among feminist critics.

Finally, we need to ask if Eagleton's proposal doesn't require us to rally behind a unicentered feminist discourse against which we pit the more powerful voices of the critical establishment struggling to repress it.

It is possible that an exploration of the relationship between feminist ideology and the structures of literary authority can point a way out of the labyrinthine circularity of power and knowledge. More than a decade has elapsed since the publication of Mary Ellmann's *Thinking About Women* and Kate Millett's *Sexual Politics*, landmark works in the development of feminist literary criticism. Since then our theoretical posture has been made an issue by male critics and also by feminist critics desiring acceptance and change. There has always been enough of a theory or sense of self-definition to foster extended debate among feminist practitioners, and even a cursory review of critical practice suggests that there is more theory to feminist criticism than meets the eye (which often chooses not to see it or doesn't know what it sees).

Standing alongside other contemporary theorists, feminists have rejected critical objectivism as an obvious consolidation of interpretive authority in the hands of a few. While much has been said here and elsewhere concerning the limitations of this outmoded view, similar biases function in finer disguise through other approaches. Not as much attention has been paid to alternative models of theory production, particularly with respect to their potential for empowering feminist critics to change the sexist ideology shaping the practice of literary criticism. Prescriptive and pluralistic criticism, however, have been explicitly debated by feminist critics.

In the mid-seventies, the notion of "prescriptive" criticism gained brief but limited popularity among some feminists. First advanced by Cheri Register, prescriptive criticism attempted to establish norms for the production of a new feminist literature: "To earn feminist approval, literature must perform one or more of the following functions: (1) serve as a forum for women; (2) help to achieve cultural androgyny; (3) provide role-models; (4) promote sisterhood; and (5) augment consciousness-raising."[14] Josephine Donovan elaborated on Register's view by explaining criticism's role in mediating between the text and the world: "Criticism is here viewed as a vehicle through which literature is prescriptively related to its social, cultural, and moral environment. . . . It proposes, at the same time, a critic who is not indifferent to the changes that are taking place. Indeed, the 'prescriptive' critic is actively engaged in encouraging the social and cultural realization of those structural changes that promote human liberation."[15]

Although prescriptive criticism was summarily dismissed by feminists,[16] it still characterizes our approach in the minds of the uninformed. It was just what every writer and critic feared: a power play on the part of women to dictate the shape and evaluation of texts. Prescriptive criticism, in retrospect, represents the first assertion of feminist critical authority. The approach argued for the direct replacement of masculinist values concerning the production of literature and criticism with feminist standards. The resistance is somewhat ironic since prescriptive criticism merely makes explicit a feminist version of the prescription implicit in most critical discourse; in a sense, it represents the deconstructive reversal. An idea presented before its time, prescriptive criticism was effectively silenced by a feminist community bent on coexistence and gradual reform.

Pluralism is another kind of response to the challenge to define feminist criticism. Annette Kolodny, for example, advocates "a playful pluralism, responsive to the possibilities of multiple critical schools and methods, but captive of none, recognizing that the many tools needed for our analysis will necessarily be largely inherited and only partly of our own making."[17] On the authority of Robert Scholes, Kolodny argues that the production of multiple readings is the only realistic strategy in the face of textual complexity. While she maintains that pluralism does not necessitate our consent to sexist criticism, she speaks against the formulation of specifically feminist methods and procedures. Perhaps more important than her insistence on pluralism is the value or goal she describes for the project of feminist criticism: "Let us generate an ongoing dialogue of competing potential possibilities—among feminists and, as well, between feminists and nonfeminist critics."[18]

The obvious benefits of critical pluralism are that, by espousing coexistence, it refuses to pass judgment on the favored theoretical systems and exempts feminist critics from having to develop a new theory. It avoids the sin of replacement—the capricious and arrogant substitution of "one mode of arbitrary action for another."[19] The equally evident disadvantage of subsuming feminist criticism under pluralism is that it would necessarily be limited to reactive and revisionary procedures circumscribed within the prevailing hierarchy of power. Kolodny weakly denies the applicability of Lillian Robinson's depiction of pluralism as "the greatest bourgeois theme of all . . . with its consequent rejection of ideological commitment as 'too simple' to embrace the (necessarily complex) truth."[20] Pluralist criticism appears liberal, tolerant, and nonthreatening, but Gayatri Spivak astutely identifies its dangers: "To embrace pluralism (as Kolodny recommends) is to espouse the politics of the masculinist establishment. Pluralism is the method employed by the *central* authorities to neutralize opposition by seeming to accept it. The gesture of pluralism on the part of the *marginal* can only mean capitulation to the center."[21] And as Jane Marcus further notes, pluralism minimizes the differences within feminist criticism, obscuring the theoretical and practical differences between "insiders"—"academic" feminist critics—and "outsiders"—black, Marxist, and lesbian feminists working outside the academy.[22]

Kolodny's essay, "Dancing Through the Minefield," incited vigorous and fairly predictable debate within the feminist community. The objection to pluralism as a direction for criticism was to a degree the least disturbing aspect of the ensuing commentary. In response to her critics, Kolodny refined her ideas and conceded that she was less wedded to the term than to her particular understanding of what it signified: "The pluralism I see as characteristic of feminism, by contrast [to Robinson's description], neither suppresses differentness and dissent, nor neutralizes it by *seeming* acceptance (or co-option). Instead, it encourages dialogue between competing possibilities and, just as important, it honors the value of having competing possibilities."[23] More problematic were the objections from feminist critics whose marginal status makes them legitimately suspicious of theoretically open dialogues as a means for arbitrating critical interpretation and cultural transformation.[24] In the minds of Third World, lesbian, working-class, and socialist feminists, pluralism, in refusing to judge, conceals and preserves the white male hegemony of the critical establishment—reservations to which we will return later in the chapter. While the objections encouraged Kolodny's reformulation of pluralism as an approach that encourages and values competing interpretations, textual possibilities still exist within a self-confirming circularity of power/ knowledge. Each reading in the moment of presentation offers itself as *the* interpretation, and the critic strives for interpretive dominance. Through its analytically shrewd method for exposing assertions of power within critical discourse, deconstruction can assist feminist criticism to exercise its political potential by refusing univocal and totalizing reductions within its own tradition as it resists such constructions in the broader field of critical theory. Eluding the circularity of power/knowledge requires yet another move—the simultaneous deconstruction of the interpretive construction.

Just as feminist criticism offers an ongoing critique of the play of sexual politics in discourse, post-structuralism, the most recent development on the critical horizon, presents feminists with both new possibilities and new problems for theory construction. Male post-structuralists might have broadened the "text milieu," as Geoffrey Hartman claims,[25] but as I pointed out earlier, they have not abandoned the gender, race, and class biases that have historically governed the processes of selection and commentary. They perpetuate the "critical discrimination" Annette Kolodny noted in 1975: "A largely male-dominated academic establishment has, for the last 75 years or so, treated men's writing as though it were the model for *all* writing. In other words, the various theories on the craft of fiction, and the formalist and structuralist models that have been based on this closed tradition, but which have been offered up as 'universals' of fictive form or even (under the influence of the psycholinguists) as emanations of yet deeper structures within human cognitive processes, may in fact prove to be less than universal and certainly less than fully human."[26]

In/Conclusion

Kolodny published this essay in *Critical Inquiry*, not in a feminist journal such as *Signs* or *Feminist Studies*, where one might expect to reach a more limited and sympathetic audience. Virtually no one heeds her caution. By denying that feminist criticism has a theory (or a theory that refuses to be a theory), most male critics presume that they can legitimately continue to survey male texts within the context of male versions of literature, philosophy, and history, and specifically within deconstruction, which itself claims to be a method or a practice of reading rather than a theory. (It should be noted that this tendency to ignore texts signed by women is shared by their French compatriots—Barthes, Foucault, and Derrida.) They are men speaking to men about men. In this respect post-structuralist criticism remains retrograde in its sexual politics, writing the denial of its desire for woman, for feminism.

While Hartman defuses the power of feminist criticism by denying it a theoretical basis for practice, Gerald Graff employs another means of silencing feminist critics. He argues that feminist criticism attempts to replace prevailing truth with its own truth and merely institutes a new order of oppression.[27] Graff's is a particularly effective strategy since it threatens the intellectual's essential belief in liberal values such as tolerance, charity, and peaceful coexistence, and plays upon our commitment to the very sentiments that pluralism purports to protect. His argument rests on men's unfounded fear that they will be robbed of power in a trick of role reversal. These feared divestings occur only when subjects are provoked to revolution. Since white non-working-class men at present occupy the positions of authority, they have only to fear that they might be persuaded, like Wittig's amazons, to give power away, to share it with others, to "authorize" woman.

The fundamental charge to feminist critics writing after post-structuralism is to move beyond the phallocentric structure of knowledge as it is reproduced through pluralism or the reversal of roles (the never equal "separate-but-equal" position). In the *Diacritics* dialogue between Peggy Kamuf and Nancy Miller, Kamuf poses the provocative question: "If feminist theory can be content to propose cosmetic modifications on the face of humanism and its institutions, will it have done anything more than reproduce the structure of woman's exclusion in the same code which has been extended to include her?"[28] Or in another statement of the problem: "Can a feminist practice on this cultural text stop there, leaving oppositional logic in place and in the place it has always occupied as the unquestioned ground and limit of thought?"[29] Following Michel Foucault's lead, Kamuf challenges us to scrutinize the basic assumptions at work in the impulses either to situate feminist thought at the center of patriarchal institutions or to construct alternative feminine-centered models.

We can push the dilemma imposed by the delimiting structures of thought even further by problematizing the nature of the self as revolutionary agent. In *The Daughter's Seduction*, Jane Gallop asks how the feminist, socialized as she is by the patriarchal culture, can bring about the overthrow of the patriar-

chy: "For if patriarchal culture is that within which the self originally constitutes itself, it is always already there in each subject as subject. Thus how can
it be overthrown if it has been necessarily internalized in everybody who could
possibly act to overthrow it?"[30] We know at the same time that this is something of a metalogical trap, that "regimes" can be and are overthrown by their
subjects. But deconstruction provokes us to ask whether or not such reversals
accomplish displacements of power relations that result in liberty, equality, or
"truth."

According to an alternative logic, feminist criticism could refuse the phallo-
morphic (singular, simple) patriarchal absolute in favor of an indefinite feminist de-centering (diverse, complex), or, as Kamuf puts it, "a necessary pluri-
vocality and plurilocality."[31] Perhaps this is one way of describing what has
been happening over the past decade with respect to feminist literary criticism's refusal to construct a theory. If so, it has occurred accidentally or
"naturally," without clearly articulated theoretical underpinnings. To refuse to
theorize could in itself be to create a theory; it can be posited as an act rather
than a re-action when related to the general as opposed to the particular. This
refusal to theorize as an activity that resists specification, in the form of
continual, conscious "de-centering" instead of being silenced or seeking an
"equal" voice, offers a specific potential for feminist criticism.

The strategy of "de-centering" or theory displacement is demonstrated in the
progression Jane Gallop works through in *The Daughter's Seduction*, particularly as she discusses Luce Irigaray. In a philosophy seminar, Irigaray finds
herself in the position of being "the authority" on women, the irony and
problematics of which Gallop explains: "To have a theory of woman is already
to reduce the plurality of woman to the coherent and thus phallocentric representations of theory. Irigaray, as professor of woman, is in the role of 'subject
of theory,' subject theorizing, a role appropriate to the masculine. . . . How
can she avoid it without simply giving up speaking, leaving authority to men
and phallocentrism?"[32] In answer to her question, Gallop elaborates the posture of resistance Irigaray adopts: "All clear statements are trapped in the same
economy of values, in which clarity (oculocentrism) and univocity (the One)
reign. Precision must be avoided, if the economy of the One is to be unsettled.
Equivocations, allusions, etc. are all flirtatious; they induce the interlocutor to
listen, to encounter, to interpret, but defer the moment of assimilation back
into a familiar model. Even if someone asks for *précisions*, even if that
someone is oneself, it is better for women to avoid stating things precisely."[33]
Therefore, we are condemned to speaking, rather than to futile silence, but in
ways always unsettling, always off the center, if the de-centering of the One is
to be accomplished.

In/Conclusion

The threat inherent in being the "subject theorizing" is the construction of theory itself, the fear of reversing and thus recapitulating the exclusive phallocentrism of the institution of knowledge. Gallop elaborates Irigaray's meaning; she "uncovers a sublimated male homosexuality structuring all our institutions: pedagogy, marriage, commerce, even Freud's theory of so-called heterosexuality. Those structures necessarily exclude women, but are unquestioned because sublimated—raised from suspect homo*sexuality* to secure homo*logy*, to the sexually indifferent *logos*, science, logic."[34] Other feminist critics have noted similar tendencies. For example, in her critique of pluralism, Jane Marcus comments on the exclusionary practices of American male critics: "If Annette Kolodny's espousal of the pluralist position from the margin may be seen as a capitulation to a misogynist power structure, Jameson's Marxist pluralism, in its refusal to deal with gender, should show those tempted to follow Kolodny's lead that male bonding transcends theoretical enmities and is more primary among American critics than the issues that divide them intellectually."[35] This "homo*logy*" of male intellectuals, symbolizing their power in the world at large, constantly presents itself to the feminist critic as a reminder of what we cannot pluralistically join or univocally replace. By unveiling the male-affiliative nature of social and intellectual institutions of culture, Irigaray (and Gallop) call for a true hetero-sexuality or an "other bi-sexuality" that "pursues, loves and accepts"[36] all that has traditionally been fixed in oppositional choices. In such a move, feminist criticism frees itself and invites critical theory in general, and deconstructive practice in particular, to make a similar choice.

Having discarded the authority of inherited theory, dodged the trap of polarization, and refused the posture of "authority," the feminist critic hopes to enter a new realm of discourse inhabited by inescapable contra/dictions. We see it illustrated in Gallop's double-columned pursuit of two paths at once.[37] We detect her uncomfortable self-scrutiny when she presents a critique of Irigaray's treatment (as compared with Lacan's) of Sade and his character Saint-Ange. Gallop asks and exclaims parenthetically, slightly off her center (page 88 of 150): "(. . . Am I charitable to phallocratic Saint-Ange, but expecting more from Irigaray? My 'step beyond' like any is phallic one-upmanship, refusing homage, refusing loyalty. Irigaray is not just my sister-rival; she is my Daddy, my Mummy. And when she is at her best, as angelic as Saint-Ange at *her* best, I love her and I get scared not knowing where the boundary lies between her and me.)"[38] As Tillie Olsen shows us so clearly in *Silences*—and even Woolf with her multiple narrators—the boundaries between "self" and "other" blur in an osmotic relationship constitutive of new, expanded, and expanding identity that never forecloses or concludes the process of constituting and differing from itself.

Crossing the Double-Cross

Gallop ends up in the inevitable position of the feminist intellectual. Having rejected the control of authorial (that is, authoritative) discourse, she explores parenthetically the unsettling position of her own irresolution:

> (A few pages back I found myself switching sides. . . . That was momentarily disconcerting. But then I began to find it gratifying. I reflected that my avowed project in this chapter—and in this book—is to avoid getting locked into a specular opposition, and that a blatant switch was perhaps a good way to practise such avoidance, since taking sides seems inevitable in any attempt to be engaged as a reader, or to engage my reader.
>
> But then, this parenthesis itself seems at once the most and the least unsettling gesture of all. It is a last-ditch attempt to regain the correct position, the correct position here being to be unsettled from any position. The real risk avoided here is the risk of being wrong.)[39]

By choosing sides and refusing to take sides, by resisting the compulsion to fix in resolution, Gallop elects instead to remain unsettled, off-center, in a de-centering posture that uncovers the phallic assumptions of texts and suggests provisional alternative possibilities. The approach that emerges in Gallop's work "might be a text that alternately quotes and comments, exercises and criticizes."[40] She cites Kristeva in support: " 'Never one without the other,' knowingly, lucidly to exercise *and* criticize power is to dephallicize, to assume the phallus and unveil that assumption as presumption, as fraud. A constantly double discourse is necessary, one that asserts and then questions. Who is capable of such duplicity? 'Perhaps a woman. . . .' "[41]

Despite Graff's allegation, or perhaps because of it, it is difficult to resist seeing replacement as the preferred strategy for the production of feminist critical theory. It would seem that the espousal of a theory of feminist criticism would settle the contentiousness of male theorists and earn feminists a place in the debate. It could situate feminist criticism at the heart of theoretical discourse, just as feminism could secure its place at the center of our socio-cultural institutions. At the same time, we know that those debates and institutions have been constructed on the weak, monological foundation of a mono-sexual discourse that is as exclusive of the otherness of women as it is oppressive of lesbians, working-class and poor women, blacks, and Third World women. Hélène Cixous's warning echoes within the feminist project: "Beware, my friend, of the signifier that would take you back to the authority of a signified!"[42] To attempt to situate ourselves at these crumbling centers of power/knowledge is to heighten our complicity.

Describing the writer's dilemma in *Writing Degree Zero*, Barthes articulates the fundamental problem faced by the revolutionary in culture. Writing exists by conventions that constitute and are constituted by history. In order to be "always new," the writer must destroy the very thing being created. Thus, Barthes concludes, "there is therefore in every present mode of writing a double postulation: there is the impetus of a break and the impetus of a coming to power, there is the very shape of every revolutionary situation, the fundamental ambiguity of which is that Revolution must of necessity borrow, from what it wants to destroy, the very image of what it wants to possess."[43] Feminist criticism, by definition, engages this struggle. It is political—that is, it necessitates a challenge to the disposition of power within the critical establishment. It is revolutionary—a destructive and reconstructive rather than just a deconstructive act. The feminist critic, in order to work toward the transformation of society, attempts a particular kind of duplicity: she works within the present order so that she can destroy it; she borrows its tools in order to subvert it.[44] As Barthes observes, "when no known language is available to you, you must determine *to steal a language*—as men used to steal a loaf of bread. (All those—legion—who are outside Power are obliged to steal language.)"[45] Women will steal words and use them to subvert the phallocentric values of "unicity, identity, linearity."[46] It is this figure of the woman as thief that Cixous plays on in the word *voler*—thief and one in flight—to which the previous chapter's epigraph refers. Woman flies, steals, and crosses over, takes the words and runs: "We've lived in flight, stealing away, finding, when desired, narrow passageways, hidden crossovers."[47]

Such an understanding of what is required produces a definition of what feminist criticism is and who can practice it. Julia Kristeva, in calling woman "an eternal dissident,"[48] speaks Freud's fear of woman as being inadequately civilized. Our essential "disloyalty to civilization," our willingness to steal and fly, constitute the source of our revolutionary potential. Feminists are those who are in the process of exorcizing the patriarchal consciousness that all of us have internalized because of our place in society; we have performed certain sometimes "hidden crossovers" with respect to the double-cross of difference. Because we have been culturally constituted as the "Other," we have the potential as a group or "class" for disloyalty. This manifests itself as feminism when a woman displays a critique of her own internalized patriarchal consciousness—an active and ongoing process. One senses a dissonance in the patriarchal world. Such a critique is difficult to formulate. Words do not say what we mean; we do not always mean what we say. We are the linguistic and conceptual captives of a phallocentric economy that depends upon our very captivity for its survival, just as, in many respects, we have been led to depend upon it. Realization of alterity, the "otherness" living inside, separates us from the illusion of equal participation under patriarchy; it guards us from the homologous structure of "knowledge" as it is.

Through a strategy of displacement, the assertion of disruptions and the admission of multivoiced contra/dictions, we can hope to protect the interests of all feminist critics. It requires work in consort rather than in opposition, but unlike pluralism, this de-centering criticism constantly takes itself apart as it takes others into itself. A commitment to such a strategy guards against the romantic illusion of sameness achieved through synthesis at the expense of denying material differences. It also protects us from prematurely privileging one feminist theory or method over another and instituting yet another political and therefore critical hegemony that is just as fiercely exclusive by virtue of its codification as what we have struggled to destroy. Our alternative, in Féral's words, is "to privilege the multiple and undermine the edifice of the law."[49] This is the general strategy, made specific with respect to gender by the feminist, that Derrida insists upon in his deconstructive practice. The double-cross of sexual difference calls for the undoing or deconstruction of the rhetoric of difference. Around such a concern the interests of feminism and critical theory converge. By substituting diversity and displacement for the Father's Law of the One and the Same, we can guard against exclusion and create the openings needed for the multivocality required if theory is to be made by and to permit the expression of all women. This position is most clearly demonstrated in the works of our writer-theorists like Woolf, Olsen, Lorde, and Rich. As Nelly Furman puts it, "to refuse the authority of a signified means rejecting the status of defined object in favor of the dynamics of becoming, and privileging the freedom of process rather than the permanence of product."[50] It entails the rejection of the insider's role, the place at the center of the literary establishment, as we try simultaneously to win that authority in an institution we ceaselessly attempt to undermine and to unsettle. It is the writer's double gesture of crossing the double-cross rather than exposing it with bravado, to deconstruct as one constructs. Feminism requires more than the narcissistic language game of criticism and challenges critical theory to discover and admit its own politics.

If we extend the reasoning presented against theory replacement and consider the historic difficulties within feminism of formulating *a theory*, we can appreciate the impossibility of a single, complete expression of the subject. Ann Rosalind Jones explains that "a monolithic vision of shared female sexuality, rather than defeating phallocentrism as doctrine and practice, is more likely to blind us to our varied and immediate needs and to the specific struggles we must coordinate in order to meet them."[51] Because racist, heterosexist, and classist biases are as pervasive as sexist assumptions, a de-centering "polylogue" is just as advantageous within the feminist community as it is between feminist and nonfeminist, man and woman. Refusing pluralism and reversal, feminism can attempt displacement and serve as the liberating wedge. It would necesarily provide a check on limitations such as those identified by Ella Grasso Patterson and Elly Bulkin in Kolodny's "Dancing

In/Conclusion

Through the Minefield," or Barbara Smith's reaction to Elaine Showalter's review essay in *Signs*: "The idea of critics like Showalter *using* Black literature is chilling, a case of barely disguised cultural imperialism."[52] If the de-centering strategy could provide the space for a true sharing of perceptions, white, middle-class, heterosexual, and academic feminists (those occupying positions of privilege, sometimes multiple privilege) could educate them-selves, in dialogue with other feminists, about their unquestioned assumptions of privilege, and we could engage collectively in feminist theorizing.

The catalogue of our injuries and insults to one another has been unending. Perhaps a theorizing process that cultivates the specificities of many voices within their own special contexts, that moves from unravelling the politics of textual discourse to undoing the oppressive politics of life's discourses, is radical enough to address the concerns Barbara Smith articulates so well in her landmark essay, "Toward a Black Feminist Criticism": "Black women's exis-tence, experience, and culture and the brutally complex systems of oppression which shape these are in the 'real world' of white and/or male consciousness beneath consideration, invisible, unknown."[53] What it comes to is that there is no singular, monovocal theory worth writing. Echoing Audre Lorde's com-ments on difference, Ann Rosalind Jones similarly warns feminists against a monolithic vision of female sexuality as the ground for constructing a feminist theory: "To the extent that each of us responds to a particular tribal, national, racial, or class situation vis à vis men, we are in fact separated from one another. As the painful and counterproductive splits along class and racial lines in the American women's movement have shown, we need to understand and respect the diversity in our concrete social situations."[54] These are the real differences we dare not obscure. We need to substitute new questions for the unfortunate, restrictive choices required by the construction of queries like these posed by Lillian Robinson: "Who speaks for the lesbian community: the highly educated experimentalist with an unearned income or the naturalistic working-class autobiographer? Or are both the *same kind* of foremother, re-flecting the community's range of cultural identities and resistance?"[55] In their place, we need to ask how each of these women represented her community, in what terms and how well? How were they different from each other and from us today? How were they situated in relation to the power/knowledge nexus of life and language? The search for answers to questions formulated in this way could also create bridges between the work of women involved in radical social and political change and the work of women in the academic institu-tions.

As long as culture is multiform rather than monolithic, and power or access to power is localized rather than diffuse, a single theoretical formulation will prove inadequate. Joanna Russ puts it well: "In everybody's present historical situation, there can be, I believe, no single center of value and hence no absolute standards. That does not mean that assignment of values must be arbitrary or self-serving. . . . It does mean that for the linear hierarchy of good and bad it becomes necessary to substitute a multitude of centers of value, each with its own periphery, some closer to each other, some farther apart. The centers have been constructed by the historical facts of what it is to be female or black or working class or what-have-you; when we all live in the same culture, then it will be time for one literature."[56] In response to the complexity resulting from multicentering moves, we need to conceive of feminist criticism, indeed as Culler suggests, all criticism, as an infinite progression that refuses to identify a center because it is always decentered, self-displacing and self-contradictory. Further, there can be no center because the boundary or circumference (of which it is supposed to be the center) cannot be determined. Fluid and in motion, feminism is an assertion of values that, like Gallop's conception of identity, "must be continually assumed and immediately called into question."[57] This progression inscribes the ongoingness of its own progress and interanimating disruptions on the way toward something that is not knowable because it is always indeterminate. From this perspective, there will never be *a theory* of feminist criticism; rather, feminist criticism will be a theorizing process, guided perhaps by an ethical dream of relationships between others. As one who dreams of what is not now, though fervently sought, I must refuse to close this question, preferring instead to write in/conclusion.

NOTES

PREFACE

1. Spivak, Translator's Foreword, 382–83.
2. Gallop, *The Daughter's Seduction*, xii.
3. Culler, *Structuralist Poetics*, 160.
4. Jacobus, "The Difference of View," 12–13.
5. Lorde, *Sister Outsider*, 118.

CHAPTER I

1. Smith, *The Winner Names the Age*, 217–18.
2. A number of contemporary feminist critics and writers have discussed the politics of literary criticism. See, for example, Katz-Stoker, "The Other Criticism," 315–27; Olsen, *Silences*, 22–46; Ellmann, *Thinking About Women*; Ozick, "Women and Creativity," 307–22; Showalter, "Women Writers and the Double Standard," 323–43.
3. Fiedler, "Literature as an Institution," 73–74.
4. Marxist critics such as Fredric Jameson in *The Political Unconscious* frequently exclude sex and race as features that also mark a text's exclusion from the literary canon. Most often Marxists consider class the fundamental term in the complex interpretive nexus of sex, race, and class. See, for example, Angela Davis's *Women, Race and Class*, in which women's complicity in race and class oppression is considered completely at the expense of knowledge concerning women as an oppressed group.

In *Sex, Class, and Culture*, Lillian S. Robinson makes a useful point concerning the politics of exclusion: "Within the limits of literature, at least, women's exclusion is clearly shared by all non-white and working-class men" (p. 4). As a Marxist feminist, Robinson is careful not to set exclusionary terms in a hierarchical relationship. As a result, she focuses more attention on women, inclusive of race and class concerns, and calls for a literature reflective of the whole culture.
5. Olsen, *Silences*, 223.
6. Louis Kampf and Paul Lauter present an excellent summary of the changes in the critic's role (Introduction to *The Politics of Literature*, 15–18). They correctly note the influence of publishing houses in shaping literary taste by virtue of their ability to determine our range of choice (pp. 45–46), in addition to the control they exercise in constituting texts. Richard Kostelanetz, in *The End of Intelligent Writing*, elaborates upon other important dimensions of the problem, including the organization of the literary marketplace and the power of advertising.
7. Stade, "Fat-Cheeks," 140–41. In this same collection, Fiedler demonstrates how canonized writers such as Emerson and Tolstoy also attacked the institution of culture (Fiedler, "Literature as an Institution," 86).

8. Lentricchia, *Criticism and Social Change*, 7.

9. Culler points out that in Lentricchia's *After the New Criticism*, which purports to be a history of critical activity from 1957–77, the emergence of feminist criticism is completely ignored: "One speculates that this is because feminist criticism, in its specifically political orientation, does what Lentricchia condemns others for failing to do and would thus expose, if he addressed it, the dubiousness of his own critical ideal" (Culler, *On Deconstruction*, 42n.).

10. Fish, *Is There a Text in This Class?*, 10–11.

11. For a discussion of Bloom's work, see Annette Kolodny, "A Map for Rereading," 451–67.

12. Abrams, "How to Do Things with Texts," 587.

13. Olsen, *Silences*, 244.

14. Woolf, *Three Guineas*, 61.

15. Ibid.

16. Fish, *Is There a Text in This Class?*, 11.

17. Ibid., 6.

18. Mailer, *Advertisements for Myself*, 433.

19. Fish, *Is There a Text in This Class?*, 296.

20. Woolf, *A Room of One's Own*, 4.

21. Fish, *Is There a Text in This Class?*, 342–44.

22. Kolodny, "Not-So-Gentle Persuasion," 5.

23. Camus, *The Rebel*, 3.

24. Quoted by Kostelanetz, *The End of Intelligent Writing*, 243.

25. Kolodny, "Not-So-Gentle Persuasion," 16.

26. Woolf, *Three Guineas*, 62.

27. Foucault, *Power/Knowledge*, 133.

28. Smith, *The Winner Names the Age*, 191.

29. Camus, *The Rebel*, 20.

30. Quoted by Olsen, *Silences*, 229.

31. Fish, *Is There a Text in This Class?*, 361.

32. George, "Stumbling on Melons," 109.

33. Abel, "Editor's Introduction," 173–74.

34. Fiedler, "Literature as an Institution," 91.

35. Fish, *Is There a Text in This Class?*, 314–15.

36. White, "Conventional Conflicts," 155.

37. Ibid., 154.

38. Foucault, *Power/Knowledge*, 133.

39. Ibid.

40. Culler, *On Deconstruction*, 61.

41. Irigaray, "When Our Lips Speak Together," 69.

CHAPTER 2

1. Woolf, *Three Guineas*, 90.

2. De Man, *Blindness and Insight*, 102–3. His chapter on Derrida's reading of

Rousseau (pp. 102–41) presents a model for interpretation which proceeds from this analysis.

3. Johnson, *The Critical Difference*, 5–6.

4. There are several other works on Freeman that have secondary significance to this study: Michele Clark's Afterword to Freeman's *The Revolt of Mother and Other Stories*, and Julia Bader's "The Dissolving Vision." Clark's purpose is to establish a very brief bio-critical context for reading a new collection of Freeman's stories. Bader's study concerns the tension between the narrative design of realism and the blurring dissolution of the local colorists in the works of Jewett, Freeman, and Gilman.

5. Foster, *Mary E. Wilkins Freeman*, 32.

6. Ibid., 141.

7. Ibid., 69–70.

8. Ibid., 142.

9. Ibid., 143.

10. Wood, "The Literature of Impoverishment," 27.

11. Foster, *Mary E. Wilkins Freeman*, 191.

12. Wood, "The Literature of Impoverishment," 14.

13. Ibid., 16.

14. Cather, Preface to *The Country of the Pointed Firs*, 9.

15. Foster, *Mary E. Wilkins Freeman*, 106, 105.

16. Ibid., 108, 109.

17. Ziff, *The American 1890s*, 293.

18. De Man, *Blindness and Insight*, 136.

19. Culler, *On Deconstruction*, 81.

20. Freeman, "A New England Nun," 79. Further references are cited in the text.

21. Wood, "The Literature of Impoverishment," 21.

22. Brand, "Mary Wilkins Freeman," 83, 89.

23. Toth, "Defiant Light," 90.

24. Westbrook, *Mary Wilkins Freeman*, 59.

25. Clark, Afterword to *The Revolt of Mother and Other Stories*, 177.

26. Donovan, *New England Local Color Literature*, 132.

27. Foster, *Mary E. Wilkins Freeman*, 172. This calls into question assertions like Wood's: "I have already spoken of the nearly empty pestiferous old house which dominated the Local Colorists' imaginations and of its iconographical links with the diseased and barren womb" ("The Literature of Impoverishment," 28).

28. Brand, "Mary Wilkins Freeman," 83.

29. Toth, "Defiant Light," 90.

30. Brand, "Mary Wilkins Freeman," 88, 89.

31. Freeman, "A Conflict Ended," 331. Further references are cited in the text.

32. Brand, "Mary Wilkins Freeman," 98.

33. Freeman, "Arethusa," 147. Further references are cited in the text.

34. Donovan, *New England Local Color Literature*, 121.

35. Ibid., 129.

36. Toth, "Defiant Light," 92.

37. Ibid.

38. Freeman, "The Revolt of 'Mother,'" 122. Further references are cited in the text.
39. Foster, *Mary E. Wilkins Freeman*, 93.
40. Westbrook, *Mary Wilkins Freeman*, 64–65.
41. Foster, *Mary E. Wilkins Freeman*, 91–92.
42. Freeman, "Mary E. Wilkins Freeman," 25, 75.
43. Williams, *Our Short Story Writers*, 170.
44. O'Connor, *The Habit of Being*, 329.
45. Williams, *Our Short Story Writers*, 170.
46. Culler, *On Deconstruction*, 81.
47. Glasser, "'She Is the One You Call Sister,'" 188.
48. Barthes, *Image-Music-Text*, 148.
49. Culler, *On Deconstruction*, 214–15.

CHAPTER 3

1. Walker, "On Refusing to Be Humbled," 2.
2. Walker, "Looking for Zora," 302.
3. See Robert Hemenway's *Zora Neale Hurston*, 104–35, for a discussion of the effects of Mrs. Charlotte Mason's patronage on Hurston's life and works.
4. Hughes, *The Big Sea*, 239.
5. Washington, "Zora Neale Hurston," 11.
6. Neal, "Zora Neale Hurston," 161. In the final chapters of *Zora Neale Hurston*, Hemenway provides a useful assessment of Hurston's political views. The critiques presented by black intellectuals are both accurately and narrowly construed; their obvious silences obscure the question of what Hurston does say as well as the black community's singular role in character assassination surrounding the false morals charge against Hurston.
7. Bethel, "'This Infinity of Conscious Pain,'" 178–79.
8. Washington, "Zora Neale Hurston," 15.
9. Ibid.
10. Rayson, "The Novels of Zora Neale Hurston," 4.
11. Neal, "Zora Neale Hurston," 164.
12. Christian, *Black Women Novelists*, 57.
13. Howard, *Zora Neale Hurston*, 94.
14. Hurston, *Their Eyes Were Watching God*, 23. Further references are cited in the text.
15. Bethel, "'This Infinity of Conscious Pain,'" 180.
16. Ibid., 181.
17. Ibid., 182.
18. Howard, *Zora Neale Hurston*, 100.
19. Hemenway, "Are You a Flying Lark or a Setting Dove?," 145. See also Abrahams' "Negotiating Respect."
20. Heath, "Difference," 82.
21. Cixous, "Castration or Decapitation?," 45.

22. Christian, *Black Women Novelists*, 58.
23. Lillie Howard presents a useful discussion of Hurston's treatment of race in *Zora Neale Hurston*, 108–10.
24. Hemenway, *Zora Neale Hurston*, 237.
25. Lorde, *Sister Outsider*, 123.
26. Abrahams, "Negotiating Respect," 78–79.
27. Borker, "Anthropology," 40.
28. Derrida et al., "Deconstruction in America," 17.
29. Derrida, *Dissemination*, 334.
30. Alice Walker achieves a similar effect through Nettie's letters in *The Color Purple*. While Walker's means are different, she accomplishes a similar goal by integrating the African presence (though some would argue that she subordinates it) into relationship with the lives of black American women today.
31. Derrida et al., "Deconstruction in America," 17.

CHAPTER 4

1. Rich, *The Dream of a Common Language*, 61.
2. Robinson, *Housekeeping*, 3. Further references are cited in the text.
3. Rich, *Diving into the Wreck*, 22–24.
4. Derrida, *Dissemination*, 357.
5. Derrida, "Differance," 158.
6. Atwood, *Surfacing*, 222.
7. Beauvoir, *The Second Sex*, 301.
8. Culler, *On Deconstruction*, 9.

CHAPTER 5

1. Showalter, "Review: Literary Criticism," 436–37.
2. Ibid., 445.
3. Kolodny, "Some Notes," 90.
4. Kolodny, "Review Essay," 420.
5. Showalter, "Towards a Feminist Poetics," 26.
6. Ibid., 39.
7. Kolodny, "Turning the Lens," 345.
8. Showalter, "Towards a Feminist Poetics," 27–28.
9. It is of course problematic to totalize and then to appropriate deconstruction for the sake of my argument; by focusing on its most widely held strategies and by making specific attributions when possible, I hope to avoid some of the worst effects inherent in my approach.
10. Showalter, "Towards a Feminist Poetics," 37.
11. Gallop, "The Ladies' Man," 30.
12. Beauvoir, *The Second Sex*, 41.
13. Millett, *Sexual Politics*, 27.

14. Wittig, "Paradigm," 115.
15. Collette Guillaumin's two-part essay, "The Practice of Power and Belief in Nature," contains the most comprehensive feminist consideration of this question.
16. Beauvoir, *The Second Sex*, xxi.
17. Ibid., xix.
18. Ibid., xvi.
19. Ibid., 301.
20. Ann Rosalind Jones and Hélène Wenzel are exceptions to this; both have noted Guillaumin's objections to interpretations of difference. For example, Jones says of the French psychoanalytic critique of *féminité*: "It reverses the values assigned to each side of the polarity [man/woman] but it still leaves man as the determining referent, not departing from the opposition male/female, but participating in it" ("Writing the Body," 255). In "The Text as Body/Politics," Wenzel clearly outlines the French feminist controversy over difference, particularly with respect to the positions assumed by Cixous, Wittig, and Guillaumin.
21. Guillaumin, "The Question of Difference," 33–34.
22. Ibid., 34.
23. Lorde, *Sister Outsider*, 45.
24. Guillaumin, "The Practice of Power, Part I," 19.
25. Ibid., 23.
26. Quintanales, "I Paid," 153.
27. Eagleton, *Literary Theory*, 135.
28. Wittig, "The Category of Sex," 64.
29. Ibid.
30. Editorial Collective, "Variations on Common Themes," 226.
31. Wittig, "The Category of Sex," 66.
32. Féral, "Antigone," 10.
33. Lewis, "The Post-Structuralist Condition," 12. In working out the perspective of this section and the next, I have been particularly indebted to David Miller's keen questions and to Philip Lewis's thoughtful exploration of deconstruction.
34. Derrida, "Differance," 129.
35. Johnson, Translator's Introduction to *Dissemination*, xiii.
36. Lewis, "The Post-Structuralist Condition," 14–15.
37. Ibid., 15.
38. Derrida, *Positions*, 41–42.
39. Derrida, *Spurs*, 65.
40. Guillaumin, "The Question of Difference," 45.
41. Lewis, "The Post-Structuralist Condition," 13; emphasis mine.
42. Ibid.
43. Derrida affirms this as a motive for deconstruction in "Deconstruction in America," 15–16.
44. Gallop, *The Daughter's Seduction*, 93.
45. Lorde, *Sister Outsider*, 111–12.
46. Culler, *On Deconstruction*, 166.
47. Editorial Collective, "Variations on Common Themes," 227.
48. Lewis, "The Post-Structuralist Condition," 18.

49. Clément, "Enslaved Enclave," 131.
50. Eagleton, *Literary Theory*, 144.
51. Derrida and MacDonald, "Choreographies," 68.

CHAPTER 6

1. Michèle Barrett's introduction to *Women and Writing*, Lillian Robinson's "Who's Afraid of A Room of One's Own" (*Sex, Class, and Culture*, 97–149), and Berenice Carroll's " 'To Crush Him in Our Own Country,' " present particularly useful commentaries on Woolf's two essays. Jane Marcus's collections, *New Feminist Essays on Virginia Woolf* and *Virginia Woolf: A Feminist Slant*, have prepared the way for startling reinterpretations of Woolf's life and work. In "Still Practice," for example, Marcus calls *A Room of One's Own* "the first modern text of feminist criticism" (p. 79). Perhaps more than any critic, Marcus has presented new understandings of Woolf's philosophy and politics, that is, of her feminism and socialism. Deborah Rosenfelt's thoughtful consideration of Olsen is especially helpful in understanding her life and work with respect to time and tradition.
2. Kamuf, "Writing Like a Woman," 286.
3. Marcus, Introduction to *New Feminist Essays on Virginia Woolf*, xiii.
4. Naomi Black revises the view of Woolf as apolitical and suggests the range of social concerns she engages in *A Room of One's Own* and *Three Guineas* as well as in her personal activities. She presents Woolf as a bridge between "the older and the newer, present-day women's movement" in "Virginia Woolf," 309.
5. Woolf, *A Room of One's Own*, 117. Further references are cited in the text.
6. Schlack, *Continuing Presences*, ix.
7. Fleishman, "Virginia Woolf," 134. Alice Fox, in "Literary Allusion as Feminist Criticism," presents a fine corrective to the notion of allusion as an expression of relatedness to tradition, arguing instead for its use as an expression of Woolf's critique of phallocentrism.
8. Marcus, "Thinking Back," 1.
9. Ibid., 3.
10. Ibid.
11. Showalter, *A Literature of Their Own*, 283.
12. Woolf, *The Pargiters*, 9.
13. Woolf, *A Writer's Diary*, 198.
14. Kamuf in "Penelope at Work" describes the text's zig-zag motion of repeated reversals as a means of demonstrating "how *A Room* frames the question of women and fiction within the field of an exclusion" (p. 8).
15. Ibid., 10.
16. Féral, "Towards a Theory of Displacement," 55.
17. Woolf, "Professions for Women," 238–39.
18. Alice Fox discusses Woolf's use of this ballad (Child No. 173) as a means of establishing sisterhood, an expression of the ideal of anonymity, and as a structure for situating the story of Judith Shakespeare ("Literary Allusion," 155–56).
19. Furman, "Textual Feminism," 50.

20. Ibid., 51.

21. Nancy Topping Bazin, in *Virginia Woolf and the Androgynous Mind*, describes this split epistemologically: "the dual nature of the author's vision is related to two opposite approaches to truth, the masculine ('knowing in terms of apartness') and the feminine ('knowing in terms of togetherness')" (p. 124). In his discussion of *A Room of One's Own* and *Three Guineas*, Rosenthal also cautions against reading Woolf's view of androgyny as an espousal of "any radically new psychological doctrine" (*Virginia Woolf*, 228).

22. Showalter, *A Literature of Their Own*, 289.

23. Spivak, "Unmaking and Making in *To the Lighthouse*," 323.

24. Jacobus, "The Difference of View," 20.

25. Johnson, *The Critical Difference*, x.

26. Barbara Currier Bell and Carol Ohmann provide a useful discussion of Woolf's resistance to omniscient narration in favor of "the common reader" persona directed at constructing community ("Virginia Woolf's Criticism," 48–60). Similarly Jane Marcus, in her article, " 'No More Horses,' " notes that the genius of Woolf's essay arises in part from her use of "a fictional narrative technique which demands open sisterhood as the stance of the reader" (p. 274).

27. Woolf, *A Writer's Diary*, 238–39.

28. Cixous, "The Laugh of the Medusa," 883.

29. Mary Jacobus considers another instance of the text's undoing as she speaks of the way Brontë's anger in *Jane Eyre* enters *A Room of One's Own*: "Editing into her writing the outburst edited out of Charlotte Brontë's, Virginia Woolf creates a point of instability which unsettles her own urbane and polished decorum. The rift exposes the fiction of authorial control and objectivity, revealing other possible fictions, other kinds of writing; exposes, for a moment, its own terms" ("The Difference of View," 17).

30. Rich, "Women and Honor," 189.

31. Ibid., 194.

32. Lillian Robinson, *Sex, Class, and Culture*, 141.

33. Showalter, *A Literature of Their Own*, 295.

34. Ibid., 294.

35. Ibid., 297.

36. Jones, "Writing the Body," 249.

37. Marder, *Feminism and Art*, 175.

38. Rosenthal, *Virginia Woolf*, 242.

39. Heilbrun, "Virginia Woolf in Her Fifties," 241.

40. Silver, "*Three Guineas* Before and After," 254.

41. Woolf, *Three Guineas*, 3. Further references are cited in the text.

42. Woolf, *A Writer's Diary*, 182.

43. Woolf, like several contemporary writers—Kristeva, Irigaray, and Féral— discovers woman's circumstance figured in Antigone who, as Woolf says in *Three Guineas*, wanted "not to break the laws, but to find the law" (p. 138).

44. Féral, "Antigone," 6–7.

45. Marder, *Feminism and Art*, 155.

46. Barthes, *Writing Degree Zero*, 87.
47. Marcus, "Thinking Back," 5.
48. Woolf, *A Writer's Diary*, 183.
49. Carroll, " 'To Crush Him in Our Own Country,' " 118.
50. Féral, "Antigone," 12.
51. Ibid.
52. Ibid.
53. Burkom and Williams, "De-Riddling Tillie Olsen's Writing," 64.
54. Olsen, *Silences*, 38–39. Further references are cited in the text.
55. Rosenfelt, "From the Thirties," 374.
56. Ibid., 388.
57. Ibid., 373.
58. Duncan, "Coming of Age in the Thirties," 221.
59. Woolf, "Introductory Letter," xv.
60. Ibid., xxxix.
61. Barthes, *Image-Music-Text*, 148.
62. Cixous, "Castration or Decapitation?," 54–55 (n. 5).
63. Beauvoir, *The Second Sex*, xxxi–xxxii.
64. Quoted in Culler, *On Deconstruction*, 173.
65. Derrida and McDonald, "Choreographies," 76.
66. Barrett, Introduction to *Women and Writing*, 13.
67. Cixous, "Castration or Decapitation?," 53.
68. Féral, "Antigone," 11.

CHAPTER 7

1. Guillaumin, "The Practice of Power, Part 1," 12.
2. Beauvoir, *The Second Sex*, 43.
3. Guillaumin, "The Practice of Power, Part 2," 89.
4. Guillaumin, "The Practice of Power, Part 1," 14.
5. Derrida, *Writing and Difference*, 39.
6. Gagnon, "Body I," 180.
7. Jane Gallop offers a provocative exploration of feminist criticism's blurring of the distinction between the literal body and the metaphorical body in "*Writing and Sexual Difference*: The Difference Within."
8. Jacobus, "The Difference of View," 12.
9. Derrida, *Writing and Difference*, 43.
10. Kamuf, "Writing Like a Woman," 286.
11. Kamuf, "Replacing Feminist Criticism," 44.
12. Miller, "Women's Autobiography in France," 271.
13. Showalter, "Feminist Criticism in the Wilderness," 187.
14. Miller, "The Text's Heroine," 49.
15. Jacobus, "The Difference of View," 13.
16. Jardine, "Gynesis," 64.

17. Jacobus, "The Difference of View," 16.
18. Johnston, *Lesbian Nation*, 68.
19. Yaeger, " 'Because a Fire,' " 955.
20. Millett, *Sexual Politics*, 116.
21. Olsen, *Silences*, 31.
22. Guillaumin, "The Practice of Power, Part 1," 27 (n. 24).
23. Jehlen, "Archimedes and the Paradox of Feminist Criticism," 582.
24. Ibid., 600.
25. Chopin, *The Awakening*, 269. Further references are cited in the text.
26. Guillaumin, "The Practice of Power, Part 2," 91.
27. Treichler, "The Construction of Ambiguity," 245.
28. In his discussion of the novel's romantic imagery, Donald Ringe discusses the way in which the sea both opens out to the infinite and closes in on the self ("Romantic Imagery," 583). Ringe's error rests in his compulsion to separate Chopin's feminist concerns from what he sees as broader "philosophic questions" (p. 588). In "The Construction of Ambiguity," Paula Treichler presents an illuminating linguistic analysis of Chopin's style in *The Awakening*.
29. Treichler, "The Construction of Ambiguity," 256.
30. Cixous, "Castration or Decapitation?," 884.
31. Atwood, *Surfacing*, 122. Further references are cited in the text.
32. Atwood, "Women's Novels," 34–35.
33. Margaret Homans gives interesting readings of *Surfacing* and other works, including *Les Guérillères* in " 'Her Very Own Howl.' " She discusses, for example, the rejection of language as an essential divestiture for Atwood's character, whose "internalization of the father's mode of repression, which wins her civilization and language, is acquired at the cost of her relation to her female body and experience" (p. 199).
34. Walker, *The Color Purple*, 17. Further references are cited in the text.
35. Irigaray, "When Our Lips Speak Together," 73. Further references are cited in the text.
36. For discussions of the complex divergence and alignments within French feminism, see Burke, "Report from Paris"; Marks, "Women and Literature in France"; Jones, "Writing the Body"; and Wenzel, "The Text as Body/Politics." Stanton, in "Language and Revolution," explores differences within French feminism and differences between American and French feminist critics.
37. Wenzel, "The Text as Body/Politics," 267.
38. Ibid., 276.
39. Wittig, *Les Guérillères*, 14. Further references are cited in the text.
40. Wenzel makes the observation that in her four works Wittig "redefines and reinvents" the major genres of canonical literature: "Under the subversive pen of Wittig, *bildungsroman*, epic poem, Bible and dictionary—all powerful tools of patriarchal discourse—contribute to the genesis of another language, from which another culture is already clearly emerging" ("The Text as Body/Politics," 285).
41. Wittig, *The Lesbian Body*, 10. Further references are cited in the text.
42. Wenzel, "The Text as Body/Politics," 281.

43. Ibid., 277.
44. Wittig and Zeig, *Lesbian Peoples*, 89. Further references are cited in the text.
45. Jagger, in *Feminist Politics and Human Nature*, comments that, in addition to defining "woman" as obsolete, Wittig and Zeig omit the term "man" from the dictionary (p. 100). Wenzel notes the redefinition of "mother" (p. 277).
46. Wenzel, "The Text as Body/Politics," 284.
47. Donzelot, *The Policing of Families*, 234.
48. Seltzer, "Reading Foucault," 78–79.
49. Piercy, *Braided Lives*, 400.
50. Gallop, "*Writing and Sexual Difference*," 289.

CHAPTER 8

1. Makward, "To Be or Not to Be," 104.
2. Showalter, "Feminist Criticism in the Wilderness," 183. Carolyn Allen's critique of this essay is particularly helpful because it reveals the inadequacies of Showalter's argument concerning "the contemporary plurality of cultures based on differences of race, class, sexual preference, age, religion, and geography, to name only some of the variables" ("Feminist(s) Reading," 300). Showalter's rebuttal follows in "Reply to Carolyn J. Allen."
3. Eagleton, *Literary Theory*, 149.
4. Ibid., 197.
5. Ibid., 201.
6. Ibid., 203.
7. Ibid., 205.
8. Ibid., 211.
9. Ibid., 212.
10. Ibid., 209.
11. Ibid.
12. Foucault, *Power/Knowledge*, 133.
13. Spivak challenges Eagleton's appropriation of an "undifferentiated, undocumented, monolithic feminist criticism" in his *Walter Benjamin; or, Towards a Revolutionary Criticism*. Her assessment is as follows: "Having praised feminist criticism . . . for its revolutionary-Marxist potential, Eagleton proceeds to trash it in three paragraphs: his main contention, feminism is theoretically thin, or separatist. Girls, shape up!" ("The Politics of Interpretation," 277).
14. Register, "American Feminist Literary Criticism," 18–19.
15. Donovan, "Afterword," 75.
16. See Annette Kolodny's discussion of Register's essay in her "Review Essay," 413–14, and her objections to the notion of prescriptive criticism in "The Feminist as Literary Critic," 827–28.
17. Kolodny, "Dancing Through the Minefield," 19.
18. Ibid.
19. Ibid.

20. Robinson, *Sex, Class, and Culture*, 11.

21. Gayatri Spivak, "A Response to Annette Kolodny," as quoted in Marcus, "Storming the Toolshed," 218 (n. 3).

22. Ibid., 217–18.

23. Gardiner et al., "An Interchange," 667.

24. The objections of feminist critics are well represented in the response to the publication of Kolodny's essay; see Gardiner et al., "An Interchange."

25. This comment was made in discussion during the Alabama Symposium on Language and Literature, "After Strange Texts: The Role of Theory in the Study of Literature," held in October 1982.

26. Kolodny, "Some Notes," 89.

27. Graff's position, advanced in discussion following the presentation of papers, Society for Critical Exchange session, SAMLA, November 1982.

28. Kamuf, "Replacing Feminist Criticism," 45.

29. Ibid., 46.

30. Gallop, *The Daughter's Seduction*, 14.

31. Kamuf, "Replacing Feminist Criticism," 47.

32. Gallop, *The Daughter's Seduction*, 63.

33. Ibid., 78.

34. Ibid., 64.

35. Marcus, "Storming the Toolshed," 220–21 (n. 11).

36. Gallop, *The Daughter's Seduction*, 150.

37. Ibid., 127–30. The double-columned representation of Gallop's reluctance to choose between the left (sinister) path of lesbian feminism and the "right" path leading to the mother is undermined as the right path graphically becomes the "right" path and overtakes the discourse that follows.

38. Ibid., 88. Gallop returns to this provocative passage in "The Mother Tongue," 152–53, her commentary on *The Daughter's Seduction*.

39. Gallop, *The Daughter's Seduction*, 103.

40. Ibid., 126.

41. Ibid., 122.

42. Cixous, "The Laugh of the Medusa," 892.

43. Barthes, *Writing Degree Zero*, 87.

44. In her critique of Myra Jehlen's "Archimedes and the Paradox of Feminist Criticism," Patrocinio Schweickart presents an interesting view of feminist criticism as a "divisive enterprise" engaged in rethinking the logic of literary criticism as a discipline in order ultimately to free it from the control of sexist domination ("Comments," 175).

45. Barthes, *Roland Barthes*, 167.

46. Féral, "Towards a Theory of Displacement," 59.

47. Cixous, "The Laugh of the Medusa," 887.

48. Julia Kristeva, *Polylogue* (Paris: Éditions du Seuil, 1977), as quoted in Féral, "Towards a Theory of Displacement," 63.

49. Féral, "Towards a Theory of Displacement," 59.

50. Furman, "Textual Feminism," 49.

51. Jones, "Writing the Body," 257.
52. Smith, "Toward a Black Feminist Criticism," 161.
53. Ibid., 157.
54. Jones, "Writing the Body," 257.
55. Robinson, "Treason Our Text," 93.
56. Russ, *How to Suppress Women's Writing*, 120.
57. Gallop, *The Daughter's Seduction*, xii.

BIBLIOGRAPHY

Aaron, Daniel. *Writers on the Left*. New York: Harcourt, Brace and World, 1961.

Abel, Elizabeth. "Editor's Introduction." *Critical Inquiry* 8 (1981): 173–78.

Abrahams, Roger. "Negotiating Respect: Patterns of Presentation among Black Women." *Journal of American Folklore* 88 (1975): 58–80.

Abrams, M. H. "How to Do Things with Texts." *Partisan Review* 46 (1979): 566–88.

Allen, Carolyn J. "Feminist(s) Reading: A Response to Elaine Showalter." In *Writing and Sexual Difference*, edited by Elizabeth Abel, 298–303. Chicago: University of Chicago Press, 1982.

Atwood, Margaret. "Happy Endings" and "Women's Novels." In *Murder in the Dark: Short Fictions and Prose Poems*, 37–40, 34–36. Toronto: Coach House Press, 1983.

———. *Surfacing*. New York: Simon and Schuster, 1972.

Bader, Julia. "The Dissolving Vision: Realism in Jewett, Freeman, and Gilman." In *American Realism: New Essays*, edited by Eric J. Sundquist, 176–98. Baltimore: Johns Hopkins University Press, 1982.

Bakhtin, Mikhail M. *The Dialogic Imagination*. Translated by Caryl Emerson and Michael Holquist. Edited by Michael Holquist. Austin: University of Texas Press, 1981.

Barrett, Michèle. Introduction to *Women and Writing*, by Virginia Woolf. Edited by Michèle Barrett. New York: Harcourt Brace Jovanovich, 1979.

Barthes, Roland. *Image-Music-Text*. Translated by Stephen Heath. New York: Hill and Wang, 1977.

———. *Roland Barthes*. Translated by Richard Howard. New York: Hill and Wang, 1977.

———. *Writing Degree Zero*. Translated by Annette Lavers and Colin Smith. New York: Hill and Wang, 1968.

Bazin, Nancy Topping. *Virginia Woolf and the Androgynous Mind*. New Brunswick, N.J.: Rutgers University Press, 1973.

Beauvoir, Simone de. *The Second Sex*. Translated by H. M. Parshley. 1952. Reprint. New York: Vintage, 1974.

Bell, Barbara Currier, and Carol Ohmann. "Virginia Woolf's Criticism: A Polemical Preface." In *Feminist Literary Criticism: Explorations in Theory*, edited by Josephine Donovan, 48–60. Lexington: University Press of Kentucky, 1975.

Bethel, Lorraine. " 'This Infinity of Conscious Pain': Zora Neale Hurston and the Black Female Literary Tradition." In *All the Women Are White, All the Blacks Are Men, But Some of Us Are Brave: Black Women's Studies*, edited by Gloria T. Hull, Patricia Bell Scott, and Barbara Smith, 176–88. Old Westbury, N.Y.: Feminist Press, 1982.

Black, Naomi. "Virginia Woolf and the Women's Movement." In *Virginia Woolf: A Feminist Slant*, edited by Jane Marcus, 180–97. Lincoln: University of Nebraska Press, 1983.

165

Bibliography

_____. "Virginia Woolf: 'The Life of Natural Happiness.'" In *Feminist Theorists: Three Centuries of Key Women Thinkers*, edited by Dale Spender, 296–313. New York: Pantheon, 1983.

Borker, Ruth. "Anthropology: Social and Cultural Perspectives." In *Women and Language in Literature and Society*, edited by Sally McConnell-Ginet, Ruth Borker, and Nelly Furman, 26–44. New York: Praeger, 1980.

Brand, Alice Glarden. "Mary Wilkins Freeman: Misanthropy as Propaganda." *New England Quarterly* 50 (1977): 83–100.

Burke, Carolyn Greenstein. "Report from Paris: Women's Writing and the Women's Movement." *Signs* 3 (1978): 843–55.

Burkom, Selma, and Margaret Williams. "De-Riddling Tillie Olsen's Writing." *San José Studies* 2 (1976): 64–83.

Camus, Albert. *The Rebel: An Essay on Man in Revolt*. Translated by Anthony Bower. New York: Vintage, 1956.

Carroll, Berenice. "'To Crush Him in Our Own Country': The Political Thought of Virginia Woolf." *Feminist Studies* 4 (1978): 99–131.

Cather, Willa. Preface to *The Country of the Pointed Firs and Other Stories*, by Sarah Orne Jewett, 6–11. 1925. Reprint. Garden City, N.Y.: Doubleday and Co., 1956.

Chopin, Kate. *The Awakening and Other Stories*. Edited by Lewis Leary. New York: Holt, Rinehart and Winston, 1970.

Christian, Barbara. *Black Women Novelists: The Development of a Tradition, 1892–1976*. Westport, Conn.: Greenwood Press, 1980.

Cixous, Hélène. "Castration or Decapitation?" Translated by Annette Kuhn. *Signs* 7 (1981): 41–55.

_____. "The Laugh of the Medusa." Translated by Keith Cohen and Paula Cohen. *Signs* 1 (1976): 875–93.

Clark, Michele. Afterword to *The Revolt of Mother and Other Stories*, by Mary Wilkins Freeman, 79–97. Old Westbury, N.Y.: Feminist Press, 1974.

Clément, Catherine. "Enslaved Enclave." Translated by Marilyn R. Schuster. In *New French Feminisms: An Anthology*, edited by Elaine Marks and Isabelle de Courtivron, 130–36. Amherst: University of Massachusetts Press, 1980.

Coward, Rosalind. *Patriarchal Precedents: Sexuality and Social Relations*. London: Routledge and Kegan Paul, 1983.

Culler, Jonathan. *On Deconstruction: Theory and Criticism after Structuralism*. Ithaca, N.Y.: Cornell University Press, 1982.

_____. *Structuralist Poetics: Structuralism, Linguistics, and the Study of Literature*. Ithaca, N.Y.: Cornell University Press, 1975.

Davis, Angela. *Women, Race and Class*. New York: Random House, 1981.

De Man, Paul. *Blindness and Insight: Essays in the Rhetoric of Contemporary Criticism*. New York: Oxford University Press, 1971.

Derrida, Jacques. "Differance." In *Speech and Phenomena and Other Essays on Husserl's Theory of Signs*, translated by David B. Allison, 129–60. Evanston, Ill.: Northwestern University Press, 1973.

_____. *Dissemination*. Translated by Barbara Johnson. Chicago: University of Chicago Press, 1981.

Bibliography

————. *Positions*. Translated by Alan Bass. Chicago: University of Chicago Press, 1981.

————. *Spurs: Nietzsche's Styles*. Translated by Barbara Horlow. Chicago: University of Chicago Press, 1978.

————. *Writing and Difference*. Translated by Alan Bass. Chicago: University of Chicago Press, 1978.

Derrida, Jacques, and Christie V. McDonald. "Choreographies." *Diacritics* 12 (1982): 66–76.

Derrida, Jacques; James Creech; Peggy Kamuf; and Jane Todd. "Deconstruction in America: An Interview with Jacques Derrida." *Critical Exchange* 17 (1985): 1–33.

Dickinson, Emily. *The Complete Poems of Emily Dickinson*. Edited by Thomas H. Johnson. 1957. Boston: Little, Brown and Co., 1963.

Donovan, Josephine. "Afterword: Critical Re-Vision." In *Feminist Literary Criticism: Explorations in Theory*, edited by Josephine Donovan, 74–81. Lexington: University Press of Kentucky, 1975.

————. *New England Local Color Literature: A Women's Tradition*. New York: Frederick Ungar Publishing Co., 1983.

Donzelot, Jacques. *The Policing of Families*. Translated by Robert Hurley. New York: Pantheon, 1979.

Duncan, Erika. "Coming of Age in the Thirties: A Portrait of Tillie Olsen." *Book Forum* 6 (1982): 207–22.

Eagleton, Terry. *Literary Theory: An Introduction*. Minneapolis: University of Minnesota Press, 1983.

————. *Walter Benjamin; or, Towards a Revolutionary Criticism*. London: Verso, 1981.

Editorial Collective of *Questions féministes*. "Variations on Common Themes." Translated by Yvonne Rochette-Ozzello. In *New French Feminisms: An Anthology*, edited by Elaine Marks and Isabelle de Courtivron, 212–30. Amherst: University of Massachusetts Press, 1980.

Eisenstein, Hester, and Alice Jardine, eds. *The Future of Difference*. Boston: G. K. Hall and Co., 1980.

Ellmann, Mary. *Thinking About Women*. New York: Harcourt Brace Jovanovich, 1968.

Féral, Josette. "Antigone or *The Irony of the Tribe*." *Diacritics* 8 (1978): 2–14.

————. "Towards a Theory of Displacement." Translated by Kristina Dragaitis. *SubStance* 32 (1981): 52–64.

Fetterley, Judith. *The Resisting Reader: A Feminist Approach to American Fiction*. Bloomington: Indiana University Press, 1978.

Fiedler, Leslie. "Literature as an Institution: The View from 1980." In *English Literature: Opening Up the Canon*, Selected Papers from the English Institute, 1979, edited by Leslie A. Fiedler and Houston A. Baker, Jr., 73–91. Baltimore: Johns Hopkins University Press, 1981.

Fish, Stanley. *Is There a Text in This Class?: The Authority of Interpretive Communities*. Cambridge, Mass.: Harvard University Press, 1980.

Fleishman, Avrom. "Virginia Woolf: Tradition and Modernity." In *Forms of Modern*

Bibliography

British Fiction, edited by Alan Warren Friedman, 133–63. Austin: University of Texas Press, 1975.

Foster, Edward. *Mary E. Wilkins Freeman*. New York: Hendricks House, 1956.

Foucault, Michel. *Language, Counter-Memory, Practice: Selected Essays and Interviews*. Edited by Donald F. Bouchard. Ithaca, N.Y.: Cornell University Press, 1977.

_____. *Madness and Civilization: A History of Insanity in the Age of Reason*. New York: Vintage, 1973.

_____. *Power/Knowledge: Selected Interviews and Other Writings, 1972–1977*. Translated by Colin Gordon et al. Edited by Colin Gordon. New York: Pantheon, 1980.

Fox, Alice. "Literary Allusion as Feminist Criticism in *A Room of One's Own*." *Philological Quarterly* 63 (1984): 145–62.

Freeman, Mary Wilkins. "Arethusa." In *Understudies: Short Stories*, 147–69. 1901. Reprint. Freeport, N.Y.: Books for Libraries Press, 1969.

_____. "A Conflict Ended." In *The Best Stories of Mary E. Wilkins*, selected by Henry Wysham Lanier, 320–35. New York: Harper and Brothers, 1927.

_____. "Mary E. Wilkins Freeman: An Autobiography." *Saturday Evening Post* (8 December 1917).

_____. "A New England Nun." In *The Revolt of Mother and Other Stories*, 79–97. Old Westbury, N.Y.: Feminist Press, 1974.

_____. "The Revolt of 'Mother.'" In *The Revolt of Mother and Other Stories*, 116–39. Old Westbury, N.Y.: Feminist Press, 1974.

Furman, Nelly. "Textual Feminism." In *Women and Language in Literature and Society*, edited by Sally McConnell-Ginet, Ruth Borker, and Nelly Furman, 45–54. New York: Praeger, 1980.

Gagnon, Madeleine. "Body I." Translated by Isabelle de Courtivron. In *New French Feminisms: An Anthology*, edited by Elaine Marks and Isabelle de Courtivron, 179–80. Amherst: University of Massachusetts Press, 1980.

Gallop, Jane. *The Daughter's Seduction: Feminism and Psychoanalysis*. Ithaca, N.Y.: Cornell University Press, 1982.

_____. "The Ladies' Man." *Diacritics* 6 (1976): 28–34.

_____. "The Mother Tongue." In *The Politics of Theory*, edited by Francis Barker et al., 49–56. Colchester: University of Essex, 1983.

_____. "*Writing and Sexual Difference*: The Difference Within." In *Writing and Sexual Difference*, edited by Elizabeth Abel, 283–90. Chicago: University of Chicago Press, 1982.

Gardiner, Judith Kegan; Elly Bulkin; Rena Grasso Patterson; and Annette Kolodny. "An Interchange on Feminist Criticism: On 'Dancing Through the Minefield.'" *Feminist Studies* 8 (1982): 629–75.

George, Diana Hume. "Stumbling on Melons: Sexual Dialectics and Discrimination in English Departments." In *English Literature: Opening Up the Canon*, Selected Papers from the English Institute, 1979, edited by Leslie A. Fiedler and Houston A. Baker, Jr., 107–36. Baltimore: Johns Hopkins University Press, 1981.

Bibliography

Gilbert, Sandra, and Susan Gubar. *The Madwoman in the Attic: The Woman Writer and the Nineteenth-Century Literary Imagination*. New Haven, Conn.: Yale University Press, 1979.

Glasser, Leah Blatt. "'She Is One You Call Sister': Discovering Mary Wilkins Freeman." In *Between Women: Biographers, Novelists, Critics, Teachers and Artists Write about Their Work on Women*, edited by Carol Ascher, Louise DeSalvo, and Sara Ruddick, 186–211. Boston: Beacon Press, 1984.

gossett, hattie. "who told you anybody wants to hear from you? you ain't nothing but a black woman!" In *This Bridge Called My Back: Writings by Radical Women of Color*, edited by Cherríe Moraga and Gloria Anzaldúa, 175–76. Watertown, Mass.: Persephone Press, 1981.

Graff, Gerald. *Literature Against Itself: Literary Ideas in Modern Society*. Chicago: University of Chicago Press, 1979.

Gubar, Susan. "'The Blank Page' and the Issues of Female Creativity." *Critical Inquiry* 8 (1981): 243–64.

Guillaumin, Collette. "The Practice of Power and Belief in Nature. Part I: The Appropriation of Women." Translated by Linda Murgatroyd. *Feminist Issues* 1 (1981): 3–28.

———. "The Practice of Power and Belief in Nature. Part II: The Naturalist Discourse." Translated by Linda Murgatroyd. *Feminist Issues* 1 (1981): 87–109.

———. "The Question of Difference." Translated by Hélène V. Wenzel. *Feminist Issues* 2 (1982): 33–52.

Heath, Stephen. "Difference." *Screen* 19 (1978): 51–112.

Heilbrun, Carolyn G. "Virginia Woolf in Her Fifties." In *Virginia Woolf: A Feminist Slant*, edited by Jane Marcus, 236–53. Lincoln: University of Nebraska Press, 1983.

Hemenway, Robert. "Are You a Flying Lark or a Setting Dove?" In *Afro-American Literature: The Reconstruction of Instruction*, edited by Dexter Fisher and Robert Stepto, 122–52. New York: Modern Language Association, 1979.

———. *Zora Neale Hurston: A Literary Biography*. Urbana: University of Illinois Press, 1977.

Homans, Margaret. "'Her Very Own Howl': The Ambiguities of Representation in Recent Women's Fiction." *Signs* 9 (1983): 186–205.

Howard, Lillie P. *Zora Neale Hurston*. Boston: G. K. Hall and Co., 1980.

Huggins, Nathan. *Harlem Renaissance*. New York: Oxford University Press, 1971.

Hughes, Langston. *The Big Sea: An Autobiography*. New York: Hill and Wang, 1963.

Hurston, Zora Neale. *Mules and Men*. 1935. Reprint. Bloomington: Indiana University Press, 1978.

———. *Their Eyes Were Watching God*. 1937. Reprint. Urbana: University of Illinois Press, 1978.

Irigaray, Luce. "When Our Lips Speak Together." Translated by Carolyn Burke. *Signs* 6 (1980): 69–79.

Jacobus, Mary. "The Difference of View." In *Women Writing and Writing About Women*, edited by Mary Jacobus, 10–21. London: Croom Helm with Oxford University Women's Studies Committee, 1979.

Bibliography

Jaggar, Alison M. *Feminist Politics and Human Nature*. Sussex: Rowman and Allanheld, 1983.

Jameson, Fredric. *The Political Unconscious: Narrative as a Socially Symbolic Act*. Ithaca, N.Y.: Cornell University Press, 1981.

Jardine, Alice. "Gynesis." *Diacritics* 12 (1982): 54–65.

Jehlen, Myra. "Archimedes and the Paradox of Feminist Criticism." *Signs* 6 (1981): 575–601.

Johnson, Barbara. *The Critical Difference: Essays in the Contemporary Rhetoric of Reading*. Baltimore: Johns Hopkins University Press, 1980.

_____. Translator's Introduction to *Dissemination*, by Jacques Derrida, vii–xxxiii. Chicago: University of Chicago Press, 1981.

Johnston, Jill. *Lesbian Nation: The Feminist Solution*. New York: Simon and Schuster, 1973.

Jones, Ann Rosalind. "Writing the Body: Toward an Understanding of *L'Ecriture Feminine*." *Feminist Studies* 7 (1981): 247–63.

Jordan, June. "Notes toward a Balancing of Love and Hatred." *Black World* 23 (1974): 4–8.

Kampf, Louis, and Paul Lauter. Introduction to *The Politics of Literature: Dissenting Essays on the Teaching of English*, 3–54. New York: Pantheon, 1972.

Kamuf, Peggy. "Penelope at Work: Interruptions in *A Room of One's Own*." *Novel* 16 (1982): 5–18.

_____. "Replacing Feminist Criticism." *Diacritics* 12 (1982): 42–47.

_____. "Writing Like a Woman." In *Women and Language in Literature and Society*, edited by Sally McConnell-Ginet, Ruth Borker, and Nelly Furman, 284–99. New York: Praeger, 1980.

Katz-Stoker, Fraya. "The Other Criticism: Feminism vs. Formalism." In *Images of Women in Fiction: Feminist Perspectives*, edited by Susan Koppelman Cornillon, 315–27. Bowling Green, Ohio: Bowling Green University Popular Press, 1972.

Kermode, Frank. *The Sense of an Ending: Studies in the Theory of Fiction*. London: Oxford University Press, 1967.

Kolodny, Annette. "Dancing Through the Minefield: Some Observations on the Theory, Practice and Politics of a Feminist Criticism." *Feminist Studies* 6 (1980): 1–25.

_____. "The Feminist as Literary Critic." *Critical Inquiry* 2 (1976): 821–32.

_____. "A Map for Rereading: Or, Gender and the Interpretation of Literary Texts." *New Literary History* 11 (1980): 451–67.

_____. "Not-So-Gentle Persuasion: A Theoretical Imperative of Feminist Literary Criticism." In Conference on Feminist Literary Criticism, *Feminist Literary Criticism*, 3–20. Research Triangle Park, N.C.: National Humanities Center, 1981.

_____. "Review Essay: Literary Criticism." *Signs* 2 (1976): 404–21.

_____. "Some Notes on Defining a 'Feminist Literary Criticism.'" *Critical Inquiry* 2 (1975): 75–92.

_____. "Turning the Lens on 'The Panther Captivity': A Feminist Exercise in Practical Criticism." *Critical Inquiry* 8 (1981): 329–45.

Bibliography

Kostelanetz, Richard. *The End of Intelligent Writing: Literary Politics in America*. New York: Sheed and Ward, 1974.

Kuhn, Thomas S. *The Structure of Scientific Revolutions*. 2d ed. Chicago: University of Chicago Press, 1970.

Lentricchia, Frank. *After the New Criticism*. Chicago: University of Chicago Press, 1980.

_____. *Criticism and Social Change*. Chicago: University of Chicago Press, 1983.

Lewis, Philip. "The Post-Structuralist Condition." *Diacritics* 12 (1982): 2–24.

Lorde, Audre. *Sister Outsider: Essays and Speeches*. Trumansburg, N.Y.: Crossing Press, 1984.

Mailer, Norman. *Advertisements for Myself*. New York: Perigee, 1976.

Makward, Christiane. "To Be or Not to Be . . . A Feminist Speaker." In *The Future of Difference*, edited by Hester Eisenstein and Alice Jardine, 95–105. Boston: G. K. Hall and Co., 1980.

Marcus, Jane. Introduction and "Thinking Back Through Our Mothers." In *New Feminist Essays on Virginia Woolf*, edited by Jane Marcus, xiii–xx, 1–30. Lincoln: University of Nebraska Press, 1981.

_____. " 'No More Horses': Virginia Woolf on Art and Propaganda." *Women's Studies* 4 (1977): 265–90.

_____. "Still Practice, A/Wrested Alphabet: Toward a Feminist Aesthetic." *Tulsa Studies in Women's Literature* 3 (1984): 79–97.

_____. "Storming the Toolshed." In *Feminist Theory: A Critique of Ideology*, edited by Nannerl O. Keohane, Michelle Z. Rosaldo and Barbara C. Gelpi, 217–35. Chicago: University of Chicago Press, 1982.

_____, ed. *Virginia Woolf: A Feminist Slant*. Lincoln: University of Nebraska Press, 1983.

Marder, Herbert. *Feminism and Art: A Study of Virginia Woolf*. Chicago: University of Chicago Press, 1968.

Marks, Elaine. "Women and Literature in France." *Signs* 3 (1978): 832–42.

Miller, Nancy. "The Text's Heroine: A Feminist Critic and Her Fictions." *Diacritics* 12 (1982): 48–53.

_____. "Women's Autobiography in France: For a Dialectics of Identification." In *Women and Language in Literature and Society*, edited by Sally McConnell-Ginet, Ruth Borker, and Nelly Furman, 258–73. New York: Praeger, 1980.

Millett, Kate. *Sexual Politics*. New York: Equinox, 1971.

Moers, Ellen. *Literary Women*. New York: Doubleday, 1976.

Neal, Larry. "Zora Neale Hurston: A Profile." *Southern Exposure* 1, 3, and 4 (1974): 160–68.

O'Connor, Flannery. *The Habit of Being*. Edited by Sally Fitzgerald. New York: Farrar, Straus, Giroux, 1979.

Olsen, Tillie. *Silences*. New York: Delacorte Press, 1978.

_____. *Tell Me a Riddle*. New York: Delta, 1960.

Ozick, Cynthia. "Women and Creativity: The Demise of the Dancing Dog." In *Woman in Sexist Society*, edited by Vivian Gornick and Barbara Moran, 307–22. New York: Basic, 1971.

Bibliography

Piercy, Marge. *Braided Lives*. New York: Summit, 1982.

Planck, Max. *Scientific Autobiography, and Other Papers*. Translated by Frank Gaynor. New York: Philosophical Library, 1949.

Quintanales, Mirtha. "I Paid Very Hard for My Immigrant Ignorance." In *This Bridge Called My Back: Writings by Radical Women of Color*, edited by Cherríe Moraga and Gloria Anzaldúa, 150–56. Watertown, Mass.: Persephone Press, 1981.

Rayson, Ann L. "The Novels of Zora Neale Hurston." *Studies in Black Literature* 5 (1974): 1–10.

Register, Cheri. "American Feminist Literary Criticism: A Bibliographical Introduction." In *Feminist Literary Criticism: Explorations in Theory*, edited by Josephine Donovan, 1–28. Lexington: University Press of Kentucky, 1975.

Rich, Adrienne. "Disloyal to Civilization: Feminism, Racism, Gynephobia (1978)." In *On Lies, Secrets, and Silence: Selected Prose, 1966–1978*, 275–310. New York: W. W. Norton and Co., 1979.

──────. *Diving into the Wreck: Poems 1971–1972*. New York: W. W. Norton and Co., 1973.

──────. *The Dream of a Common Language: Poems 1974–1977*. New York: W. W. Norton and Co., 1978.

──────. *The Will to Change*. New York: W. W. Norton and Co., 1971.

──────. "Women and Honor: Some Notes on Lying (1975)." In *On Lies, Secrets, and Silence: Selected Prose 1966–1978*, 186–94. New York: W. W. Norton and Co., 1979.

Rideout, Walter B. *The Radical Novel in the United States, 1900–1954*. New York: Hill and Wang, 1956.

Ringe, Donald A. "Romantic Imagery in Kate Chopin's *The Awakening*." *American Literature* 43 (1972): 580–88.

Robinson, Lillian S. *Sex, Class, and Culture*. Bloomington: Indiana University Press, 1978.

──────. "Treason Our Text: Feminist Challenges to the Literary Canon." *Tulsa Studies in Women's Literature* 2 (1983): 83–98.

Robinson, Marilynne. *Housekeeping*. New York: Bantam, 1982.

Rosenfelt, Deborah. "From the Thirties: Tillie Olsen and the Radical Tradition." *Feminist Studies* 7 (1981): 371–406.

Rosenthal, Michael. *Virginia Woolf*. New York: Columbia University Press, 1979.

Russ, Joanna. *How to Suppress Women's Writing*. Austin: University of Texas Press, 1983.

Schlack, Beverly Ann. *Continuing Presences: Virginia Woolf's Use of Literary Allusion*. University Park: Pennsylvania State University Press, 1979.

Schweickart, Patrocinio. "Comments on Jehlen's 'Archimedes and the Paradox of Feminist Criticism.'" *Signs* 8 (1982): 170–76.

Seltzer, Mark. "Reading Foucault: Cells, Corridors, Novels." *Diacritics* 14 (1984): 78–89.

Showalter, Elaine. "Feminist Criticism in the Wilderness." *Critical Inquiry* 8 (1981): 179–205.

──────. *A Literature of Their Own: British Women Novelists from Brontë to Lessing*. Princeton, N.J.: Princeton University Press, 1977.

Bibliography

————. "Reply to Carolyn J. Allen." In *Writing and Sexual Difference*, edited by Elizabeth Abel, 304–7. Chicago: University of Chicago Press, 1982.

————. "Review: Literary Criticism." *Signs* 1 (1975): 435–60.

————. "Towards a Feminist Poetics." In *Women Writing and Writing about Women*, edited by Mary Jacobus, 22–41. London: Croom Helm, 1979.

————. "Women Writers and the Double Standard." In *Woman in Sexist Society*, edited by Vivian Gornick and Barbara Moran, 323–43. New York: Basic, 1971.

Silver, Brenda R. *"Three Guineas* Before and After: Further Answers to Correspondents." In *Virginia Woolf: A Feminist Slant*, edited by Jane Marcus, 254–76. Lincoln: University of Nebraska Press, 1983.

Smith, Barbara. "Toward a Black Feminist Criticism." In *All the Women Are White, All the Blacks Are Men, But Some of Us Are Brave: Black Women's Studies*, edited by Gloria T. Hull, Patricia Bell Scott, and Barbara Smith, 157–75. Old Westbury, N.Y.: Feminist Press, 1982.

Smith, Lillian. *The Winner Names the Age: A Collection of Writings by Lillian Smith.* Edited by Michelle Cliff. New York: W. W. Norton and Co., 1978.

Spivak, Gayatri Chakravorty. "The Politics of Interpretation." *Critical Inquiry* 9 (1982): 259–78.

————. Translator's Foreword to "Draupadi," by Mahasveta Devi. *Critical Inquiry* 8 (1981): 381–92.

————. "Unmaking and Making in *To the Lighthouse.*" In *Women and Language in Literature and Society*, edited by Sally McConnell-Ginet, Ruth Borker, and Nelly Furman, 310–27. New York: Praeger, 1980.

Stade, George. "Fat-Cheeks Hefted a Snake: On the Origins and Institutionalization of Literature." In *English Literature: Opening Up the Canon*, Selected Papers from the English Institute, 1979, edited by Leslie A. Fiedler and Houston A. Baker, Jr., 107–36. Baltimore: Johns Hopkins University Press, 1981.

Stanton, Domna C. "Language and Revolution: The Franco-American Dis-Connection." In *The Future of Difference*, edited by Hester Eisenstein and Alice Jardine, 73–87. Boston: G. K. Hall and Co., 1980.

Throne, Sara R. "Virginia Woolf's Feminist Identity and the Parthenogenesis of Female Culture." *University of Michigan Papers in Women's Studies* 2 (1975): 146–61.

Toth, Susan Allen. "Defiant Light: A Positive View of Mary Wilkins Freeman." *New England Quarterly* 46 (1973): 82–93.

Treichler, Paula A. "The Construction of Ambiguity in *The Awakening*: A Linguistic Analysis." In *Women and Language in Literature and Society*, edited by Sally McConnell-Ginet, Ruth Borker, and Nelly Furman, 239–57. New York: Praeger, 1980.

Turner, Darwin. *In a Minor Chord: Three Afro-American Writers and Their Search for Identity.* Carbondale: Southern Illinois University Press, 1971.

————. "The Negro Novelist and the South." *Southern Humanities Review* 1 (1967): 30–33.

Walker, Alice. *The Color Purple.* New York: Harcourt Brace Jovanovich, 1982.

————. "On Refusing to Be Humbled by Second Place in a Contest You Did Not Design: A Tradition by Now" and "Looking for Zora." In *I Love Myself When I Am*

Bibliography

Laughing . . . And Then Again When I Am Looking Mean and Impressive: A Zora Neale Hurston Reader, edited by Alice Walker, 1–5, 297–313. Old Westbury, N.Y.: Feminist Press, 1979.

Washington, Mary Helen. "Zora Neale Hurston: A Woman Half in Shadow." In *I Love Myself When I Am Laughing . . . And Then Again When I Am Looking Mean and Impressive: A Zora Neale Hurston Reader*, edited by Alice Walker, 7–25. Old Westbury, N.Y.: Feminist Press, 1979.

Wenzel, Hélène Vivienne. "The Text as Body/Politics: An Appreciation of Monique Wittig's Writing in Context." *Feminist Studies* 7 (1981): 264–87.

Westbrook, Perry D. *Mary Wilkins Freeman*. New York: Twayne, 1967.

White, Hayden. "Conventional Conflicts." *New Literary History* 13 (1981): 145–60.

_____. "Michel Foucault." In *Structuralism and Since: From Lévi-Strauss to Derrida*, edited by John Sturrock, 81–115. Oxford: Oxford University Press, 1979.

Williams, Blanche Colton. *Our Short Story Writers*. New York: Moffat, Yard, and Co., 1920.

Wittig, Monique. "The Category of Sex." *Feminist Issues* 2 (1982): 63–68.

_____. *The Lesbian Body*. Translated by David Le Vay. New York: William Morrow and Co., 1975.

_____. *Les Guérillères*. Translated by David Le Vay. New York: Avon, 1973.

_____. "Paradigm." In *Homosexualities and French Literature: Cultural Contexts/Critical Texts*, edited by George Stambolian and Elaine Marks, 114–21. Ithaca, N.Y.: Cornell University Press, 1979.

Wittig, Monique, and Sande Zeig. *Lesbian Peoples: Material for a Dictionary*. New York: Avon, 1979.

Wood, Ann Douglas. "The Literature of Impoverishment: The Women Local Colorists in America 1865–1914." *Women's Studies* 1 (1972): 3–45.

Woolf, Virginia. *Between the Acts*. 1941. Reprint. London: Penguin, 1953.

_____. "Introductory Letter to Margaret Llewelyn Davies." In *Life As We Have Known It*, by Co-Operative Working Women, edited by Margaret Llewelyn Davies, xv–xxxix. 1931. Reprint. New York: W. W. Norton and Co., 1975.

_____. "The Leaning Tower." In *The Moment and Other Essays*, 128–54. New York: Harcourt, Brace and Co., 1948.

_____. *The Pargiters*. Edited by Michael Leaska. New York: Harcourt Brace Jovanovich, 1977.

_____. "Professions for Women." In *The Death of the Moth and Other Essays*, 235–42. 1942. Reprint. New York: Harcourt Brace Jovanovich, 1970.

_____. *A Room of One's Own*. New York: Harcourt, Brace and World, 1929.

_____. *Three Guineas*. New York: Harcourt, Brace and World, 1938.

_____. *A Writer's Diary: Being Extracts from the Diary of Virginia Woolf*. Edited by Leonard Woolf. 1953. Reprint. New York: Harcourt Brace Jovanovich, 1973.

Yaeger, Patricia S. " 'Because a Fire Was in My Head': Eudora Welty and the Dialogic Imagination." *PMLA* 99 (1984): 955–73.

Ziff, Larzer. *The American 1890s: Life and Times of a Lost Generation*. New York: Viking, 1966.

INDEX

Index

Index

Index